PRINCIPLES AND PRACTICES OF MANAGEMENT

PRINCIPLES AND PRACTICES OF MANAGEMENT

Khushboo Manoj

CENTRUM PRESS
NEW DELHI-110002 (INDIA)

CENTRUM PRESS
H.O.: 4360/4, Ansari Road, Daryaganj,
New Delhi-110002 (India)
Tel: 23278000, 23261597, 23255577, 23286875
B.O.: No. 1015, Ist Main Road, BSK IIIrd Stage,
IIIrd Phase, IIIrd Block, Bangalore-560085 (INDIA)
Tel: 080-41723429
Email: centrumpress@gmail.com
Visit us at: www.centrumpress.com

Principles and Practices of Management

First Edition, 2011 2015

ISBN 978-93-80921-12-9

PRINTED IN INDIA

Printed at Balaji Offset, Delhi.

Contents

Preface

The book Principle and practice in Management is a balanced mixture of theoretical concepts and practical guidance about management that involves training and development approaches, based on best practice used by companies, public sector organisations, training institutions, business schools and management consultants in various countries around the world.

The book provides a guidelines for implementing and maintaining effective training and development programs in organizations. The intent is to capture theoretical advances made in training over the last ten years and apply insights from this work as a foundation for grounding processes such as strategic planning and needs assessment, training design and media selection, training delivery, transfer of training and training evaluation, and long-term maintenance of learning programs in organizations.

The book provides clear-cut guidance and a systematic approach for planning, establishing, managing, operating, and evaluating a management development program. Human resources professionals will be able to design and implement a program that increases the organization's ability to respond to change. It also helps individuals realize their career goals

1

Concept of Management

AN OVERVIEW

Management is an activity process composed of some basic functions, for getting the objective of any enterprise accomplished through the efforts of its personnel. Wherever and whenever objectives are to be achieved through organized and co-operative endeavour, management becomes essential for directing and unifying the group efforts towards a common purpose.

As human aims and beliefs are mostly realised through the establishment of diverse associations in our society, management is universally needed for operating all such organisation. Management, viewed as a functional concept, is of equal necessity to the educational religious, charitable and other non-business institutions as it is required for business Organizations.

Furthermore, the greatest and the most comprehensive of our social organizations, viz., the Government of all types needs management as others require, perhaps more than all other social organizations. That the Government without requires a management process has been apply pointed out in the statement: A Government without good management is a house built on sand.

Put in short, management is an essential accompaniment of all social organizations, and it is to be found everywhere as a distinct, separate and dominate activity. The nature and significance of the activity do not change even if it is called administration in some social in situations and management in others. Management is the only activating element of any enterprise for getting things done through it personnel. The job of management is to provide dynamic leadership that combines the productive but passive resources into a fruitful organization. Not only does it adapt itself to existing opportunities, restrictions and pressures, but it exercises a positive influence as well as to make the future events favourable for the enterprise.

With a view to getting the expected results and seeing that things happen as they should, management has to become a creator of the economy rather then its creature. Management forges ahead through innovations in operating situation and the adoptian of far-sighted planning. It visualize the future, initiates changes and achieves the purpose of any enterprise under highly dynamic conditions.

As an activity process, management plans the future course of action, organizes people and their work, directs the operation an controls the performance, and thus ensures the accomplishment of enterprise objectives. Adaptations and innovations permeate through each of these phases of the management process. Management acts as a creative and invigorating force in the organization.

It creates result that is bigger than the sum total of efforts put in by the group. Management adds real plus value to the operation of any enterprise by enlisting as little extra value out of each person. It provides new ideas, imaginations and visions to the group working an integrates its efforts in such a manner as to account for better results. It ensures a smooth flow of work in the organization by focusing on strong points, neutralizing weak link, overcoming difficulties and establishing team spirit. Management strives to secure the maximum result by the use of minimum resources.

Management is old as civilization and it has been of some concern to organized society thought civilized history. Various examples exist today to remind us the result of the organized activities of the past. However, the principles of such organized activities are either not available or not applicable in present day social structure. In fact, no organised effort towards developing management principles was carried on before the present century and most of the earlier contributions towards increasing the efficiency of organised groups were scattered. Another significant point in the context of the development of thought is that the contributions have been made by practicing managers as well as academicians. Thus the total contribution is the result of practical experience as well as the organised researches. If we analyse various thought from period point of view, the role of organised researches successively increase in the development of management principles.

For the sake of analysis, the management thoughts have been classified as:

- Systems approach.
- Human relations approach, and
- Classical Approach

This classification is based on the grouping of various thoughts which have similarity in the approach of how managers get the things done. The classification in not very rigid suggesting that the thoughts can be classified in some other ways. Before we proceed to the study of management in an organised way, let us have a look on the early contributions mostly in scattered way.

SYSTEM APPROACH OF MANAGEMENT

The systems approach, also labeled as modern theory of management, is a relatively new approach though neither the terms management and organisation nor the system is a new concept.Over the past tow decades or so the systems approach has emerged as vigourous and lively. Now, we are bombarded with reference to system in various walks of life. Everything is a system and the system thinking is the by work.

We have entered a period that forces man to find more accurate answers to questions involving the 'wholeness' of an operation. This age of synthesis forces management to think out in new and different ways- as suggested by the systems approach. In this view the whole is not merely a combination of the system but distinct from it s parts. Before analyzing how an organisation functions as a system, it is imperative to analyse the concept, and working of the system. A system is defined as the assemblage of things connected or interdependent, so as to form a complex unity; a whole composed of parts in orderly arrangement according to some scheme or plan. This has been defined as 'an organised' or complex whole; an assemblage or combination of things or parts forming a complex unitary whole.

Various authors on systems approach have attempted to develop a generalized theory which can be applied to any system-physical, biological, or social. They have termed is as General Systems Theory (GST). The theory is concerned with developing a systematic, theoretical framework for describing the empirical world. Buckley describes its role as such, 'A which functions as a whole by virtue of the inter-dependence of its parts i called a system and the method which aims at discovering how this is brought about in widest variety of systems has been called General Systems Theory. General Systems Theory seeks to classify systems by the way their components are organised and to derive the laws, or typical patterns of behaviour, for the different classes of systems singled but by the taxonomy.

The first basic stage in system management is the determination of organisation system. Since organisation is a deliberate and purposive creations, the basic objectives of the organisation should be determined before its creation. Determination of objectives is important because every attempt is directed towards realization of these objectives. In the second stage,each element of the organisation is arranged in some combination to provide desired results. Systems design provides the overall framework for implementing systems concepts. It includes strategic and comprehensive planning for the entire organisational system, as well as the development of operation and facilitating sun-system. The third stage-operation and control-refers to conversion of inputs into outputs. Inputs may be in the form of information, materials, and energy. The inputs are allocated to plan, though it is possible to eliminate parts of the planning required during operations by designing system with predetermined input allocation structuring the system to operate in a specified fashion and with more predictable results. Operation of the system requires some sort of control, that is, a mechanism for output or related characteristics, comparing he measurement with the standard, and activating the unit to adjust inputs to correct the deficiency. This is necessary to maintain the equilibrium of the system near the ideal point. The fourth stage pertains to review and evaluation, that is, to ascertain how well the system has performed. This is different from the control in the sense that control refers to operating efficiency, while the concept of review and evaluation is more comprehensive, and always relates the functioning of the system to its objectives. The review and evaluation occur at periodic intervals during the life cycle of a system and lead to design changes in the present system or recommendations for changes which may be operated in future systems

HUMAN RELATION APPROACH OF MANAGEMENT

The classical approach which focused attention on the mechanical an physiological variables of organisational functioning was tested on the field to increase the efficiency of organisations.Surprisingly, positive aspects of these variables could not evoke positive response in work behaviour, and researchers tried to investigate the reasons for human behaviour at the work. They discovered that the real cause of human behaviour was something more than physiological variables.

Such findings generated a new phenomenon about the human behaviour and focused attention of the human beings in the organisations. As such, this new approach his been called 'human approach of management'.Even in the writings of classical approach, notably, Taylor, Fayol, Henry Gantt, Follet, Urwick, and others, the human element in the organisation was recognised, but they emphasised it very little. The human relations approach was born out o fa reaction to classical approach and during the last four decades, a lot of literature on human relations had been developed.

The essence of the human relations contributions is contained in two points:

1. Organisational situation should be viewed in social terms as well as in economic and technical terms,
2. The social process of group behaviour can be understood in terms of clinical method analogous to the doctor's diagnosis of the human organism.

Among human relations approach, there are many contributions and many more researches are being carried on. These include contributions form famous 'Hawthorne Experiments', many sociologists-Bakke, Selznic, Homans, dubin, and Dalton; many psychologists-McGregor, Likert, Argyris, March and Simon, Leavitt, Blake, Sayles, Brown, etc. There will be relatively lengthy discussion of the results and implications of the Hawthorne studies because of their historical importance to the behavioural approach to the analysis of management problems. In fact, for the first time, an intensive and systematic analysis of human factor in organisations was made in the form of Hawthorne experiments.

CONTRIBUTION OF HENRY FAYOL OF CLASSICAL APPROACH

Perhaps, the real father of modern management theory is Henry Fayol. He was a French mining engineer, who after obtaining engineering degree joined a French coal firm as technician in 1880. Fayol observed the organisational functioning from manager's point of view.

He found that all activities of the organisation could be divided into six groups:

- Technical (relating to production)
- Commercial (buying, selling, and exchange)
- Financial (search of capital and its optimum use)
- Accounting (including statistics)
- Managerial (planning, organisation, command, co-ordination and control).

He points out that these activities exist in every organisation. He further observes that first five activities.

Fayol has divided his approach of studying management in three parts:

1. Managerial qualities and training.
2. General principles of management,
3. Elements of management.

Management in all business and human organization activity is the performance of getting people together to accomplish desired goals and objectives. Management comprises planning, organizing, staffing, leading or directing, and controlling an organization (a group of one or more people or entities) or effort for the purpose of accomplishing a goal. Resourcing encompasses the deployment and manipulation of human resources, financial resources, technological resources, and natural resources.

Because organisations can be viewed as systems, management can also be defined as human action, including design, to facilitate the production of useful outcomes from a system. This view opens the opportunity to 'manage' oneself, a pre-requisite to attempting to manage others. Management can also refer to the person or people who perform the act(s) of management.

The verb *manage* comes from the Italian *maneggiare* (to handle — especially tools), which in turn derives from the Latin *manus* (hand). The French word *mesnagement* influenced the development in meaning of the English word *management* in the 17th and 18th centuries.

Some definitions of management are:

- Organisation and coordination of the activities of an enterprise in accordance with certain policies and in achievement of clearly defined objectives. Management is often included as a factor of production along with machines, materials, and money. The management guru Peter Drucker, the basic task of a management is twofold: marketing and innovation.
- Directors and managers who have the power and

> responsibility to make decisions to manage an enterprise. As a discipline, management comprises the interlocking functions of formulating corporate policy and organizing, planning, controlling, and directing the firm's resources to achieve the policy's objectives. The size of management can range from one person in a small firm to hundreds or thousands of managers in multinational companies. In large firms the board of directors formulates the policy which is implemented by the chief executive officer.

Mary Parker Follett, who wrote on the topic in the early twentieth century, defined management as "the art of getting things done through people". She also described management as philosophy. One can also think of management functionally, as the action of measuring a quantity on a regular basis and of adjusting some initial plan; or as the actions taken to reach one's intended goal. This applies even in situations where planning does not take place.

From this perspective, Frenchman Henri Fayol considers management to consist of seven functions:

1. Planning
2. Organizing
3. Leading
4. Coordinating
5. Controlling
6. Staffing
7. Motivating

Some people, however, find this definition, while useful, far too narrow. The phrase "management is what managers do" occurs widely, suggesting the difficulty of defining management, the shifting nature of definitions, and the connection of managerial practices with the existence of a managerial cadre or class.

One habit of thought regards management as equivalent to "business administration" and thus excludes management in places outside commerce, as for example in charities and in the public sector. More realistically, however, every organization must manage its work, people, processes, technology, etc. in order to maximize its effectiveness. Nonetheless, many people refer to university departments which teach management as "business schools." Some institutions use that name while others employ the more inclusive term "management." English speakers may also use the term "management" or "the management" as a collective word describing the managers of an organization, for example of a corporation. Historically this use of the term was often contrasted with the term "Labour" referring to those being managed.

In for-profit work, management has as its primary function the satisfaction of a range of stakeholders. This typically involves making a profit, creating valued products at a reasonable cost (for customers), and providing rewarding employment opportunities (for employees). In nonprofit management, add the importance of keeping the faith of donors. In most models of management/governance, shareholders vote for the board of directors, and the board then hires senior management. Some organizations have experimented with other methods (such as employee-voting models) of selecting or reviewing managers; but this occurs only very rarely. In the public sector of countries constituted as representative democracies, voters elect politicians to public office.

Such politicians hire many managers and administrators, and in some countries like the United States political appointees lose their jobs on the election of a new president/governor/mayor. Difficulties arise in tracing the history of management. Some see it (by definition) as a late modern (in the sense of late modernity) conceptualization. On those terms it cannot have a pre-modern history, only harbingers (such as stewards). Others, however, detect management-like-thought back to Sumerian traders and to the builders of the pyramids of ancient Egypt.

Slave-owners through the centuries faced the problems of exploiting/motivating a dependent but sometimes unenthusiastic or recalcitrant workforce, but many pre-industrial enterprises, given their small scale, did not feel compelled to face the issues of management systematically. However, innovations such as the spread of Arabic numerals (5th to 15th centuries) and the codification of double-entry book-keeping (1494) provided tools for management assessment, planning and control. Given the scale of most commercial operations and the lack of mechanized record-keeping and recording before the industrial revolution, it made sense for most owners of enterprises in those times to carry out management functions by and for themselves.

But with growing size and complexity of organizations, the split between owners (individuals, industrial dynasties or groups of shareholders) and day-to-day managers (independent specialists in planning and control) gradually became more common.

While management has been present for millennia, several writers have created a background of works that assisted in modern management theories.

Sun Tzu's The Art of War

Written by Chinese general Sun Tzu in the 6th century BC, *The Art of War* is a military strategy book that, for managerial purposes, recommends being aware of and acting on strengths and weaknesses of both a manager's organization and a foe's.

Niccolò Machiavelli's The Prince

Believing that people were motivated by self-interest, Niccolò Machiavelli wrote *The Prince* in 1513 as advice for the leadership of Florence, Italy. Machiavelli recommended that leaders use fear—but not hatred—to maintain control.

Adam Smith's The Wealth of Nations

Written in 1776 by Adam Smith, a Scottish moral philosopher, *The Wealth of Nations* aims for efficient organization of work through Specialization of labour. Smith described how changes in processes could boost productivity in the manufacture of pins. While individuals could produce 200 pins per day, Smith analysed the steps involved in manufacture and, with 10 specialists, enabled production of 48,000 pins per day.

19TH CENTURY

Classical economists such as Adam Smith (1723 - 1790) and John Stuart Mill (1806 - 1873) provided a theoretical background to resource-allocation, production, and pricing issues. About the same time, innovators like Eli Whitney (1765 - 1825), James Watt (1736 - 1819), and Matthew Boulton (1728 - 1809) developed elements of technical production such as standardization, quality-control procedures, cost-accounting, interchangeability of parts, and work-planning. Many of these aspects of management existed in the pre-1861 slave-based sector of the US economy. That environment saw 4 million people, as the contemporary usages had it, "managed" in profitable quasi-mass production.

By the late 19th century, marginal economists Alfred Marshall (1842 - 1924), Léon Walras (1834 - 1910), and others introduced a new layer of complexity to the theoretical underpinnings of management. Joseph Wharton offered the first tertiary-level course in management in 1881.

20TH CENTURY

By about 1900 one finds managers trying to place their theories on what they regarded as a thoroughly scientific basis. Examples include Henry R. Towne's *Science of management* in the 1890s, Frederick Winslow Taylor's *The Principles of Scientific Management* (1911), Frank and Lillian Gilbreth's *Applied motion study* (1917), and Henry L. Gantt's charts (1910s). In 1912 Yoichi Ueno introduced Taylorism to Japan and became first management consultant of the "Japanese-management style". His son Ichiro Ueno pioneered Japanese quality assurance.

The first comprehensive theories of management appeared around 1920. The Harvard Business School invented the Master of Business Administration degree (MBA) in 1921. People like Henri Fayol (1841 - 1925) and Alexander Church described the various branches of management and their inter-relationships. In the early 20th century, people like Ordway

Tead (1891 - 1973), Walter Scott and J. Mooney applied the principles of psychology to management, while other writers, such as Elton Mayo (1880 - 1949), Mary Parker Follett (1868 - 1933), Chester Barnard (1886 - 1961), Max Weber (1864 - 1920), Rensis Likert (1903 - 1981), and Chris Argyris (1923 -) approached the phenomenon of management from a sociological perspective.

Peter Drucker (1909 – 2005) wrote one of the earliest books on applied management: *Concept of the Corporation* (published in 1946). It resulted from Alfred Sloan (chairman of General Motors until 1956) commissioning a study of the organisation. Drucker went on to write 39 books, many in the same vein.

H. Dodge, Ronald Fisher (1890 - 1962), and Thornton C. Fry introduced statistical techniques into management-studies. In the 1940s, Patrick Blackett combined these statistical theories with microeconomic theory and gave birth to the science of operations research.

Operations research, sometimes known as "management science" (but distinct from Taylor's scientific management), attempts to take a scientific approach to solving management problems, particularly in the areas of logistics and operations. Some of the more recent developments include the Theory of Constraints, management by objectives, reengineering, Six Sigma and various information-technology-driven theories such as agile software development, as well as group management theories such as Cog's Ladder.

As the general recognition of managers as a class solidified during the 20th century and gave perceived practitioners of the art/science of management a certain amount of prestige, so the way opened for popularised systems of management ideas to peddle their wares. In this context many management fads may have had more to do with pop psychology than with scientific theories of management.

Towards the end of the 20th century, business management came to consist of six separate branches, namely:

1. Human resource management
2. Operations management or production management
3. Strategic management

4. Marketing management
5. Financial management
6. Information technology management responsible for management information systems

21ST CENTURY

In the 21st century observers find it increasingly difficult to subdivide management into functional categories in this way. More and more processes simultaneously involve several categories. Instead, one tends to think in terms of the various processes, tasks, and objects subject to management.

Branches of management theory also exist relating to nonprofits and to government: such as public administration, public management, and educational management. Further, management programmes related to civil-society organizations have also spawned programmes in nonprofit management and social entrepreneurship. Note that many of the assumptions made by management have come under attack from business ethics viewpoints, critical management studies, and anti-corporate activism.

As one consequence, workplace democracy has become both more common, and more advocated, in some places distributing all management functions among the workers, each of whom takes on a portion of the work. However, these models predate any current political issue, and may occur more naturally than does a command hierarchy. All management to some degree embraces democratic principles in that in the long term workers must give majority support to management; otherwise they leave to find other work, or go on strike.

Despite the move towards workplace democracy, command-and-control organization structures remain commonplace and the *de facto* organization structure. Indeed, the entrenched nature of command-and-control can be seen in the way that recent layoffs have been conducted with management ranks affected far less than employees at the lower levels of organizations. In some cases, management has even rewarded itself with bonuses when lower level employees have been laid off.

MANAGEMENT TOPICS

BASIC FUNCTIONS OF MANAGEMENT

Management operates through various functions, often classified as planning, organizing, leading/directing, and controlling/monitoring:

- *Planning*: Deciding what needs to happen in the future (today, next week, next month, next year, over the next 5 years, etc.) and generating plans for action.
- *Organizing*: (Implementation) making optimum use of the resources required to enable the successful carrying out of plans.
- *Staffing*: Job Analyzing, recruitment, and hiring individuals for appropriate jobs.
- *Leading/directing*: Determining what needs to be done in a situation and getting people to do it.
- Controlling/Monitoring, checking progress against plans, which may need modification based on feedback.

These functions are closely interlinked and interwoven in character. All executives or mangers, regardless of their area and position,a are o discharge these functions. These functions are the identifying marks by which a manger can be differentiated form a non-manager. Of the four functions, however, the upper or top executives are mostly preoccupied with the first two functions-planning and organization, while the lower-ranking executives are largely busy with direction and largely busy with direction and control. But the thinking functions of planning and organisation cannot be separated in to water-tight compartments from the doing functions of direction and control.

Irrespective of their levels and spheres of activity, executives are required to perform all the four functions in varying degrees:

- *Planning*: Is the rational and orderly thinking about ways and means for the realization of certain goals. It involves thought and decision pertaining to a future course of action. It anticipates and precedes action rather than making a reflective thinking abut the past events. Absence of planning before doing implies rashness, imprudence or shortsightedness in the performance of work. Before undertaking any work, is to be done, and who is to do the work. In considering these points, managers have to clarify objectives or goals and to evolve policies and procedures for guiding those who do the work; they have to chart the proposed lines of action with proper time schedules for the execution of work. For providing a factual basis for future action, managers have to map out a programme indicating the best course of action to be followed, fixing the targets and standards of work performance there in and evolving the strategies and remedies for possible hindrances to the smooth flow of work. In other words, programmes provide a complete road map for the guidance of managers to get things done through operators. In a sense, planning and decisions making are synonymous. Like decision making, planning is made for providing guide to action in problem areas. There is much common ground between the steps planning and of decision making-diagnosis of the problem, development of alternative, evaluation of alternative and selection of the best course of action. The decision phase of planning is so important that many writers have treated planning as a synonym of decision making.

- *Organization*: Provides the mechanism or apparatus for purposive, integrated and co-operative action by two or more persons with a view to implementing any plan. With a few persons, organization calls for the allocation of tasks to individuals and the requires the efforts of many people, several departments come into existence under the charge of different managers who are tied together neatly by authority relationships for integrated action. That is, organization involves the division and subdivision of activities, into departments, sections and jobs as well as the integration of activities and positions into a co-ordinated whole. The division of activities entails three thing, viz., determination of total activities, grouping of such activities and assignment of jobs to both managers and operators. The integration of activities is effected through positions which are bound together in a consistent pattern by the fabric of inter-relationships among enterprise functions, jobs and personnel. Delegation of authority is the cement that holds the positions together as one entity. The concept of organization has a number of implications.

- *First, it has two aspects*: Technical or mechanistic aspect pertaining to activities and social or humanistic aspect pertaining to people. For the personal contentment and social satisfaction of people, organization calls for the matching of jobs with individuals and vice-versa. Secondly, as a mechanism for action, organization is required to be changed when either the volume and nature of action or the personnel change. Although some amount of reorganization takes place with every personnel change, upper-level personnel change is more significant in effect. Thirdly, delegation of authority takes place not only between management members, but it extends to operators as well. In addition to managerial jobs, the operating jobs are also put to the same process of delegation.
- *Direction*: Is largely a function of human relations and motivation. This function is, of course, denoted variously by different writers, such as command, leadership, motivation, execution or actuating. The organizational mechanism is to be energized, activated or put into action for carrying out the management plan. This is what is actually done through directing function to set the organization in motion. But human beings are not inanimate cogs in a machine; they have emotions, aspirations, sentiments, capacity to participate or to withhold

such participation. Like a machine, they could not be ordered to do a predetermined work. With the purpose of inducing the members of the organization to put forth their best endeavour, managers direct the employees through the medium of leadership, guidance, supervision, communication and counselling. Direction involves personal and social-group relationships. The working terms are inspired and motivated to do the work willingly and whole-heartedly because of providing desirable job satisfaction and wanted team spirit.

- *Control*: Ensures qualitative and quantitative performance of work in the organization for completing plans and achieving objectives. Under the control function, measuring standards or yardsticks are established and communicated to managers so that they can regulate employee performance and can work by self-control. Moreover, control brings to light any management lapses that hinder satisfactory work progress, and thus it provides the managers with an opportunity to take remedial action before it is too late. The control function furnishes new data and facts that enable the managers to verify the accuracy of their decisions with regard to planning, organizing and directing functions. Controlling as a process involves measurement, evaluation and correction of performance in the light of standards established through planning. That planning and controlling are inter-dependent can be explained form the nature of either functions. As control forces events to conform to plans, three can exist no control without planning. Likewise, plans are not capable of self-achieving without the exercise of controlling function. In the past, control was work-focused rather than work-focused,

Areas and categories and implementations of management:

- Accounting management
- Agile management

- Applied Engineering (field)
- Association management
- Capability Management
- Change management
- Conflict management
- Commercial operations management
- Communication management
- Constraint management
- Cost management
- Crisis management
- Critical management studies
- Customer relationship management
- Decision making styles
- Design management
- Disaster management
- Distributed management
- Earned value management
- Educational management
- Engineering Management
- Environmental management
- Facility management
- Financial management
- Forecasting
- Human resources management
- Hospital management
- Hospitality management
- Hotel management
- Information technology management
- Innovation management
- Interim management
- Inventory management
- Knowledge management
- Land management
- Leadership
- Logistics management
- Lifecycle management
- Marine fuel management
- Marketing management

- Materials management
- Office management
- Operations management
- Organization development
- Perception management
- Practice management
- Programme management
- Project management
- Process management
- Performance management
- Product management
- Public administration
- Public management
- Quality management
- Records management
- Relationship management
- Resource management
- Restaurant management
- Risk management
- Rural management
- Skills management
- Social entrepreneurship
- Spend management
- Strategic management
- Stress management
- Supply chain management
- Systems management
- Talent management
- Time management
- Technology Management

2

Functions of Manager

Managers striving to meet their own department's goals often must overcome resistance born of competing agendas among staff in other business units, such as HR, accounting, and sales. These managers need to help everyone see that they are really all striving for the same corporate objectives. Essentially, they must succeed at team building. What is needed to resolve pervasive workplace conflicts is some smart decoding to unlock insight and understanding.

CHALLENGE S

Security organizations today are faced with inevitable conflicts in team building. These conflicts require creative resolutions that may be outside the security manager's toolbox. Even the most experienced managers have to approach each new conflict with renewed understanding, because no two conflicts are the same. A common mistake that security managers make is giving in to the tendency to settle for a superficial understanding of things. They do this because time is scarce and they have to understand and fix organizational problems and conflicts quickly and effectively so they are ready for another top priority.

Managers are also hardwired, as are all human beings, to seek the easiest route to peace in the workplace. Sound research reveals that the human brain functions more as an efficiency machine than a truth finder. It turns out that our brains want quick, easy, and simple certainty and will settle for artificial, incomplete truth just for the sake of closure. Take the usual level of understanding of something like a meeting, for example. It is rare for managers to go past the words they hear. They rarely try to understand how and why the other person is using these particular words, what they mean to the other person, or whether they accurately represent the original ideas and intentions.

Many security managers with too much work and too little time often just listen to a conversation in order to respond, rather than to really understand. It often takes aggressive listening to pick up the nuances in the speaker's manner. Other issues that frequently interfere with understanding include distractions such as impatience, personal agendas, more pressing priorities, noise, and bad timing.

For example, there is a natural conflict between the service goals of the operations department and the revenue-generating goals of the sales department. To really understand the operations versus sales conflict well enough to resolve it with a creative compromise, the manager will have to listen well enough to hear the sales person's frustrations and obstacles about the keen competition she is trying to overcome. Simultaneously, the manager will have to understand the operations leader's failed attempts to recruit the right employees and to fill odd schedules at low pay rates.

In the best situations, the company will have some sales people with previous exposure to the operations side of the house. There is nothing like doing someone else's job to increase personal empathy for the difficulties that are involved. In other cases, conflicts among departments may arise from frustrations much like that of police officers catching the bad guys and then being frustrated that the courts release them to the streets so quickly. The manager should help each of the parties to focus on doing their duties to the best of their abilities, without wasting time worrying about what happens that is outside of their control.

The manager must not ignore it. It is often through the process of patiently working out what is the underlying cause of a conflict that the solution to a difficult problem can be found. Working through a conflict can also help all those involved to get to the next stage of development in self-awareness, team building, and productivity. Finding this purpose is not easy because there are too many distractions getting in the way. These include all the noisy symptoms of turnover, sick-leave abuse, business cancellations, decreasing revenue, employee grievances, and low morale. Managers must look past these symptoms to decode the conflict.

In the sales versus operations conflict, the answer may simply be to focus each department on considering how what it does will affect the other side of the equation. Thus, if sales brings clients in indiscriminately, servicing them may not be possible. Therefore, sales may need to develop and follow more qualifying business development rules. Improved communications between the two conflicting groups is also generally advisable.

UNDERSTANDING

People need to feel that they are understood—and that takes considerable unselfish time and effort on the team's part. We all have probably reversed the order in seeking to be understood ourselves first, before we are willing to try to understand the other person. But that never gets results, especially when you are trying to build a team.

In the case of sales staff versus operational staff, both need to show a little empathy for the difficulty of each other's jobs. In cases where one group seems to be making unreasonable demands on, for example, the security department, it may be that the internal or external client does not understand why the demand is unreasonable or there may simply be a miscommunication about what the client is really requesting.

CONTEXT

Certain conditions create problem behaviour, and these conditions must be understood. Most people are not inherently mean, unmotivated, conniving, dumb, or cruel. Certain conditions can, however, provoke such behaviour. When managers learn to recognize these conditions, they can often put an end to them—and to the unpleasant behaviour that is generating conflict. In the case of a conflict between sales and operational staff, for example, the manager must to take the time to see what conditions—beyond the normal adversarial relationship—may be responsible for fueling the problem. The manager may find one particularly difficult new account was the proverbial straw that broke the camel's back or that three people quit without notice and thus put holes in the operations manager's schedule. And worse yet, these incidents may not have been openly communicated between the two groups, leaving sales to think that operations was simply inept.

The reality is that misunderstood emotions often hide the real issues that need to be resolved in these sorts of conflicts. And, of course, egos can create defensive communication and make matters worse. In the example of a demanding client, whether in-house or external, the manager may need to do some more homework and rapport building to better understand the client's true motivations. Just spending more time with clients to understand the pressures they are under may also do the trick.

ACTION

So what can a security manager do to mitigate the damage when employees are in the middle of a fierce conflict? The simple answer is to encourage all stakeholders in the conflict to focus on trying to clearly understand three areas of their team relationship, by asking and answering these three critical questions:

- What can I do to understand the other team members better?
- What are the conditions that are creating the problem behaviour we are all involved in?
- What am I failing to learn from this conflict?

By answering these three questions, the manager can get beyond the symptoms and assess the underlying problem. Understanding any conflict is three-quarters of its resolution. Fixing symptoms in team conflict isn't the help that is needed from the manager, because that approach doesn't work. The only thing that does work is to take the time and make the commitment to truly understand the conflict and the people who are in it and teaching them how to do the same. In a sense, team building can be a test of everyone's character and a chance to see how creative the team can be in resolving the conflict.

Ultimately, conflicts can never be solved without all stakeholders understanding the respective roles of the other players and the underlying cause of the problem.

3

Is Managing a Science or Art?

Is effective management an art or a science? Can it be both? How, exactly, should we think about the management of an organization? For years now, an often spirited art-versus science debate has ranged through an extensive body of literature on organizational management, and many subfields of management, including organizational behaviour and leadership.

An art-versus-science dialogue flourishes in business administration and related areas such as banking. The debate also continues in public administration and related areas such as health administration. Edward O. Wilson is not known as a contributor to the literature on management.

His early work is on the study of social insects, particularly ants. When he wrote Sociobiology: The New Synthesis, he inaugurated the scientific study of animal societies and communication. All told, he is the author of 18 books, and two of them, On Human Nature and The Ants, received the Pulitzer Prize.

He is currently Pellegrino University Research Professor and Honorary Curator of Entomology of the Museum of Comparative Zoology at Harvard. The Unity of Knowledge, Wilson entered the management as art versus science debate, simply because his book is about everything.

Consilience means a "jumping together," which is what Wilson wishes would happen with the natural and social sciences, the arts, politics, ethics, and every other form of human knowledge. He believes that all real phenomena, from galaxies and planets to people and subatomic particles, are based on material processes that are ultimately reducible to a small number of fundamental natural laws that explain everything. All explanations for everything are causal and all causes are material.

Wilson laments the increasingly complex, specialized, and fragmented state of human knowledge today and argues that the progress of science has always been a story of increasing consilience.

Is management an art or a science? If Wilson's belief in a unified theory of everything is correct, maybe we should be asking a much larger question. Is a consilience of all of our ways of thinking about management feasible?

WILSON'S DESCRIPTION OF SCIENCE

Science is extraordinary. With the aid of science, we can visualize matter across 37 orders of magnitude, from the largest galactic cluster to the smallest known particle. When science is done correctly, it can advise us in all of our day-to-day decisions and actions.

Wilson only acknowledges one resource limitation on the pursuit of scientific knowledge, a lack of data. Wilson is a natural scientist and, for him, science is not a philosophy or belief system. Science is science. It involves the expansion of sensory capacity by instruments, the classification of data, and the interpretation of data guided by theory. Scientific theories are falsifiable. They "are constructed specifically to be blown apart if proved wrong, and if so destined, the sooner the better".

Science is a method of doing things. It "is the organized, systematic enterprise that gathers knowledge about the world and condenses the knowledge into testable laws and principles". There are five "diagnostic features" that distinguish real science from pseudoscience.

The first is the repeatability of research results, preferably by independent investigators. The second is a reporting of research as simply and elegantly as possible. Third, scientific findings are subject to universally accepted and unambiguous scales of measurement. Fourth, scientific research stimulates new learning and new knowledge. And finally, science is consilient. Research results can be connected and proved consistent with one another.

Astronomy, biomedicine, and physiological psychology possess all of the features of real science. Astrology, ufology, creation science, and Christian Science do not. Wilson is silent on the matter, but there is certainly plenty of other support for placement of a science of management among the former and not the latter "sciences."

MANAGEMENT AS A SCIENCE

The origin of a modern science of management can be traced to the work of Frederick Taylor and Luther Gulick. However, when James D. Thompson helped launch the first issue of Administrative Science Quarterly, he remarked that "the possibility of a science of administration is only now coming to be taken seriously".

Thompson envisioned an applied science built from a combination of both deductive and inductive techniques for the development of logical, abstract, tested systems of thought. A science of administration would "be distinguished from administrative lore by the methods used to build that knowledge of administration".

From its struggle to be taken seriously in the 1950s, the science of management and administration has become a principal component of management theory and practice in the 1990s.

It is prominent in the academic literature and in business school classrooms. In public administration, a "new" science of administration is establishing a presence with the literature of traditional administrative science.

WILSON'S DESCRIPTION OF THE ARTS

Wilson thinks that the creative arts and science are very different from one another. Scientific knowledge is useful to us because it provides us with objective, verifiable knowledge about the real world around us. The creative arts, broadly defined, are also beneficial, but in a different way. They are in tune with our underlying "human nature," which Wilson say is an inborn ensemble of instinctive or "epigenetic rules" tha govern our behaviour.

Epigenetic rules are hereditary predispositions in ou mental development that are anchored in neural pathways ir our brain and are prescribed by our genes. Natural selectior favours epigenetic rules for behaviours that foster our survival for example, parental investment in children, territoriality taboos against incest, and keeping contractual agreements Taken together, these norms of behaviour or action become the elements of human cultures.

Artistic expression, then, arises from and resonates with our human nature. Wilson argues that creativity, ethics, culture, in fact all products of the mind, are materially grounded in physiochemical activities of the brain in interaction with the human body.

Emotions link artistic expression and human nature. If we see a movie that encourages or condones incest, it arouses a feeling of disgust because the images on the screen trigger a negative emotional response linked to one of the underlying epigenetic rules (the incest taboo) that define human nature. A knowledge of words, images, archetypes, and abstractions that resonate with our epigenetic rules helps us make decisions that support our survival as social beings.

MANAGEMENT AS ART

When viewed as an art, effective management is a remarkable, but natural, expression of human behaviour. It is intuitive, creative, and flexible. Lee G. Bolman and Terrence E. Deal, authors of Reframing Organizations: Artistry, Choice, and Leadership, see managers as leaders and artists who are able to develop unique alternatives and novel ideas about their organizations' needs.

They are attuned to people and events around them and learn to anticipate the turbulent twists and turns of organizational life: Artistry in management is neither exact nor precise. Artists interpret experience and express it in forms that can be felt, understood, and appreciated by others. Art allows for emotion, subtlety, ambiguity. An artist reframes the world so that others can see new possibilities.

Modern organizations rely too little on art in their search for attributes like quality, commitment, and creativity. "The leader as artist relies on images as well as memos, poetry as well as policy, and reflection as well as command". Like management science, management as art is also well established in the general literature on management and leadership.

It is also prominent in business administration and public administration.

SEARCH FOR CONSILIENCE À LA WILSON

Wilson assumes that all phenomena are based on material processes that are causal and, "however long and tortuous the sequences," ultimately reducible to the laws of physics. A consilience of knowledge about the management of organizations would demand a vision capable of sweeping from whole societies to an individual human brain. It would involve both reduction and synthesis.

To dissect something into its elements is consilience by reduction, and to reconstitute it is consilience by synthesis. Wilson offers an example of consilience in practice from his early research on ants.

To explain communication within an ant colony (e.g., an internal alarm alerting an entire colony to an attack by a predator), Wilson and his associates studied an ant colony across four levels of organization, from superorganism (the whole colony), then reductively to organism (individual ants), to glands and sense organs, and finally to molecules (pheromones).

He also worked in the opposite direction (synthesis) when he predicted the meanings of signals observed in the colony (e.g., "alarm, danger" versus "food, follow me") by linking various signals to matching changes in the molecular composition and concentration of individual ant pheromones. The result was a comprehensive or "holistic" study of ant communication. Follow the lead of Wilson, and the strategy in the search for consilience in management theory and practice would require the pursuit of coherent cause-and-effect explanations for all relevant phenomena across multiple levels of organization from society to neuron.

The cutting edge of investigation would be reductionism. And dealing with increasing complexity from the brain, to an organization, to society as a whole would be the major challenge in the search for consilience in approaches to the management of organizations.

MORE INCLUSIVE SEARCH FOR CONSILIENCE

Wilson readily acknowledges the limited reach of conventional scientific thinking when he notes that "at each level of organization, especially at the living cell and above, phenomena exist that require new laws and principles, which still cannot be predicted from those at more general levels". Part of this limitation may be rooted in a reluctance to make a distinction between complex systems-between non-living systems, living systems, and living systems with people in them.They differ from one another.

Probing the differences would open the door to new kinds of data and new ways to think about complex systems, especially complex human systems. Although Wilson's search for consilience is courageous and sweeping, he is too confined to traditional theoretical perspectives from the physical sciences.

Several years ago, Paul Diesing said that if we knew the whole truth our "predictions would always be correct; but since all existing theories (and approaches) are incomplete and partly false, it is better to bring together a variety of partial theories to better approximate the whole truth". Wilson unnecessarily limits his consideration of all of the ways we come to understand things.

Playwright Tom Stoppard contends that "science and art are nowadays beyond being like each other. Sometimes they seem to be each other". For Wilson, the arts were a necessary "prescientific" step in our evolutionary quest for knowledge.

But he argues that, unlike science, the arts do not contribute anything truly concrete and verifiable to our knowledge of reality.

In fact, he thinks that a future consilience of scientific knowledge may include an explanation of art. Wilson unnecessarily minimizes the ability of human imagination, like that commonly exhibited in the arts and in the sciences-in symbols, images, and metaphor-to contribute anything tangible to a consilience or "jumping together" of all the ways in which we come to understand and explain the world.

MANAGING HUMAN SYSTEMS

When management is considered a science, the knowledge that a manager uses to keep an organization moving effectively in a given direction largely has its origin in rigorous scientific research acquired in strict adherence to the scientific method. When management is viewed as art, knowledge about how to keep an organization moving successfully in the right direction is in tune with primal human nature and springs from a manager's intuition, imagination, and creativity.

It is apparent that inclusion of the well established and enduring body of literature and research that addresses management as an art in a consilience with our accumulated knowledge about the scientific management of organizations will require a significant change of Wilson's rules for consilience.

While it is true that the great successes of the natural sciences have been achieved by reducing and explaining physical phenomena in terms of their constituent elements, organizations involve human perceptions, interactions, emotions and feelings-all things that cannot be dissected and reassembled to explain how an organization works. And while mathematics is the "natural language" of physics, it is not the natural language of organizations.

If a consilience of the art and science of management is to happen, it will require a greater general willingness to think about organizations as complex, nonlinear human systems, and it will require an open-minded exploration of the as yet unproven explanatory power of metaphor as a theoretical concept. New scientific theories evolving out of a variety of disciplines, including physics, biology, and computer science, are generating new ways to think about organizations as living nonlinear human systems.

Human systems possess the dynamism and other characteristics of non-living nonlinear systems (e.g., the weather) and the familiar features of other living systems, including the ability to grow, recreate themselves, and die. And, because human systems include people, the metaphor generated and used exclusively by people is a unique feature of all living human systems.An organization, like all human systems, is made up of an extremely varied collection of "parts" that, taken together, form the organization's tangible or material basis of existence.

The parts of a typical organization include managers, employees, offices, equipment, written policies and procedures, e-mail, logos, memos, and an almost infinite variety of other things. An organization exists as highly interactive and meaningful relations between all of the parts that constitute it in interaction with elements of its environment.

An organization cannot be successfully reduced or dissected with the instruments of physics or chemistry, which are the sciences of matter. A living human organization is not entirely quantifiable or explainable by the methods of the conventional physical sciences. The concept of emergent properties or behaviours is critical to understanding an organization as a complex, living nonlinear system. The emergent behaviour of living systems may be expressed by the behaviour of the elements of a system in interaction with one another and the environment, but the emergent behaviour of a system is not a property of any individual element and it cannot be explained as a summation of the properties of those elements.

Examples include behaviour in such diverse nonlinear living systems as Wilson's ant colonies, the Department of Defence, traffic jams, and the Dow Jones composite stock market index. Like all living organisms, organizations contain within themselves a way to control relationships between their parts and relationships between their parts and the environment.

In a biological system, DNA is the instrument or plan that distributes the control of interactive relationships between the parts of the system to the parts themselves. The resulting relationships between parts of the living system (muscle groups, nervous system, organs, etc.) then express life, the emergent behaviour unique to all living organisms. The property of "aliveness" can be traced to an organism's DNA. The corresponding mechanism or internal frame of reference that distributes control of interactive relationships to the elements or parts of an organization is a common body of metaphor (CBM).

Through metaphor, our understanding of things is acquired, defined, and organized in terms of our existing knowledge of things already retained in our minds as remembered images, ideas, symbols, and stereotypes. We come to know things in terms of what is already known to us. Our understanding of ourselves and the world around us, in turn, guides our behaviour.

Acquired through shared experiences, an organization's unique CBM influences the way organization members characteristically interact with each other and with other people, and how they interact with elements of the physical environment.

In more conventional terms, an organization's CBM is comparable to its culture. "A culture may be conceived as a network of beliefs and purposes in which any string in the net pulls and is pulled by others, thus perpetually changing the configuration of the whole". Like organizational cultures, a CBM defines and, at the same time, is defined in interactive relationships between the parts of an organization.

Over time, the resultant interactive relationships between parts of an organization, in interaction with a CBM and with the features of the organization's environment, express the identity of an organization as a living human system.

Organizations are physical systems like the weather, Wilson's ant colonies, and other complex systems, but the vital presence of a common body of metaphor or CBM distinguishes human organizations from other complex systems.

Wilson may be correct when he assumes that all tangible phenomena are based on material processes that are causal and, however long and tortuous the sequences, such phenomena are ultimately reducible to the laws of physics; but like it or not, an organization is more than physical phenomena and causal relationships.

Certainly, in its early stages at least, a consilience of knowledge about the management of organizations will have to consider the inclusion of knowledge beyond that obtained exclusively from research grounded in the traditional sciences.

COMPLEXITY THEORY AND METAPHOR

At first glance, complexity theory and the concept of metaphor seem particularly well suited to the task of developing new ways to think about organizations as complex human systems. However, Wilson thinks that the value of both the theory and the concept is, at best, very uncertain. If he is correct, they will contribute little if anything to a consilience of our knowledge about the management of organizations.

Wilson knows that all living systems are complex and he acknowledges the work of a group of computer-oriented "complexity theorists" who are searching for precise mathematical models or algorithms to explain the emergence of such phenomena as cells, ecosystems, and minds. He writes that he is impressed by their sophistication and spirit, and his heart is with them, but his mind is not, "at least not yet".

Wilson thinks that, so far at least, complexity theorists lack data, their propositions need more detail, and their ceases tell us little that is really new. His real concern, however, is that none of the elements of complexity theory has anything like the generality and adherence to factual detail that he would like to see in a true scientific theory. Living systems are complex, but after giving all due respect to complexity theory, Wilson still thinks that "the laws of physics and chemistry . . .

are enough to do the job, given sufficient time and research funding". If Wilson is skeptical about complexity theory, he sees even less scientific value in the concept of metaphor. This is curious, because he recognizes the importance of metaphor, especially in the creative arts.

And when he writes about culture, he could easily be writing about a CBM or common body of metaphor. "Culture, rising from the productions of many minds that interlace and reinforce one another over many generations, expands like a growing organism into a universe of seemingly infinite possibility".

It "is historical; includes ideas, patterns, and values . . . is based upon symbols; and . . . each society creates culture and is created by it". The inborn ability to generate metaphors with ease and move them fluidly from one context to another is a special human adaptive power granted to the arts by the genetic evolution of the brain. But Wilson argues that art is the antithesis of science because it has no scientific meaning or value.

Metaphor does not lend itself to reduction and cause-and-effect scientific analysis. Therefore, by its very nature, metaphor cannot precisely explain why anything occurs and cannot contribute anything meaningful to a consilience of factual knowledge about the management of organizations. Is a consilience of the art and science of managing organizations possible?

Maybe. Wilson believes that the search for a consilience of all scientific knowledge will provide coherent explanations for all relevant phenomena across multiple levels of complexity, from neuron and brain, to organization, and to society as a whole. He begins with the assumption that all tangible phenomena are based on material processes that are ultimately reducible to the laws of physics.

All explanations are causal and all causes are material. Unfortunately, his beginning assumptions are far too restrictive to guide the formative stages of a consilience of our knowledge about organizations and other complex human systems. Art and science both foster new and creative ways to understand organizations and communicate what we know about them. They both generate and employ metaphors of management that help us form our perceptions, assumptions, and new ideas about organizations. Both inspire our imagination.

Research in the art and science of management will continue systematically to gather knowledge about the behaviour of people in organizations and try to present that knowledge in new and testable theories, concepts, and hypotheses. But future research also must be pursued with enough flexibility to permit the emergence and investigation of entirely new knowledge about organizations and the way we manage them.

4

Ethics and Responsibilities of Managers

Recently, considerable attention has been paid to ethical issues in the public and private sectors, specifically, in developing and administrating codes of ethics as means for improving and promoting the moral behaviour of the organization's members. A code of ethics is a statement of principles that describes desirable professional conduct and guides individuals in resolving ethical problems. Almost all organizations and professional organizations have codes of ethics, yet there is no agreement as to how useful and effective they are.

Some researchers maintain that business and government executives regard codes as a valuable way of promoting ethics. Others contend that codes are irrelevant to practitioners, not useful for promoting ethical conduct, or self-serving mechanisms designed to promote the economic interests of the professions.

Moreover, others criticize them because they are not based on systematic moral reasoning or firmly grounded in a well-developed ethical theory and for being overly legalistic and restrictive and that they do little to foster the internalization of the values and norms they are designed to promote.

These criticisms, but focuses on the problem of internalization. Without effective internalization a code is a meaningless document that at best can only expect blind obedience to its precepts. The argues that effective internalization is most likely to occur when members of an organization clarify and construct their integrated values systems and when the code is formulated and adopted through a process of democratic participation.

If codes are formulated and disseminated through a shared collective process and thus reflect the collective values of organizational members, the likelihood of a successful assimilation of the code's content is increased.

Unlike codes of ethics in business, which are designed primarily to promote organizational effectiveness and professional courtesy, codes of ethics in public service organizations are designed to protect and serve the "public interest." Serving the public implies a fiduciary undertaking, which places high responsibility on the part of public servants. The public servant is entrusted with power because of the belief that he or she possesses the personal integrity and professional competence to safeguard the public affairs and to promote the public good.

Codes of ethics in public service organizations should serve at least three purposes:

- Educate the public about the mission of the organization;
- Foster an ethical climate;
- Provide guidance for resolving ethical problems:
  - Codes articulate the organization's values, norms, and obligations to the public. They announce to the public that the organization seeks to operate within a specific set of ethical boundaries, and as such they facilitate public scrutiny, providing forums that allow citizens to question officials about their practices. The public's familiarity with the code's provisions inspires confidence and trust in the public service.
  - Codes of ethics in public service organizations do not provide strict guidelines on how to avoid or resolve common ethical dilemmas, and at time ignore crucial ethical issues. For example, Article III, Section 3, of the ASPA Code of Ethics provides that "public servants should

demonstrate personal integrity by which he or she is committed to guard against conflict of interest or its appearance: for example, nepotism, improper outside employment, misuse of public resources or the acceptance of gifts." What is personal integrity, and how is one to avoid a conflict between a person's private gain and that same person's official duties in a position of trust? The code does not specify the meaning of personal integrity and what precaution one has to employ to guard against conflicts of interest.

- Let me specify the differences between personal integrity and conflict of interest. Personal integrity suggests both honesty and coherence to the self. As Philip Selznick observes, "To performance with integrity is to have values and take them seriously .... To strive for integrity is to ask: What is our direction? What are our unifying principles? And how do these square with the claims of morality?" Philip Selznick suggests that the idea of integrity presume a core of morally justifiable commitments that need to be discovered and articulated.
- Similarly, Dobel asserts that personal integrity describes a condition whereby individuals can hold multiple commitments and balance among them in a morally defensible manner. Dobel claims that personal integrity presupposes the existence of central values that people have acquired independently prior to roles taken in their professional life and they can evolve and change in light of accumulated personal and professional experience. Both Dobel and Selznick imply that personal commitments need to be discovered, clarified, and reestablished.
- This requires an application of a method that permits clarification of personal values resulting in a construction of a clear cohesive value

system. This allows people to give plausible justification of their choices and to integrate various dimensions of their lives in a manner consistent with their most basic commitments.

- Conflict of interest occurs when personal interests come into conflict with an obligation to serve the interest of another. Some conflict is unavoidable, since at times interests of employees invariably differ from those in the organization.
- However, one way to minimize conflicts is to be aware of the potential for conflict. Many conflict-of-interest situations can be avoided if individuals exercise self-control in the face of strong temptations and situational pressures and are able to separate personal from professional interests.
- It is true that personal integrity enhances one's capacity to deal effectively with conflicts of interest or even avoid them. Yet it should be clarified in the code that the two concepts (*i.e.*, personal integrity and conflict of interest) are distinct and not identical, and that codes of ethics should provide a detailed explanation and operational guidance about crucial ethical issues, to avoid misinterpretation and misrepresentation.
- Codes should be accompanied with a set of commentary that elaborates central concepts, rules, principles, and provisions specifying how professionals should act. And, before applying these codes, public service administration is required to go through a stepwise procedure that might facilitate internalization of the code's provisions.
- Codes of ethics are formulated by a select group of policy makers who do not consult "line" employees when drafting the codes. These codes reflect policy makers' own personal views and

existing organizational rules, but not necessarily the experiences of a cross section of employees. Hosmer, for instance, argues that senior managers write codes as a way of influencing the way employees think, and that codes can be seen as managerial efforts to control subordinates. There is a substantial body of research on business ethics that support his view. Our argument is that ownership and shared commitments are key ingredients for a successful assimilation of codes of ethics. Consequently, codes should be developed by a process that involves as many members of the organization as possible, members who actively explore and articulate the true authentic values that should be incorporated in the code.

– Given the considerable size and complexity of government, it would be impossible to draft a simple code that could be applied effectively and fairly across all agencies. Codes designed for the police are not likely to be useful for schoolteachers or health care providers. Although all government employees may be civil servants and share many concerns about their work, many also belong to different professions within the civil service whose sense of vocation is defined by their professional identities. Each profession dictates rules that are derived from roles distinct to each profession. When each profession has distinctive types of expectations and requirements and thus designs a unique code of ethics, it generates a great deal of diversity in codes and results in a lack of communication among different governmental agencies and in misrepresentation of the entire civil service domain. With such a great diversity of codes of ethics it is difficult to reach a common ground that unifies all members of the public service organization, and that serves as a basis for drafting a code that can be applied effectively across all units and departments in the public service sector. However, by means of a democratic process, an attempt must be made to reach a common ground despite existing differences, expectations, and interests. Efforts should be directed towards establishing a unified core set of values that is acceptable to the majority of civil servants.

- Codes are ineffective in dealing with systematic corruption where an organization purports to embrace a code of ethics, but whose internal practices violate it. The cultural component embedded in an organization has a powerful effect on the ethical conduct of organization's members, and thus professional codes of ethics do not prevent unethical behaviour.
- When public servants face ethical problems, they rely upon their subjective understanding and interpretation of existing normative cultural structures, and do not necessarily consult the legal or ethical requirements. Rather, public servants follow deep-rooted existing social norms, which inspire them to performance as they do.
- These existing social norms compose the organizational culture, which serves as a vehicle for imparting and maintaining the enduring values that animate life in the organization. The actual rules of practice may be an elaboration of the espoused rules or may be incongruent with them. Codes do not reflect the collective values of organizations' members; they are imposed as an external guidance.
- Efforts should be made to incorporate employees' values so that there is a congruity between an organization's values and its

members' values. In other words, formulation of codes of ethics requires understanding and consideration of the cultural component and should reflect the diverse values system expressed by employees.

- Codes are designed for public relations purposes. They are self-serving in protecting the economic interests of the profession rather than protecting the public from unethical behaviour. Administrators are concerned with the public image the organization produces and not so much with the assimilation and internalization of ethical values. Codes become powerful tools in the hands of managers who are trained to elevate the organization's competitive advantage, to enhance institutional prestige, and to mystify institutional behaviour. In their efforts to gain public support and legitimacy organizations create a code that in part is a "myth" of a service orientation that stems from professional ideology that maintains that professionals adhere to the ideal of service to all of humanity. Codes are simply public relations pieces furthering a professional ideology disguising their primarily self-serving machinations. Codes become an artificial means of supposedly gaining public trust.
- However, an authentic trust relationship can be developed when positive attitudes about the other's motives exist. Trust emerges when an individual or the public perceives that the trustee (*i.e.*, the civil service organization) intends to perform an action that is beneficial. Thus, instead of using the code of ethics as a manipulating device, organizations should concentrate on ameliorating the mutually beneficial relationship with the public by letting the public participate in the formulation process of the code's provisions.

- Organizations need to set up a mechanism by which issues of public concern are given voice and are reflected in the code. This could occur by permitting participation of public representatives in the decision-making process, voicing their views and values about critical issues that are at stake and to reassure that the "public interest" is sufficiently served by the public organization. Through this method the organization could enhance and regain public confidence and trust. The participatory democratic process fosters an open debate about what the "public interest" is and allows the organization to respond in good faith to the public needs.
- The last point of criticism is about how codes of ethics deal with two interrelated issues: acceptability (*i.e.,* if the code is acceptable by all members of an organization) and enforceability (*i.e.,* if an organization has an enforcement mechanism for implementing the code and secure commitment). In a recent study conducted by Bowman and Williams, 750 public servants were surveyed. The researchers found that 90% of the respondents believed that codes of ethics could be effective if they meet two conditions, acceptability and enforceability. If administrators and employees accept codes, and if the organization has an effective enforcement mechanism that secures compliance, then they may encourage public servants to comply with the code. Acceptability refers to the performance of getting people to conform to the ideal identified in the code of ethics. Enforcement refers to processes whereby disciplinary actions are taken against members who are found to be guilty of code violations and alternatively to a system of rewards granted for members who exhibit a proper behaviour.

There is no point in formulating a code if it does not contain a consistent and vigourous enforcement process. I argue that acceptability and enforcement of the code's provisions are interconnected and are both generated through a collaborative participatory democratic process. The code's provision can be acceptable to employees only when employees feel that they are part of the formulation process of the code. Each member in the organization is in pursuit of a common value ground that serves as a base from which a shared code of ethics is established.

Acceptability can be generated if the managers reach out to their employees and public representatives, educate them about the values and norms of the organization, and invite them to participate in a group discussion and to express their values. Only by becoming active participants in the formulation process of codes of ethics will acceptability of the code's guidelines among the groups' members grow.

Likewise, if the codes' provisions are accepted and internalized, then the enforcement process is less needed. Instead of focusing on sanctioning or rewarding members for their actions, efforts should be directed towards transforming individuals' values system to reach the point when employees have modified their values system and have taken the accepted norms or rules as their own.

The prime goal should be to secure acceptability and enforcement through educational strategies that direct members of the organization to internalize the code's provisions and promote self-discipline and self-control. The more self-control employees exhibit, the less organizations need to oversee employees' ethical conduct and enforce discipline. Overall, the ultimate purpose of codes is to get members to internalize the spirit of their provisions. To sum up, together these seven sets of criticisms reveal deep skepticism about the relevancy and effectiveness of codes of ethics. Indeed many of the critics cited in this section have little or no use for codes. Some think they are ineffective but harmless, while others think they are counterproductive and dangerous.

But all agree they rarely achieve their stated purposes. Given these problems, there are two choices. Either codes should be abandoned altogether because at best they are ineffectual and at worst they are used by the organization to mystify the public. Alternatively, the positive values of codes can be taken seriously and we can search for a way to overcome these seven sets of criticism and design a plan for effective formulation and implementation of a code of ethics.

I believe that there is enough evidence to suggest that codes can work. Our central point is that codes are most likely to work when the values they promote are internalized, and members of the organization adopt their central messages. The focus of the following discussion is on the process of internalization. We elaborate in the meaning of the concept of internalization and then propose a schema that facilitates internalization of code of ethics.

The argues that internalization of the code's provisions is most likely to occur under two interrelated conditions:

1. When members of an organization clarify, articulate, and establish integrated values systems.
2. When the ethical code is formulated and adopted as a consequence of a participatory democratic process that permits a collective contribution of each member in the group to the formulation of a code. The end result should be that members of the organization are able to relate the code's provisions to their own personal integrated values systems. Let me first focus on the concept of internalization.

INTERNALIZATION

Internalization is a central concept in all three branches of moral psychology, cognitive developmental theories of moral judgment, social learning theories of moral behaviour, and psychoanalytic theories of motivational process.

Although all three approaches may provide important insights, the psychoanalytic theory developed by major figures such as Hartmann, Loewold, Schafer and others is most useful in helping to understand how codes can be put into practice.

Hartmann views internalization in terms of a biological, evolutionary, and adaptive functioning of an organism. He characterized it as the reciprocal relationship between an individual's inner world and his or her environment. Hartmann, internalization involves four separate processes: "adaptation, differentiation, mastery and synthesis." Internalization occurs when the individual withdraws from the external world and then returns to it with improved mastery and greater ability to integrate the new stimuli. Prior to internalization of an external stimuli, that is, a new value or norm, individuals need to undertake two steps: First they need to seclude themselves from the imposed external stimuli.

A detachment from external pressure enables one to examine his or her inner world and clarify personal experience composed of set of values and dispositions, and to see if there is a congruence between one's values system and the new imposed value. After stepping back from the situation and reflecting on one's personal values and perspectives, the second step is to return back to the situation and confront it with greater control over the course of the event, that is, to decide either to adapt the new imposed value, hold to it with improved mastery and improved ability to justify it, or alternatively, reject the new value and stick with the old values system. Internalization is best occurred when a cohesive and integrated values system is established and thus enhances one's capacity to cope effectively and confidently with environmental determinants. Loewald argues that internalization is a process of transformation by which relationship and interactions between the individual and his or her environment are changed.

The external relationship is transformed into an internal relationship, which constitutes the character composed of habits, dependencies, interests, and values. Schafer views internalization as processes by which the subject transforms real or imagined characteristics of his or her environment into the inner world. Internalization is closely related to a learning process by which a modification of one's behaviour on the basis of previous behaviour takes place. Behaviour is understood to include thinking, feelings, and other subjective processes. Internalization becomes real when the acquisition of a new norm is completed and when individuals have taken the norms or rules on as "their own" and are not dependent on external forces to initiate them or force them to adhere to them. Based on these definitions internalization can be viewed as a process of change by which an individual's inner world is transformed as a result of a reciprocal interaction with the environment. Both individuals in an organization and organizations need to undergo substantial changes.

Individuals should change their belief systems, and organizations need to change the way they make decisions and the priority they give to ethical considerations. Neither of these changes is easy. Successful change in individuals and organizations requires two conditions: the first is that individuals in an organization must be aware of their subjective experience composed of personal values, interests, preferences, and implicit theories about the self and about the others. This subjective experience shapes individuals' social conduct and serves at the same time as a basis from which change emerges.

The individuals' ability to change their behaviour and to internalize new evidence or a new set of norms is largely dependent on whatever implicit theories and values they have at their disposal, and if their experience matches the external world. The process of internalization is an experiential learning process that focuses on a continuous reciprocal interaction between the individuals' inner world and external world. Individuals are not simply passive reactors to external influences; they select, organize, and transform the stimuli that impinge on them, and this results in a revision of their implicit theories and adoption of a new type of behaviour.

The second condition is that if an organization wishes to induce change, it is beneficial to use the group as an effective mechanism for exerting a strong influence on the actual ethical behaviour exhibited by each member in the group. There is evidence that indicates that when individuals interact in a group, they often produce group decisions that are characterized by a high level of moral reasoning than when they performance alone. A modification of behaviour on an individual basis is not enough to produce change, especially when groups, not individuals, decide the content of the code of conduct. To conclude, if organizations wish to regulate the ethical behaviour of their employees and consequently produce an effective internalization process, they must take into consideration these two necessary conditions, that is, the individual subjective experience and the group dynamics factor.

THE PROPOSED PLAN

Following the process of change two subsequent processes may emerge, a self-exploratory process in which the individual clarifies his or her convictions and values and a group dialogue that generates a shared value system. These two factors are interconnected. There is no point in participating in a group discussion without a preparatory stage by which each individual clarifies values and integrates them into a well-defined cohesive system. If one has to persuade the other about the wrongs or the rightness of a particular type of behaviour, he or she has to feel confident about his or her implicit theories and moral points of views. Moreover, as an individual's own values are clarified, he or she may also gain greater appreciation of others' views.

The self-exploratory process involves values clarification. Rokeach, values have two important functions: They serve as internal standards that guide behaviour, keep evaluating reality, distinguish between right and wrong, and provide guidance in resolving conflicts; and they are motivational forces that push individuals towards attaining their goals. Clarifying values—whether individually or in groups—helps individuals and groups sort through, analyse, and assign priorities to the range of existing values. For example, through this process, one might discover that harmony and tolerance are far more important values than excellence and competitiveness. This in turn might affect how one would structure organization and formulate codes of ethics. Just these concerns arise in the current debate about privatization of public services. Too little attention has been focused on the potential impact of privatization on employee rights and the decision to privatize does not concern the employees' interests. To date the debate has been shaped by free-market economic theory that emphasizes the values of profit making, competitiveness, and efficiency.

Although important, these values may not coincide with the employees' concerns with harmony, tolerance, and decency. In the rush to privatization, public administrators have not been successful in articulating the traditional values of public service and have had difficulties defining what makes the public sector distinctive. All administrators impose too often new values that reflect a new organizational trend, and assume that the employees will instantaneously internalize these new values. Yet, lingering the employees' values may result in employees being resistant and noncommitted to new organizational goals and missions.

When leaders should make an effort to institute many changes in an organization, they should also transform employees' values in ways that generate a fit between the new organizational values and the employees' existing values systems. In their efforts to pursue collective objectives they should collaborate with their employees, learn from their experience and their value-laden knowledge, and jointly construct a common values framework that is acceptable for the majority of employees and serves as a basis for establishing a collective vision of change.

To be effective codes must depend on successful internalization that involves clarification of one's values and participatory group decision-making processes. What are the processes or methods by which values can be retraced and clarified? There are at least three strategies for eliciting and clarifying personal values: narrative inquiry, application of a case study approach, and generating a value journal. Narrative inquiry, can illuminate one's authentic life experience and permit examination, evaluation, and justification of values, preferences, and feelings in a personal context. As such it can reveal the origins of one's experiences and actions and identify values that govern one's lives. Narrative inquiry is very useful when examining relationships between fundamental values and currently expressed preferences. It forces one to join issues and defend (and perhaps alter) preferences in light of these values. Thus, narrative inquiry helps to establish a clear and integrated value system. In the context of employment and organization it can help nurture individual integrity, and the integration of personal values and professional goals.

Typically, narrative inquiry operates as follows: The employee selects a critical incident that has occurred during his or her professional life. Following the description of the event, significant values, feelings, and thoughts emerge. By focusing on one crucial incident (that reflects a selective portion of one's life experience), it is possible to discover the causes of the incident, justify emerging values, and find out whether these values are likely to fail or to cohere with the individual's entire life project.

Reflection upon one's life story allows the individuals to examine the relationship between basic values and current preferences and to make connection between the specific incident to other life events. A narrative allows the individual to reflect on these emerging values, evaluate them, redefine them, and establish an integrated value framework. Narrative inquiry can be used independently or with the assistance of an external facilitator.

A second strategy that is useful in clarifying values is the case-study approach. This involves presentation by an external facilitator (e.g., the leader) of vignettes or hypothetical scenarios that probe individuals' thought processes and reveal their hidden values and assumptions about problems presented in the scenarios. The confrontation with a hypothetical case creates a situation in which individuals must respond with a moral point of view. The case study serves as external stimuli that triggers individuals' internal world and reference to past experiences and thus allows them to establish their own ideas and moral views about the problems posed in the case study. A third way that facilitates clarification of values is a development of a value journal. Based on the value statements that emerge from the individual's narratives, and the value statements that arise while the individual responds to the presented case study, it is possible to draw comparisons and gradually develop a value journal. Comparing the two sets of values permits identification of differences or similarities in the employees' value statements.

This method requires the assistance of the leader or the manager who examines with the employee issues of consistency and validity of each value. The leader and the employee can jointly evaluate the values and determine their priorities. The evaluation process allows exploring how and why certain values emerge, what their level of importance 15, and which of them have personal significance and are worth pursuing. This method fosters the reconstruction of an integrated value system.

All of these three methods—narrative inquiry, the case study approach, and the value journal—facilitate the value clarification process, which we have argued is the first necessary condition for effective internalization. The next requirement for effective internalization is a group discussion. Group discussion permits exchange of ideas and moral points of view among an organization's members. It is through this process that a code of ethics can be constructed. Group discussion is highly successful in insuring voluntary adherence to a code's provisions and that the values in the code will be internalized. The code should be determined by all those members in the group who are to be affected by it and should certainly not be imposed by executives or senior administrators.

If successful, this process should lead participants—administrators, employees, and public representatives—to feel ownership in the code, and that they have played an integral role in a creative endeavor of great significance, which implies collective responsibility and personal liability for one's conduct. Ownership leads to a greater commitment to obey the code's rules and provisions. The determination of the code's provisions should be conducted by means of a democratic process that permits the legitimate interests and concerns of various affected groups (*i.e.*, members of the organization and public representatives) to be recognized and reflected in the code.

Each group member presents his or her view while attempting to persuade others about their particular oral point of view. Members of the group convey the merits of their positions and to persuade others in the group that adhering to their particular ethical perspectives and personal held values is going to be advantageous to the organization, employees, and the overall organizational growth. At this point the two interrelated conditions specified (*i.e.*, personal values clarification and group discussion) link together. That is, in order to persuade other members in the group about the rightness of one's position it is necessary to establish credibility and reinforce the personal position clearly and vividly. For this, individuals must prepare themselves in terms of clarifying personal positions, goals, and attitudes; eliciting some supporting evidence; and developing sound and justifiable arguments. One cannot advocate a new value or idea without learning, reflecting, and clarifying one's values and perspectives.

Therefore, it is imperative to go first through the first phase—the self-discovery process—and then engage in a dialogue aiming to convince others that one's values are important and should be incorporated in a shared code of ethics. The combination between the two phases, that is, clarification of personal values and active participation in a group discussion, is needed for effective internalization.

Effective internalization is about advocating your own personal values but at the same time testing them and revising them in light of other values systems expressed by other colleagues. Individual members of the organization can transform their values through their interaction with their environment (*i.e.*, other members in the group). We have described an elaborated multistage process from individual values clarification to the collective construction of a code of ethics. One reasonable question is how does an organization deal with the fact that once constructed codes are reviewed and rewritten only once in a great while? How do individuals renew their commitment to the codes they once helped construct? How do new members absorb the ethos of the codes? These are challenging and difficult questions.

Our response is that organizations should hire individuals whose ethical norms are congruent with the existing code. This can be done through "psychological contracts" that specify the reciprocal obligations and expectations between employees and the organization. This has worked well in other contexts, and it is likely to be successful with codes as well. Officials who recruit potential employees can learn about the candidates' values and interests and at the same time communicate the values embedded in an organization code of ethics. The psychological contract will keep clarifying this process. Despite the psychological contract's importance in selecting and hiring the right people, by itself a contract is insufficient to ensure an integrated ethical climate governed by a collective shared code of ethics.

It must be supplemented by an ongoing critical review of the ethical code and the organization's mission. This is due to external environmental pressures coming from the public or customers who impose new ethical demands on the organization. The public scrutinizes the ethical conduct of organization members and indirectly impacts the organization's values and mission. Codes of ethics in the public sector play a pivotal role. Their function is to enhance public servants' ethical conduct and to convey to the public that public officials are genuinely committed to pursuing an honourable public service reflecting the public good.

In order for public servants to pursue the code's provisions effectively they need to follow the codes' content out of persuasion and internalization and not out of fear and sanctions. That formulation and administration of codes of ethics should involve the following two steps: The first step concerns an understanding, clarification, and articulation of personal values and commitments of each member in the organization. This process amplifies one's capacity to balance among competing claims, values, and needs. The individuals detach themselves from external stimuli and carefully examine their own inner world composed of values and gradually establish an integrated and well-defined values system. This reflective process elevates moral awareness and results in an integrated moral self, capable of exercising self-restraint and self-discipline and regaining personal mastery.

The second step involves a democratic participatory process whereby each member provides his or her values input, discusses the merits of his or her position, and contributes collectively to the formulation of a code. Discovering, articulating, and determining the meaning of the principles and norms embedded in the code requires a cooperative venture, which involves public representatives, administers, and employees. A corporate approach that emphasizes the positive contribution of each member into the formulation process of the code is more likely to result in a higher level of compliance and effective implementation.

5

Evolution of Management Thought

Work flow working leadership is a form of firm-level entrepreneurship; this is our central thesis. What, then, do we mean by "entrepreneurship" at the level of the firm? Our definition of "entrepreneurship" in this context has three components. First, it is activity that seizes profit opportunities without regard to resources currently controlled. Second, it expands existing resource bundles through enhanced learning, synergies, or factor input completion (e.g., bootstrapping).

These resource expansions result in rent. Third, it promotes change and innovation leading to new combinations of resources, including new process technologies and new work systems. The managerial activity that creates new combinations typically takes place in organizational contexts characterized by teamwork, empowered operating level employees, organic structures, and fluid, informal networking.

NEW RESOURCE COMBINATIONS AND ORGANIZATIONAL ENTROPY

On the face of it, all three components of our definition, as well as the attendant managerial activities, are fairly well developed in the literature. We believe, however, that the nature of input completion in the work system is not well understood. The work system has a ceaseless need for enhancements, due to the fundamental, profound problem of coordination. Again, on the face of it, the concept of coordination is unproblematic. Often, however, it is barely understood, and more often it is misconstrued, because it tends to be seen as the concern of planning, organizational structure, and hierarchical politics. These lenses are those of Generally Approved Management Principles, or GAMP. GAMP, the widely accepted scientific management, command, motivate and control model, fails to recognize the persistent need for everyday initiatives by middle managers for "continuous mutual adaptation and retrofitting" of work flows. The planning and control mentality fails to acknowledge that "without substantial managerial inputs of interest and energy and initiative, work inevitably degrades".

GAMP fails to catch this because it does not account for their realities of work flows. Managers, and field researchers, find that vertical and horizontal interfaces between tasks and job responsibilities are never neat. In practice, managers' roles are ambiguous and overlapping. Managerial roles entail extensive and complex interdependencies, but discrepant goals, incentives, and orientations. The interconnections among teams and supervisory units are difficult to stabilize. Changes in one task ripple throughout a system of tasks. Two sources of instability are particularly noteworthy. First, there is the problem of sub-optimization.

There are countless discretionary performance choices in which optimality for the small group is system degrading. The subtle complexity of interfaces that results is not accounted for in supervisory or engineering task specifications. Second, these are constantly in flux as managers seek to be responsive to changing product mix, customization requests, technology modifications, and pressures to meet new performance targets. In most large organizations, these stresses are exacerbated by excessive complexity and buildup of staff.

WORKING LEADERS

Ambiguous interfaces and other sources of entropy are held, within GAMP, to be abnormal, exceptions to programmable work. But these sources of entropy are, we hold, the norm. They remain unresolved by plans or programmed work. They can be resolved only by creative interventions by people who we call "work flow" entrepreneurs - middle managers who fine-tune coordination and create core operating competencies. These are people like Max of "MIDA" and Kay Cohen of "Process Chemicals". Without their initiative in getting resources redistributed, job and group boundaries changed, and upper management rules and policies modified, their organizations would not have achieved the high levels of effectiveness they were seeking.

People such as these are, in the title words of Sayles, "working leaders." Working leaders are operating-level managers who take initiatives based on their "capacity to make fast-paced tradeoffs (each involving embedded people and technology issues) focusing on the ever-changing needs of coordination and the overall system".

The Kay Cohen case emphasises the ways in which working leaders create lateral and horizontal linkages to use resources that they do not directly control. This case shows how integrating the semi-autonomous work flow stages requires adept, entrepreneurial managers who can bend rules, get constraining staff groups to change specifications, and arrange compromises and consensus among dispersed interdependent supervisory units (many of whom will report to different functional or regional managers).

Their integration role requires continuous negotiation, moving from one source of stalemate or inefficient interconnection to another, along the work flow chain and among the many staff and technical groups that typically have "hands in" the system parameters. A great deal of creative improvisation is required: an entrepreneurial, not a bureaucratic view of the managerial role.

Entrepreneurial networking within the firm is needed because, as one of us argued some years ago, "organizations are changing into structures where lateral relations predominate, where there are tremendous numbers of overlapping networks of servicing, staff, and specialized interest groups. In order to get your job done, you, as the manager, must influence large numbers of people, over most of whom you have zero authority". Around the same time,

William Foote Whyte recognized the role of informal networking in the work of "engineers as internal entrepreneurs": How can engineers cope with . . . changing group membe-rship and changing task assignments? [They] develop what we might call an entrepreneurial role. . . . The leader of an engineering project group . . . does not wait passively to see what management has to assign him [or] his current associates. If he feels that he [has] an effective working team, he will make every effort to keep that team together. . . . He keeps in touch with influential individuals [and outside] activities . . . and [potential] profitable lines of investment. . . . He then conspires with his work group to do a little . . . "bootlegging".

FINDING, FORGETTING, AND REINVENTING WORK FLOW ENTREPRENEURSHIP

Work flow initiatives by working leaders create new systems of work flows, and hence new resource combinations. These new combinations create competitive advantage through work systems that work better than those of other firms. At this time, there is very substantial interest in this approach to competition, expressed in approaches such as reengineering, the horizontal corporation, world-class manufacturing, or lean production. Enumerating all of these approaches from this point on would be too unwieldy; as suggested, focus on reengineering, with references to other practices in the strategic management of operations.

THE IMPORTANCE OF OPERATIONS AND OF WORK FLOWS

Anthropologically oriented studies did not foresee all the ideas to be found in reengineering, but they captured most of the core ideas. A foundational concept shared by both is that operations are important. This concept is implicit in the view of "work flow as the basis for organization design", as well as in the detailed attention to specific operations systems, such as in Richardson. Field studies and reengineering also share the view that, within operations, work flows are critically important. This was a theme of much anthropologically oriented research. Field studies highlighted the degree of uncertainty in what the researchers called lateral or horizontal relations (in contrast to vertical or hierarchical relations). Because jobs did not automatically fit or complement each other, there was the need for much more lateral interaction than management theory had envisioned.

Traditional leadership and organization theory always distinguished between the managerial challenge of non-routine work like R&D, where there might well be substantial "lateral" interaction, and what was presumed to be the clearly prescribed work of most production operations, the machine bureaucracies. For example, in Perrow's influential Complex Organizations: Work-oriented interaction was almost always "vertical"; the "horizontal" were fun and games or protest actions.

The literature on corporate entrepreneurship has also tended to focus more on the vertical, bottom-up championing process than on the horizontal activities of working leaders. The importance of coordinating lateral ties that was apparent in much field research ran counter to prevailing scientific management ideas, which focused instead on specialization and task design. A well-known study that demonstrated the field-research finding was by the British Tavistock Clinic, in an Indian setting: An Indian textile mill seeking to modernize and attain the advantages of specialization and scientifically engineered work standards "re-engineered" the work.

Twelve tasks were prescribed for the mill. The mill was subdivided into units of 240 looms. For each such unit, work was subdivided such: The highest skilled worker, a weaver, would tend 30 looms; the next highest skilled, a "battery filler" served 50 looms. And the third most skilled, the "smash hand" had 80 looms to service. The other nine job classifications had from 120-240 looms to work on, depending on the difficulty of their particular task. As one could predict, the mill failed to attain its predicted productivity. The Tavistock researchers found, not surprisingly, that there were countless coordination problems. These had been unpredicted by the engineers who conceived these 12 differentiated tasks as autonomous. Instead there was the need for almost continuous interaction among employees in order to facilitate the right sequence of task performance since many of the breakdowns and servicing requirements were random.

Resupplying, repairing and resetting the looms thus required teamwork and mutual cooperation. It was obviously a naive assumption of the engineering work standards that a weaver, for example, would have five-eighths of a "battery filler" for his or her looms.

A PROCESS VIEW OF WORK

The Tavistock were also discovered in practice by managers. About this same period IBM began experimenting in one of its upstate New York plants - the plant of our opening vignette - with reducing specialization by enlarging jobs, and found the results impressive in improving coordination. One reason for their success, apparently, was the prescient development of lean or world-class manufacturing practices such as simplified work flows. Another was the limitations of the scientific management and bureaucratic practices that were replaced.

Our reading of the earlier studies suggests that individual field-research-based case studies over almost half a century were disclosing that many presumed machine-like technologies actually contained many inherent sources of breakdown and imperfection. Fifty years later, both researchers and practitioners were still relearning these simple findings. All the efforts to simplify jobs and optimize work at the task level have been an abysmal failure. Reengineering, for example, replaces complex processes and simple jobs with simple processes and complex jobs.

The price to be paid in coordination problems, for bureaucratic complexity, was revealed by the wide range of organizational pathologies that field researchers uncovered. Many of these findings were summarized in Whyte's, Organizational Behaviour. Field studies were disclosing that there could be substantial coordination problems within management itself. Particularly, the rapid multiplication of staff and support groups led to struggles over who should do what and who should defer to whom, struggles that sapped management time and effectiveness. In the 1940s students of industrial relations began to recognize another cost of complexity. Unions could exploit management's infatuation with specialization. So-called "working to rule" would devastate overall performance even when all employees were correctly doing their jobs. Craft jobs that had been subdivided in order to provide lower training and wage costs could be difficult to coordinate. The result could be higher employment levels and total labour costs than would have resulted from allowing employees to do more well-rounded, more highly skilled jobs.

Costs of coordination due to excessive complexity and susceptibility to working-to-rule are two reasons that scientific management did not work. Another reason was its failure to manage the boundaries between management jurisdictions or the barriers of time and space. Sayles (unpublished files) observed a large service organization in the 1950s that had increased the amount of specialization in carpenter jobs in maintenance. In one absurd example, the replacement or addition of a door required that specialists in door jambs, door locks, door closers, and door "bodies" coordinate their work in time and space. The reality was a great deal of waiting time. It was rare that the jamb and closer specialists, for example, would be free and converge at the fight place and the right time. Clearly, coordination problems were not unique to R&D or to high-tech environments.

The cease was that management needed to undertake a kind of work floor "social engineering" to avoid logical specialization becoming destructive of efficiency. The solution was for first line managers to build teams whose critical problems of interdependence could be solved by continuous exchange (of information, assistance, or even job modification). Proximity, common goals, and common supervision facilitate the creation of self-maintaining small systems. "A single supervisor" takes responsibility for "a single flow." His or her responsibilities are determined by an understanding of "processes" in the work flows. Whatever the apparent, functional character of work, Chapple and Sayles argued, the fundamental unit of organization is a "process". For in all work flows, "there is a beginning, when the process starts, something is done, and the process ends. . . . Something comes in the door, something is done to it, and it moves on its way out another door to the customer."

"Organizations keep discovering the advantages of having interdependent functions encapsulated within an organizational unit. . . . This obvious advantage of organizing on the basis of interdependence rather than functional specialty could only be missed by a GAMP-trained manager who still believed that all communications must flow through the common boss".

Why have these had to be rediscovered? One reason is that they never met with wide acceptance. They stood in direct contrast to GAMP and scientific management. Our worldviews affect how we process information. For example, the Tavistock studies, such as Rice's, were widely cited and disseminated in schools of business. These studies clearly challenged all the traditional assumptions about neatly prescribed autonomous jobs. But they had little impact on conceptions of managerial work and what was organizationally problematic. For more than twenty years the findings of studies like these were distorted by the well-accepted paradigms of management and industrial psychology.

These took as given that:

- The jobs of both workers and managers can be specified clearly and unambiguously such that they do not overlap,
- Increasing specialization by subdividing existing tasks or adding more specialists has no consequential organizational cost.

To facilitate high levels of teamwork, which were unspecified in traditional job descriptions but called for in practice, perspicacious and energetic managers were needed. But they were not being produced by U.S. management development processes. The latter presumed that the deft handling of power and authority (vis-a-vis subordinates and superiors) was what was most problematic. Management thought was biased towards vertical, formal authority, and against lateral, informal influence. Hence, findings in field research about intra-management conflict were interpreted in traditional terms. Rather than viewing these, at least in some measure, as coordination issues, academic writers interpreted the rich case data in terms of familiar hierarchical power struggles and organizational "politics".

Within the management academy, a powerful influence affecting the interpretation of field research findings was the discipline of psychology. In the 1960s, U.S. business schools strove to overcome their academically stigmatized pasts, becoming more Mandarin than the Mandarins. Viewed through the lens of psychology, the field research was not seen as challenging existing paradigms of scientific management concerning highly autonomous, well-bounded jobs. Rather, the studies were "reinterpreted" to be consistent with existing theories of psychic deprivation inherent in industrial jobs.

The field study data was then "transmuted" into a motivational context. More specialized jobs injured motivation because they provided less job satisfaction. Employees working within groups gained more social satisfaction from group membership. And work teams could improve performance insofar as they reduced the need for managerial order-giving. This reduced the sting of authority.

There was little or no recognition, in this revisionist reading, of the crucial role that teams could play in coping with the inherent ambiguities in work or the likelihood that jobs would overlap and therefore require a great deal of mutual give and take if a high level of quality and efficiency was to be attained. To be sure, there are job satisfaction issues embedded in the studies cited, but the primary "discovery" of the anthropological-style field work of those decades was lost. That "discovery" was that the appearance of precisely interlocked jobs was more myth than reality. Just as important, if not more important, than the "inside" of a task was the "outside" - that is, the interface between and among tasks. Getting work done in such a way that the task performance of individuals is mutually complementary and not contradictory is one of the major challenges of management. This "dark side" of specialization was what got lost in the motivational reinterpretation of those field studies.

Management are ill at ease dealing with technology; they are more comfortable with problems of individuals and hierarchy. The problems at managerial levels are taken to be external: finding the right strategy and competitive behaviour. Management are more at ease with grand strategizing, or strategy "content." In practice, strategy content centres on extremely broad-brush decisions about which professors can, purportedly, offer prescriptive advice.

LEARNING FROM EXPERIENCE

Field researchers are unlikely to offer grand strategic advice. However, they can claim that their grounded case studies may challenge existing paradigms. Quantitative techniques, particularly survey research, typically are employed deductively, testing hypotheses derived from accepted models of reality. This style of research can be justified on the grounds that it can discover potentially useful principles that have not been discovered in, and cannot be disclosed by observation of, practice. However, deductive researchers typically fail to challenge the dominant paradigms of practice, such as GAMP, because they do not start with the premise that we do not know what is managerially problematic. The result is that deductive research, far from challenging the dominant paradigm, reinforces it.

In contrast, field research is essentially an inductive method. The researcher seeks to comprehend "reality" by carefully observing and interviewing, and then inductively seeking regularities. Field research, at its best, does not take for granted what is problematic, what are the critical variables to which the manager should attend (for goal attainment), and what are consequential interrelationships in organizational behaviour. The armchair academic simply knows that the middle manager's everyday work, in large firms, cannot be entrepreneurial. We have looked and found otherwise. Ironically, field researchers learned about the limits of GAMP by direct interaction with managers, but managers did not, in the aggregate, learn from them. And little in the U.S. managers' environment would induce them to alter their bureaucratic mindset. For so many years after World War II American managers found it easy to believe that the stultifying principles of scientific management were still applicable. Many larger companies were oligopolies; profits came relatively easily. It appeared as though only financial/strategic decision making mattered. Getting the "real work done," the work of operations, was straightforward, rationalistic industrial engineering. Industrial psychologists reassured them that the only real problems were motivational, relating to job satisfaction (and supervisory insensitivity).

Thus, it is not surprising that American management did not view operating excellence as a particular challenge. New paradigms surrounding systems and operations only got accepted by academics and managers when competitive pressures became severe. The relatively recent emphasis in the corporate world and academia on operating effectiveness as a management strategy challenges the comfortable presumption that "new" research data from case and field studies serve to modify or change well-accepted management belief systems (paradigms).

Almost fifty years ago data began emerging challenging the scientific management emphasis on specialization and suggesting that coordination was much more problematic than most managers presumed. However, until a significant share of consumer electronics manufacturing shifted to Asia (although American invention had been preeminent) and the American auto industry suffered very painful losses in income and market share, little attention was paid to execution in American industry or American business schools. Our account raises questions about the efficiency with which new knowledge is created and disseminated in the management and organization studies fields. The research stream we report on did not have an apparent impact on management thinking until the 1990s, and even then its insights went unacknowledged. Possibly we ought not to be surprised by this. This is scarcely the first time that management writings have failed to be used by practitioners. But this attitude seems to us too defeatist. Therefore, we raise the question, how can we avoid such amnesia in the future?

Understanding organizations requires more than attention to cognition and to affect, studied at a distance; it requires attention to work flow patterns and to informal politics, studied up-close. We demonstrate this point with a social network analysis of an entrepreneurial firm.

AVOIDING AMNESIA IN MANAGEMENT THOUGHT

We have argued that academic amnesia is caused by selective perception, which in turn is caused by particular disciplinary approaches. Morgan has argued that we ought to use multiple approaches, or "metaphors," because all of them reflect organization. An organization is simultaneously a "machine," a "political system," a "culture," and so on. We agree. But a question remains: is the organization, qua polity, materially distinct as a "real" entity, from the organization qua culture, qua work system, qua personality system? In social network terms, this question can be expressed in terms of multiplexity.

MULTIPLEX NETWORKS, MULTIPLE METAPHORS

Social networks have multiple, distinct relational or transactional contents. For example, actors may have ties of friendship, political activism, kinship, and economic exchange. Following Wasserman and Faust, as suggested, refer to these and other content domains as "relations." Although we assume that most actors within an organization are involved in multiple relations, and thus have multiplex ties with one another, the term "multiplexity" technically refers to redundancy among these relations, such that no further information about network structure is obtained by knowing about more than one type of tie. Thus, if we wish to find out if it matters whether or not we view organizations through only one disciplinary lens, we ask if the social networks of the organization are multiplex. If they are, disciplinary perspectives make no difference. The same object is merely viewed from a different angle. If, however, the structure of networks differs materially between the relations, disciplines matter. The objects that are viewed are not the same.

METHOD: INTEGRATING ETHNOGRAPHIC DATA WITH NETWORK ANALYSIS

Many, perhaps most, network studies have not attempted to distinguish relations, and most efforts to do so have been seriously limited. There is, however, some evidence that small organizations are not multiplex (*i.e.*, that their relations are not merely redundant). Johnson and Miller concluded that "kinship data, economic exchange data, or co-residence data alone would have led us to a biased interpretation of the social structure of the fishermen" studied. Brajkovich studied an entrepreneurial organization; unlike Johnson and Miller, he did not obtain most of his data from observations. He found relatively little multiplexity, but did find it between what he called work networks and work activities.

What remains to be done, to answer our question, is to measure organizational activity from the perspectives of major disciplinary traditions. The substantive focus of each tradition can be construed as a relation, in the sense in which we use this term. In order to measure relations, we used the data on an entrepreneurial company, called MIDA. These data, upon which Stewart had based his 1989 ethnography, were indexed using the Ethnograph software package. This enabled us to count each instance in which any actor was the sender of a tie with respect to any index word, to any other actors in the firm.

The index words were categorized as distinctively referring to either:

- The "heart" (the affective or personality system),
- The "head" (cognition),

- The "polity" (power and influence)
- The "machine" (the work and economic-related system).

COMPARING DISCIPLINARY LENSES

How different are the network structures of the four different relations? Does the Affective/Personality relation, which psychologically oriented scholars might study, differ much from, say, the Work relation, which is the basis of work flows and reengineering? This question can be posed as one of network roles, or patterns of similarities in ties among actors. Across the four relations, are actors similar, in their pattern of ties, to the same other actors? We treated this question as one of structural equivalence, which means we focused on the extent to which actors "have identical ties to and from all other actors in the network", across the four relations. One of the earliest and most widely used analytical techniques for determining structural equivalence is CONCOR. CONCOR is an iterative procedure in that the outcome of one correlation becomes input to the next, and a convergent procedure because it ultimately partitions actors until they are positively correlated with those within the same position, and negatively correlated with those in other positions.

In the dendograms, "those actors who are connected by [unbroken strings of Xs higher] in the diagram are closer to being perfectly structurally equivalent, whereas subsets of actors who are joined only [lower down] in the diagram are less structurally equivalent (or not equivalent at all)". Inspecting these dendograms for differences is time consuming. One way to summarize the differences is to say that, if an actor is maximally (*i.e.*, level 5) equivalent to another actor, there is little tendency to be closely equivalent to that actor in the other three relations. The 23 actors are, in at least one relation, maximally equivalent to 94 other actors, an average of 4.1 per actor. For these same dyads, there are only 26 cases in which they are maximally equivalent in one of the three other relations, an average of 1.0 per actor. There are 96 cases in which they are maximally distinct (level 1) in another relation, for an average of 4.2 per actor. Perhaps the clearest way to express the distinctions among the relations is with correlations of structural equivalences. The four relations are more highly correlated than one would anticipate by chance. After all, they all reflect "takes" on a unitary stream of social action, within the same, relatively small set of actors. However, in only one of the six comparisons is the correlation above 50%. In most comparisons, there is less in common than not in common between relations. The lenses have not just seen different angles, but to a considerable extent different organizations. In making this claim, we distinguish statistical from substantive significance. As suggested, demonstrate this distinction by examining two of the most similar relations, those of Work/Economic Activity and Affect/Personality. These relations are not statistically significantly different, with a correlation coefficient of 0.47. However, important sets of ties differ between them. (Note that we here refer to direct ties, not to similarities in patterns of ties, as reflected in the CONCOR analysis.)

In the former relation, there is one particularly strong tie, between Peter and William, with a moderately strong tie between Fred and Wally. In the latter, there is one particularly strong tie, between Peter and Hector, with moderately strong ties between Peter and Max, Peter and William, and Peter and Carol, and ties that are nearly as strong between Hector and Howard, Peter and Howard, Ralph and Max, and Fred and Zhong-shi. We also find many differences if we inspect the degree (number of ties) of each actor. For example, Hector is connected to nine actors, generally weakly, in the Work relation. He is connected to six, one very strongly, in the Affective relation. This is true in general of several other actors; Yong-sheng has six connections in Work and one in Affect. The four relations are more correlated than expected by chance, but it is very hard to consider them the same.

IMPLICATIONS

Methodologically, all four of these relations were constructed from ethnographic field data. In our view it would be impossible to capture these relations, or other more subtle and private relations such as negativity, by any other means. Even if actors were willing to give frank answers to an outside researcher about all of their ties, they would be cognitively incapable of making the distinctions. If, as we have argued, the relations are meaningfully different, and if, as we have admittedly assumed, the relations all have importance, there is only one methodological cease. Up-close field research is needed. Research of this kind led to the work flow insights of the postwar generation of American industrial ethnography. Its misperception by armchair academics engendered amnesia.

Currently we witness a new generation of field researchers in management, as demonstrated by this issue. Naturally, we find this development encouraging. But we do have two concerns. First, there is little in-depth ethnography in this issue, or in entrepreneurial studies. The reason may be that ethnography takes too long for the publish-or-perish Mandarinism of business schools. This may account for the popularity of rapid appraisal approaches, reflected in this issue, such as grounded theory based on interviews, and network analysis based on questionnaire data.

Our second concern is that, even if this generation does learn much that is worth knowing, their work, like that of their academic predecessors, may be misperceived and forgotten as well. There are suggestions for ways to avoid this fate by cumulating field-research-based knowledge. First, if we as researchers venture to muddy our boots in the field, we should keep our eyes and ears wide open.

"In the observations and interviews" of the Hawthorne researchers, "shorthand sociological and psychiatric concepts are repeatedly substituted for actual first-order abstractions: the who does what to whom, when, and where, of the anthropological field method". Clearly, the latter, not the former, is what we counsel. As suggested, not learn about the subtleties of work flows, informal political networks, or sundry other matters, with stringent sensory lenses.

6

Decision Theory

In business, there are various theories for making decisions. Various alternatives are evaluated in the context of the organisational objectives.

For this evaluation purpose, normally three approaches are considered:

1. *Marginal Theory*: This approach has been suggested by economists. This emphasises the maximization of profit. The profit is maximum where marginal costs of inputs are equal to marginal revenues from outputs. Marginal cost is the additional cost which is incurred for taking one additional outputs. Marginal cost is the additional cost which is incurred for taking one additional output. Similarly, marginal revenue is earned by selling one additional unit of output. When marginal costs revenues differ, the profit cannot be maximum because, in that case, either more additional revenues can be earned at less additional cost, or additional revenues earned would be less than additional costs. In the first case, profit is maximized by additional output, and in the second case, it is maximized by reduction in output.
2. *Mathematical Theory*: This theory suggests the decision-making through building mathematical models. The models are constructed taking all factors affecting a decision, With the development of operations research add computers for handling complex mathematical models, this approach is commonly used by large-sized organisations where

decision-making problem is very complex. Mathematical techniques have given basis for analyzing difficult situation; however, the role of experience and foresightedness in selecting an alternative cannot all together be avoided. Various techniques such as venture analysis, games theory, probability theory, waiting theory, linear programming, etc., are utilised for decision model building.

3. *Psychological Theory*: The marginal and mathematical theories emphasise on maximization of profits which is the treatment of a manger as 'economic man'. Some hold the view that good organisations do not want profit maximization, rather they want maximization of satisfaction. Thus, manager is not an economic man, but an administrative man. The former selects best alternative which combines various things. The manager in the latter approach involves in finding out an alternative only when the profits go the satisfactory level. The satisfactory level may bot be maximum profits.

How the appropriateness of a strategy is to be measured of Evaluation of a Strategy Management Science, Operations Research/Mathematical School/ Decision Theory Approach Management Science (MS) is an important element in management education, playing an important role in the analysis and solution of complex problems. MS is a requisite area of study in most business curricula, the topic of many well-attended seminars, and the focal point of much academic research. Perhaps the most important reason for its existence is to facilitate better and more objective decisions by practicing managers.

Unfortunately, there is growing skepticism concerning the extent to which MS has succeeded in this endeavor. For MS, the traditional gap between what practitioners expect and what theoreticians provide has widened alarmingly. MS is losing its appeal to the business community, and its usefulness in practice has been questioned. What has been happening to MS?

Despite the growth in the field, why are practitioners becoming more and more reluctant to embrace its concepts? MS is a collection of selected quantitative techniques for objectively analyzing and solving business problems. Its role is to help practitioners solve complex problems frequently encountered in all fundamental areas of a business.

The cornerstone of MS includes various mathematical models that encompass calculus, linear and matrix algebra, statistical and simulation techniques, and the like. The use of MS requires a structured approach comprising a set of logical steps. Some of the important steps are problem identification, data collection, model selection and validation, and implementation. While Operations Research, more popular in engineering curriculum, has made substantial contributions to Management Science, the latter includes broader topical areas essential for business management education.

Without doubt, the field of management science has made substantial progress over the past several decades. At the same time, however, its popularity within the business community has steadily decreased. Its objective has become muddled, and its users less certain about its relevance. In the process of advancing our knowledge and expanding the discipline, researchers and academicians have inadvertently abandoned the original focus of MS. The emphasis, in both classrooms and research journals, has shifted from applications to theoretical refinements. MS has fallen prey to misdirection because it has concentrated on the interests of theoreticians while ignoring those of practicing business managers.

As Wren, Buckley, and Michaelsen have reported, the teaching of Management Science has taken a more theoretical direction over the past few decades. Consequently, considerable doubt has emerged in the business community concerning the potential of MS as an effective decision making tool. It is now necessary for the proponents of MS to develop new approaches so that MS can have a stronger role in business applications and fulfill the expectations it once promised. A number of factors are responsible for the failure of MS to adequately address the concerns of practitioners.

Those are:

- *Internal Consistency*: Internal consistency refers to the cumulative impact of individual policies on corporate goals, and in a well-worked-out strategy, each policy fits into an integrated pattern. A strategy must be judged o the basis of its relationships to other policies and goals of the organisation. The internal consistency is important in the sense that it identifies those areas where strategic decisions will eventually have to be made. In the absence of such internal consistency, management may be forced to make a choice without enough time either to search for or to prepare attractive alternatives.
- *Consistency with the Environment*: The strategy should be consistent with the environment, that is, this should make sense with respect to what is going on outside. Consistency with the environment has both static an dynamic aspects. In a dynamic sense, it implies judging the efficacy of strategy with the changing environment. In a dynamic sense, it implies judging the efficacy of strategy with the changing environment. Failure to have a strategy consistent with the environment can be costly to the organisation.
- Appropriateness in the Light of Available Resources: The strategy should be appropriate in the light of available resources Resources are those things that help an organisation achieve its objectives. There are two basic issues which management must decide in relating strategy and resources. These are: what are the critical resources ? Is the proposed strategy appropriate for available resources ? The three resources most frequently identified as critical are money, competence, and physical facilities. The orgnaisation can asses the quantity of these critical resources an appropriate strategy.In fact, critical strategy decision involves deciding:
  - How much of th organisation's resources to commit to opportunities, currently perceived,

  - How much to keep uncommitted as a reserve against the appearance of unanticipated demands.
- *Satisfactory Degree of Risk*: Strategy and resources, taken together, determine the degree of risk which the orgnaisation is undertaking. Thus, each organisation must decide the degree of risk it can take. This in turn, depends upon several factors. *These are*:
  - The amount of resources whose continued existence or value is not assured;
  - The length of th time or periods to which resources are committed;
  - The proportion of resources committed to a single venture.

  The greater is th quantity of these, th greater is the degree of risk involved. Strategy and risk should be correlated because, on the one hand, high payoffs are associated with the high-risk strategies, on the other, high risk strategies may present threat to the existence of the organisation, if things go wrong.
- *Appropriate Time Horizon*: A good strategy not only provides what objectives would be achieved, it also indicates when objective would be achieved. This is due to the fact that a significant part of every strategy is the time horizon on which it is based. In choosing an appropriate time horizon, the orgnaisation must pay careful attention to th goals being pursued. Goals have time-based utility and must be established far enough in advance to allow the orgnaisation to adjust to them. Larger the size of th organisation, the further its strategic time horizon must extended, since its adjustment time is longer. The importance of an extended time horizon derives not only from the fact that an orgnaisation changes slowly and needs time to modify its strategy accordingly, it also derives from the fact that there is a considerable advantage in a certain consistency of strategy maintained over long periods of time.

- *Workability*: The strategy must have enough degree of workability. The workability of a strategy can be measured in terms of results which are obtained. However, the results measure two factors: the strategy selected and the skill with which it is being executed. If the results are not up to standards, both these factors can be examined. Another approach for judging the workability of a strategy is to assess its contribution to organisational progress.

This can be done by finding out:

- The degree of consensus which exists among executives concerning organisational goals and policies;
- The degree to which major areas of managerial choices are identified in advance;
- To the extent to which resources requirements are discovered well before the last minute.

Evaluation of a Strategy

These are, of course, many factors determining organisation's success or failure. But a valid strategy can gain extraordinary results for the organisation whose general level of competence is only average. A valid strategy will yield growth, profit, or whatever the objectives managers have established. Thus, appropriate strategy is necessary for every organisation.

Strategy Formulation

Strategy consists of a set of long-range decision which establish actions to exploit opportunities or combat threats in response to environmental forces and developments. These decisions are the result of a complex decision-making process designed to establish organisational goals and long-range plans for resource allocation. Process involved in strategy formulations is the same as discussed in policy formulation; however, a major difficulty in th strategic decision process is the identifying and analyzing the factors bearing on the problem. The issue is further complicated by the inter-dependence of the variables.

Difference between Policy and Strategy

A major distinction between policy and strategy is that former is a guide to the thinking and action of those who make decisions, while strategy concerns the direction in which human and physical resources will be deployed and applied in order to maximise the chance of achieving a selected objective in th face of difficulties. Policy is contingent decision, whereas strategy is a rule for making decision. A contingent even is recognised because it is repetitive, but the time of its specific occurrence cannot be specified.

It is not worth while to require a new decision on what should be done each time when a contingency arises. It is better to prescribe, in advance, the response to be made whenever a specified contingency occurs. This is done through policy formulations. Specification of strategy is forced under conditions of partial ignorance when alternatives cannot be arranged and analysed in advance.

The strategy decision is taken under the conditions where all the facts are not known, which may not be lasting because of the further knowledge of the facts. The distinction between policy and strategy is made in the context of delegation or implementation. The implementation of policy can be delegated downward in the organisation, while the strategy cannot, since it requires a last-minute executive decision.

Characteristics of Strategy

The definition of strategy suggests the following:

- Strategy is the right combinations of factors. This requires not only the isolation of the components of the situation, but also an evaluation of their relative importance.
- Strategy relates the business organisation to its environment. Strategy decisions are primarily concerned with external, rather than internal, problems of the organisation.
- Strategy is relative. It is an action to meet a particular conditions, to solve a certain problem or to attain a desired objective. It may take many forms, for almost

every situation varies and, therefore, requires a somewhat different approach.

- Strategy may require contradictory action. A manager may take a course of action today and revises or retraces his steps tomorrow because of changes in situations.
- Strategy is forward looking, it has to do orientation towards the future. Strategy is required in a new situation. Nothing new requiring solution can exist in the past, so strategy is relevant only to the future.

Step of Policy Formulation

Policy formulation, therefore, cannot be viewed as totally objective and programmable process.

The policy formulation essentially consists of the following step:

- Understanding an analyzing of the present environment, both external and internal
- Identification of policy alternatives to achieve th goals in the anticipated environment
- Examination of th alternatives
- Elaboration of the consequences of various alternatives-prescription of goals attainment levels
- Effect of alternatives and consequences on preferred values and norms
- Selection of policies

Policy Formulation

A policy is formulated by the managerial decision. As such it involves the various stages of a decision-making process. The basic difference in a policy decision is that former involves a standing decision which is duded again over a considerable period of time, the latter decision is taken within the framework of a policy decision. The policy formulation maybe classified into tow groups. One group deals with the policy formulation in various managerial functions: planning, staffing, directing and controlling. Other group involves policy formulation in respect of business organisation's various functions: production, marketing, finance, and personnel.

Policy originate from interplay of goals and perceive attainments through a course of action. Perception of attainment through policy alternative is influenced by the external an internal environment, policy maker's value system, expertise, and judgment.

Some Kinds of Characteristics of a Sound Policy

These are certain characteristics of a sound policy, however, which are universally applicable:

- *Relationship to Objectives*: The policy should facilitate the attainment of organisation objectives. In the formulation of a general policy, those functions or activities which do not facilitate the objectives should be eliminated.
- *Planned Development*: The policy must be a planned development rather than the result of opportunistic decision made on the spur of the moment. It may not be possible on solve every problem of the orgnaisation on the basis of established policy because many new situations arise, but the routine activities should be carried on in a manner dictated by the policy.
- *Clarity*: The policy should be clear, definite and explicit, leaving no scope for misinterpretation. This should minimize the number of cases where decisions are based on personal judgment.
- *Written*: The policy should be in written form as far as possible. A written policy generally becomes more clear and definite and its communication is more easy. It creates an atmosphere in which individual actions may be taken with confidence. Besides, it speeds up administration by reducing repetition to routine a d brings consistency in the organisation. The claim that a written policy creates rigidity and lack of creativity dos not hold good as flexibility remains in it.
- *Consistency*: The policy should make for consistency

in the operation of an organisation. The functions and activities in the policy must be in agreement. Furthermore both, general or specific policies must result in stability over a considerable period of time.

- *Flexibility*: The clearly defined and consistent policy does not mean that it is stable and permanent which is unalterable. If the objectives, premises or major plans change, a policy should also be changed to meet the new situations. For this purpose, constant review of the situations should be made, and the changes in them should be incorporated in a policy.
- *Communication*: The policy should be clearly communicated in the organisation so that individuals who have to take decisions in the framework of a policy understand it clearly. It is well-established fact that what people do not understand they cannot use correctly and are likely to distrust. Mere issuance of a written policy is not enough, the ambiguity in it must be removed and the objective of policy formulation mus be conveyed.
- *Control*: The policy, to b effective, must be controlled which requires its periodical review bing uptodate, reflecting organisational objectives and plans in changing situations, consistency, flexibility, understanding, interpreting, and applicability.

Types of Policies

Numerous policies are formulated and observed in a business organisation. Their classification is made on the basis of their sources and scope.

The understanding of various policies helps in formulating as well as observing them:

- *Source of Policies*: As to the source of their formulation, policies may be classified as originated, appealed, implied an externally imposed.
  - *Originated Policy*: An originated policy is that which is formulated by the managers in the organisation for their subordinate's action as well

as their own action. Such a policy flows form higher level because such a policy is originated in the broad framework of the objectives which are set and defined by top management. This policy may be broad giving a general guidance for the action or may be spelled so completely as to leave little scope for definition and interpretation.

- *Appealed Policy*: Appealed policy arises from the appeal made by a subordinate to his superior for deciding an important case. The need for such an appeal may arise because th particular case has not been covered by earlier policies. The appeals are taken upward and decisions made on them set a kind of common law to be followed by others. Appealed policies are mostly incomplete, unco-ordinated and confused. As such, if frequent appeals are made, the managers should visualize their policy formulation, its communication and interpretation so that guidelines become clear and specific.
- *Implied Policy*: Sometimes, policies are not clearly stated, and the actions of managers, particularly at higher levels, provide guidelines for actions at the lower levels. These actions might be constituting policy. Or sometimes, the orgnaisation have clearly expressed policies for its image, but it is unable to enforce these. In such a case, the action of a decision-maker, consciously or unconsciously, depends upon their own guidelines, prejudices and whims. Moreover, in the absence of any specific guideline, decision is based on individual interpretation of actions observed in the orgnaisation crating chaos.
- *Imposed Policy*: Imposed policy arises from th influence of some outside forces like government, trade unions, and trade associations. In the

present social structure, external variables affect the functioning of a business organisation to a great extent. These variables may impose th specific policy or conditions may be created to adopt a particular policy. In India, the rise of public sector and government regulations create such situations.

- *Scope of Policies*: The various policies on their scope in an organisation may be classified as basic policies and general or departmental policies. The basic policies are used by the top management for its own guidance. The general polices are used uniformally through the various units of the orgnaisation, while departmental policies are specific to particular departments such as marketing, production, finance, personal, and purchase policies. The policies may be based on the classification of basic managerial functions, such as planing, organising, staffing, directing, and controlling policies.

POLICY AND STRATEGY

Every organisation involves a complicated pattern of decisions-form broad decisions about the objectives of the organisation to specific decisions about day-to-day processes Some of the decisions do have a long-term effect and many decisions are made within the context of earlier decisions because they provide guidelines for subsequent decisions. Two such parts of planning-policy and strategy-are very important in all the organisations.

Advantage of O.R. Techniques or Tools

These tools are widely applicable to problems in many industries, though not necessarily the best tolls, but are widely known because they have the great advantage of generalized versatility.

- *Probability Theory*: The probability theory is based upon the inference form experience that certain things are likely to happen in accordance with a predictable pattern. There may be some deviation from the predicted pattern, however, the deviation from such a pattern is within fairly predictable margin Thus, probability theory provides base for ascertaining future events which helps in decision-making. There are a few discrete and continuous probability distributions which occur often in practical application. These are binomial, poisson, uniform, rectangular, exponential, normal, and beta distributions.

- *Games Theory*: In daily life, various games are played where players try to win. In normal games, each player or players in group try to choose a course of action which will frustrate opponents' action as well as win the game for them. Similarly while formulating the strategy in business, an attempt is made to maximise profit. Though the games theory started in the 20th century, the mathematical treatment of games was started by publication of the famous boom 'Theory of Games and Economic Behaviour' by John Von Neumann and Morgenstern in 1944. The theory is very useful in actual planning and future development and this theory can have a remarkable impact on the scientific approach to strategic planning in competitive situation.
- *Queueing Theory*: This is also known as waiting theory. This theory uses mathematical techniques to balance the costs of waiting lines versus the cost of preventing waiting lines by increased service. A group of items waiting to receive service, including those receiving the service, is known as queue. A queue exists because the demand for a limited service exceeds the availability of the service. A reasonably long waiting line may result in loss of customers to the organisation while opening of further facility to serve all customers may result in idle time. Queuing theory is usefully utilised in business decisions, more profitably in banks, booking offices, automobile repair shops, aeroplanes waiting for the runway to be cleared and others.

- *Replacement Theory*: This theory suggested the determination of the time when items of plant should be replaced. The replacement of items is necessary because the efficiency of an item deteriorates with time, or sometimes the item may fail completely. Replacement, on the one hand, requires investment, on the other, saves operating cost which otherwise is more while using old parts Thus, problem arises when the part should be replaced so that cost is minimum.

  The replacement problems arise in three conditions:

  1. Replacement of items that fail completely and are expensive to be replaced
  2. Replacement of items whose efficiency deteriorates with time
  3. Replacement of items because of obsolescence. In all such cases, the problems are decided profitably by replacement theory.

- *Network Analysis*: The network analysis is, perhaps, the most useful O.R. Technique. A network can be defined by a set of points or nodes that are connected by links or lines. The links in a network are generally characterized in terms of time, cost or distance involved in traversing them. There are two most commonly used methods of network analysis-critical path method (CPM) and project evaluation and review technique, though schedule charts as suggested by Gantt are also used.
- *Mathematical Programming*: Mathematical programme-ming is mostly used for determining the optimum combination of limited resources to obtain a desired goal. Linear programming is one of the most important tolls in mathematical programming for solving such problems.
- *Linear Programming*: It is based on the assumption that a linear or straight line relationship exists between variables and that limits of variations can be well defined. The technique is useful in solving the

problems of production planning, shipping rates and routes utilization of warehousing facilities, transportation, etc. There are various ways of allocating the scarce resources, however, out of these, only one might be optimum. For example, in a workshop, there are five different types of machines, each with different types of machines, each with different cost structure and capacity. Thus, foreman may face a problem as how the work on these machines should be allocated so that the total cost of production is minimum. If he has to allocated 10 activities, the number of ways would be 5 or ten crores. This problem he can solve by application of liner programming. Besides linear programming, there are techniques of mathematical programming. Many of these have been developed from linear properties. These involve a considerable increase in the amount of calculation required to find an optimum solution.

- *Other Tools*: There are a number of other tolls used in O.R. Some of these are Survo theory, Information theory, Symbolic logic, Value theory, Multiple regression analysis, Factor analysis, Incremental analysis, Monto Carlo method. etc.

OR Procedures

O.R. Provides optimum solution of any problem by going through the following process:

- *Specifying the problem*: Specifying the problem is probably the most difficult and important stage of O. R. Procedures. At this stage, the knowledge of whole tam drawn from various disciplines-mathematics, statistics, economics, accounting, etc, is used. The clear formulation of the problem is necessary so that the objective can be established, factors can be analysed, models can be chosen for analysis, and alternatives can be sear ched for.
- *Building the Model*: After the problem is specified, the

next step is to build a model which describes the relationships between various factors on which the solution of the problem depends. An O.R. Model is mathematical or theoretical or theoretical description of various variables of a system representing some aspects of a problem. The building of a model requires quantitative data which can be obtained from existing records, from experiments and surveys, or from estimates on th basis of parallel action, and the analyzing of the data with the help of statistical and mathematical tools.

- *Testing of Model*: There are a number of ways for solving a problem and O. R. models should be evaluated in the context of optimum solution. An optimum solution is one which maximizes or minimizes other performance of any measure in a model subject to the conditions and constraints in it. If the model is a good representation of th system, the optimum solution of th model must improve the system's performance. The testing of a model should be carried on in the context of various alternative models.
- *Implementation*: The optimum solution obtained in this process may be applied to actual conditions. The decisions are enforced by managers who should be communicated in a language comprehensible to them. Thus, it is reverse process of O.R., that is, the conversion of mathematical language into a simple one. The performance of the total system should be evaluated in order to find out the validity of the solution.

7

Approach and Planning

SYSTEM APPROACH

A system is commonly defined as a group of interacting units or elements that have a common purpose. The units or elements of a system can be cogs, wires, people, computers, and so on. Systems are generally classified as open systems and closed systems and they can take the form of mechanical, biological, or social systems.

Open systems refer to systems that interact with other systems or the outside environment, whereas closed systems refer to systems having relatively little interaction with other systems or the outside environment. For example, living organisms are considered open systems because they take in substances from their environment such as food and air and return other substances to their environment.

Humans, for example, inhale oxygen out of the environment and exhale carbon dioxide into the environment. Similarly, some organizations consume raw materials in the production of products and emit finished goods and pollution as a result. In contrast, a watch is an example of a closed system in that it is a relatively self-contained, self-maintaining unit that has little interacts or exchange with its environment.

All systems have boundaries, a fact that is immediately apparent in mechanical systems such as the watch, but much less apparent in social systems such as organizations. The boundaries of open systems, because they interact with other systems or environments, are more flexible than those of closed systems, which are rigid and largely impenetrable. A closed-system perspective views organizations as relatively independent of environmental influences. The closed-system approach conceives of the organization as a system of management, technology, personnel, equipment, and materials, but tends to exclude competitors, suppliers, distributors, and governmental regulators.

This approach allows managers and organizational theorists to analyse problems by examining the internal structure of a business with little consideration of the external environment. The closed-system perspective basically views an organization much as a thermostat; limited environmental input outside of changes in temperature is required for effective operation. Once set, thermostats require little maintenance in their ongoing, self-reinforcing function. While the closed-system perspective was dominant through the 1960s, organization scholarship and research subsequently emphasized the role of the environment. Up through the 1960s, it was not that managers ignored the outside environment such as other organizations, markets, government regulations and the like, but that their strategies and other decision-making processes gave relatively little consideration to the impact these external forces might have on the internal operations of the organization.

Open-systems theory originated in the natural sciences and subsequently spread to fields as diverse as computer science, ecology, engineering, management, and psychotherapy. In contrast to closed-systems, the open-system perspective views an organization as an entity that takes inputs from the environment, transforms them, and releases them as outputs in tandem with reciprocal effects on the organization itself along with the environment in which the organization operates.

That is, the organization becomes part and parcel of the environment in which it is situated. Returning for a moment to the example of biological systems as open-systems, billions of individual cells in the human body, themselves composed of thousands of individual parts and processes, are essential for the viability of the larger body in which they are a part. In turn, "macro-level" processes such as eating and breathing make the survival of individual cells contingent on these larger processes. In much the same way, open-systems of organizations accept that organizations are contingent on their environments and these environments are also contingent on organizations. As an open-systems approach spread among organizational theorists, managers began incorporating these views into practice.

Two early pioneers in this effort, Daniel Katz and Robert Kahn, began viewing organizations as open social systems with specialized and interdependent subsystems and processes of communication, feedback, and management linking the subsystems. Katz and Kahn argued that the closed-system approach fails to take into account how organizations are reciprocally dependent on external environments. For example, environmental forces such as customers and competitors exert considerable influence on corporations, highlighting the essential relationship between an organization and its environment as well as the importance of maintaining external inputs to achieve a stable organization.

Furthermore, the open-system approach serves as a model of business activity; that is, business as a process of transforming inputs to outputs while realizing that inputs are taken from the external environment and outputs are placed into this same environment. Companies use inputs such as labour, funds, equipment, and materials to produce goods or to provide services and they design their subsystems to attain these goals. These subsystems are thus analogous to cells in the body, the organization itself is analogous to the body, and external market and regulatory conditions are analogous to environmental factors such as the quality of housing, drinking water, air and availability of nourishment.

The production subsystem, for example, focuses on converting inputs into marketable outputs and often constitutes a primary purpose of a company. The boundary subsystem's goal is to obtain inputs or resources, such as employees, materials, equipment, and so forth, from the environment outside of the company, which are necessary for the production subsystem. This subsystem also is responsible for providing an organization with information about the environment. This adaptive subsystem collects and processes information about a company's operations with the goal of aiding the company's adaptation to external conditions in its environment. Another subsystem, management, supervises and coordinates the other subsystems to ensure that each subsystem functions efficiently. The management subsystem must resolve conflicts, solve problems, allocate resources, and so on.

To simplify the process of evaluating environmental influences, some organizational theorists use the term "task environment" to refer to aspects of the environment that are immediately relevant to management decisions related to goal setting and goal realization. The task environment includes customers, suppliers, competitors, employees, and regulatory bodies. Furthermore, in contrast to closed-systems, the open-system perspective does not assume that the environment is static. Instead, change is the rule rather than the exception. Consequently, investigation of environmental stability and propensity to change is a key task of a company, making the activities of an organization contingent on various environmental forces. As an open system, an organization maintains its stability through feedback, which refers to information about outputs that a system obtains as an input from its task environment. The feedback can be positive or negative and can lead to changes in the way an organization transforms inputs to outputs.

Here, the organization acts as a thermostat, identified previously as an example of a relatively closed-system. The difference between closed-systems and open-systems, then, is in the complexity of environmental interactions. Closed-systems assume relatively little complexity; a thermostat is a simple device dependent mainly on temperature fluctuations. Conversely, open-system such as the human body and modern organizations are more intricately dependent on their environments. The point is that closed-systems versus open-systems do not represent a dichotomy, but rather a continuum along which organizations are more open or less open to their environments. The key defining variable governing this degree of openness is the complexity of the environment in which the organization is situated. Managers must take into consideration their organization's position along the open-closed continuum. The Linux computer operating system, for instance, is "open-source" and Red Hat, Inc., the corporation selling the bundled revisions-the multiple inputs from geographically dispersed users-represents an organization that would cease to exist if it were not for an open-systems perspective. Thus, stable environments with low complexity are more consistent with a relatively closed-system or mechanistic management style, while rapidly-changing environments are more consistent with flexible, decentralized, or "organic" management styles

MCKINSEY'S 7-S APPROACH

McKinsey's 7S Model that was created by the consulting company McKinsey and Company in the early 1980s. Since then it has been widely used by practitioners and academics alike in analysing hundreds of organisations. The explains each of the seven components of the model and the links between them. It also includes practical guidance and advice for the students to analyse organisations using this model.

The McKinsey 7S model was named after a consulting company, McKinsey and Company, which has conducted applied research in business and industry. All of the authors worked as consultants at McKinsey and Company; in the 1980s, they used the model to analyse over 70 large organisations. The McKinsey 7S Framework was created as a recognisable and easily remembered model in business. The seven variables, which the authors term "levers", all begin with the letter "S":

These seven variables include structure, strategy, systems, skills, style, staff and shared values. Structure is defined as the skeleton of the organisation or the organisational chart. The authors describe strategy as the plan or course of action in allocating resources to achieve identified goals over time.

The systems are the routine processes and procedures followed within the organisation. Staff are described in terms of personnel categories within the organisation (e.g. engineers), whereas the skills variable refers to the capabilities of the staff within the organisation as a whole. The way in which key managers behave in achieving organisational goals is considered to be the style variable; this variable is thought to encompass the cultural style of the organisation. The shared values variable, originally termed superordinate goals, refers to the significant meanings or guiding concepts that organisational members share.

The shape of the model was also designed to emphasise the interdependency of the variables. This is emphasised by the model also being termed as the "Managerial Molecule". While the authors thought that other variables existed within complex organisations, the variables represented in the model were considered to be of crucial importance to managers and practitioners. The analysis of several organisations using the model revealed that American companies tend to focus on those variables which they feel they can change (e.g. structure, strategy and systems) while neglecting the other variables. These other variables (e.g. skills, style, staff and shared values) are considered to be "soft" variables. Japanese and a few excellent American companies are reportedly successful at linking their structure, strategy and systems with the soft variables. The authors have concluded that a company cannot merely change one or two variables to change the whole organisation. For long-term benefit, they feel that the variables should be changed to become more congruent as a system. The external environment is not in the McKinsey 7S Framework, although the authors do acknowledge that other variables exist and that they depict only the most crucial variables in the model. While alluded to in their discussion of the model, the notion of performance or effectiveness is not made explicit in the model.

DESCRIPTION OF 7 SS

Strategy: Strategy is the plan of action an organisation prepares in response to, or anticipation of, changes in its external environment. Strategy is differentiated by tactics or operational actions by its nature of being premeditated, well thought through and often practically rehearsed.

It deals with essentially three questions:

1. Where the organisation is at this moment in time,
2. Where the organisation wants to be in a particular length of time and
3. How to get there. Thus, strategy is designed to transform the firm from the present position to the new position described by objectives, subject to constraints of the capabilities or the potential.

Structure: Business needs to be organised in a specific form of shape that is generally referred to as organisational structure. Organisations are structured in a variety of ways, dependent on their objectives and culture. The structure of the company often dictates the way it operates and performs. Traditionally, the businesses have been structured in a hierarchical way with several divisions and departments, each responsible for a specific task such as human resources management, production or marketing. Many layers of management controlled the operations, with each answerable to the upper layer of management. Although this is still the most widely used organisational structure, the recent trend is increasingly towards a flat structure where the work is done in teams of specialists rather than fixed departments. The idea is to make the organisation more flexible and devolve the power by empowering the employees and eliminate the middle management layers.

Systems: Every organisation has some systems or internal processes to support and implement the strategy and run day-to-day affairs. For example, a company may follow a particular process for recruitment. These processes are normally strictly followed and are designed to achieve maximum effectiveness. Traditionally the organisations have been following a bureaucratic-style process model where most decisions are taken at the higher management level and there are various and sometimes unnecessary requirements for a specific decision (e.g. procurement of daily use goods) to be taken.

Increasingly, the organisations are simplifying and modernising their process by innovation and use of new technology to make the decision-making process quicker. Special emphasis is on the customers with the intention to make the processes that involve customers as user friendly as possible.

Style/Culture

All organisations have their own distinct culture and management style. It includes the dominant values, beliefs and norms which develop over time and become relatively enduring features of the organisational life. It also entails the way managers interact with the employees and the way they spend their time. The businesses have traditionally been influenced by the military style of management and culture where strict adherence to the upper management and procedures was expected from the lower-rank employees. However, there have been extensive efforts in the past couple of decades to change to culture to a more open, innovative and friendly environment with fewer hierarchies and smaller chain of command. Culture remains an important consideration in the implementation of any strategy in the organisation.

Staff

Organisations are made up of humans and it's the people who make the real difference to the success of the organisation in the increasingly knowledge-based society. The importance of human resources has thus got the central position in the strategy of the organisation, away from the traditional model of capital and land. All leading organisations such as IBM, Microsoft, Cisco, etc put extraordinary emphasis on hiring the best staff, providing them with rigorous training and mentoring support, and pushing their staff to limits in achieving professional excellence, and this forms the basis of these organisations' strategy and competitive advantage over their competitors. It is also important for the organisation to instil confidence among the employees about their future in the organisation and future career growth as an incentive for hard work.

SHARED VALUES/SUPERORDINATE GOALS

All members of the organisation share some common fundamental ideas or guiding concepts around which the business is built. This may be to make money or to achieve excellence in a particular field. These values and common goals keep the employees working towards a common destination as a coherent team and are important to keep the team spirit alive. The organisations with weak values and common goals often find their employees following their own personal goals that may be different or even in conflict with those of the organisation or their fellow colleagues.

USING THE 7S MODEL TO ANALYSE AN ORGANISATION

A detailed case study or comprehensive material on the organisation under study is required to analyse it using the 7S model. This is because the model covers almost all aspects of the business and all major parts of the organisation. It is therefore highly important to gather as much information about the organisation as possible from all available sources such as organisational reports, news and press releases although primary research, e.g. using interviews along with literature review is more suited. The researcher also needs to consider a variety of facts about the 7S model. Some of these are detailed in the paragraphs to follow.

The seven components are normally categorised as soft and hard components. The hard components are the strategy, structure and systems which are normally feasible and easy to identify in an organisation as they are normally well documented and seen in the form of tangible objects or reports such as strategy statements, corporate plans, organisational charts and other documents. The remaining four Ss, however, are more difficult to comprehend. The capabilities, values and elements of corporate culture, for example, are continuously developing and are altered by the people at work in the organisation. It is therefore only possible to understand these aspects by studying the organisation very closely, normally through observations and/or through conducting interviews. Some linkages, however, can be made between the hard and soft components. For example, it is seen that a rigid, hierarchical organisational structure normally leads to a bureaucratic organisational culture where the power is centralised at the higher management level.

It is also noted that the softer components of the model are difficult to change and are the most challenging elements of any change-management strategy. Changing the culture and overcoming the staff resistance to changes, especially the one that alters the power structure in the organisation and the inherent values of the organisation, is generally difficult to manage. However, if these factors are altered, they can have a great impact on the structure, strategies and the systems of the organisation. Over the last few years, there has been a trend to have a more open, flexible and dynamic culture in the organisation where the employees are valued and innovation encouraged.

This is, however, not easy to achieve where the traditional culture is been dominant for decades and therefore many organisations are in a state of flux in managing this change. What compounds their problems is their focus on only the hard components and neglecting the softer issues identified in the model which is without doubt a recipe for failure. Similarly, when analysing an organisation using the 7S model, it is important for the researcher to give more time and effort to understanding the real dynamics of the organisation's soft aspects as these underlying values in reality drive the organisations by affecting the decision-making at all levels. It is too easy to fall into the trap of only concentrating on the hard factors as they are readily available from organisations' reports etc.

However, to achieve higher marks, students must analyse in depth the cultural dimension of the structure, processes and decision made in an organisation. For even advanced analysis, the student should not just write about these components individually but also highlight how they interact and affect each other. Or in other words, how one component is affected by changes in the other. Especially the "cause and effect" analyses of soft and hard components often yield a very interesting analysis and provide readers with an in-depth understanding of what caused the change.

SOURCES FOR DATA ON MCKINSEY'S 7S MODEL

The main source of academic work on the 7S model has to be the writings of Waterman *et al.*, and Pascale and Athos who came up with the idea and applied it to analyse over 70 large organisations. Since then, it has been used by hundreds of organisations and academics for analytical purposes. Many such case studies can be obtained from the academic journals and the books written on the topic.

PLANNING

Planning in organizations and public policy is both the organizational process of creating and maintaining a plan; and the psychological process of thinking about the activities required to create a desired goal on some scale. As such, it is a fundamental property of intelligent behaviour. This thought process is essential to the creation and refinement of a plan, or integration of it with other plans, that is, it combines forecasting of developments with the preparation of scenarios of how to react to them.

An important, albeit often ignored aspect of planning, is the relationship it holds with forecasting. Forecasting can be described as predicting what the future will look like, whereas planning predicts what the future should look like. The term is also used to describe the formal procedures used in such an endeavor, such as the creation of documents diagrams, or meetings to discuss the important issues to be addressed, the objectives to be met, and the strategy to be followed. Beyond this, planning has a different meaning depending on the political or economic context in which it is used. Two attitudes to planning need to be held in tension: on the one hand we need to be prepared for what may lie ahead, which may mean contingencies and flexible processes. On the other hand, our future is shaped by consequences of our own planning and actions.

Planning is a process for accomplishing purpose. It is blue print of business growth and a road map of development. It helps in deciding objectives both in quantitative and qualitative terms. It is setting of goals on the basis of objectives and keeping in view the resources. A plan should be a realistic view of the expectations. Depending upon the activities, a plan can be long range, intermediate range or short range. It is the framework within which it must operate. For management seeking external support, the plan is the most important document and key to growth. Preparation of a comprehensive plan will not guarantee success, but lack of a sound plan will almost certainly ensure failure.

PURPOSE OF PLAN

Just as no two organizations are alike, so also their plans. It is therefore important to prepare a plan keeping in view the necessities of the enterprise. A plan is an important aspect of business.

It serves the following three critical functions:

1. Helps management to clarify, focus, and research their business's or project's development and prospects.
2. Provides a considered and logical framework within which a business can develop and pursue business strategies over the next three to five years.
3. Offers a benchmark against which actual performance can be measured and reviewed.

IMPORTANCE OF THE PLANNING PROCESS

A plan can play a vital role in helping to avoid mistakes or recognize hidden opportunities. Preparing a satisfactory plan of the organization is essential. The planning process enables management to understand more clearly what they want to achieve, and how and when they can do it.

A well-prepared business plan demonstrates that the managers know the business and that they have thought through its development in terms of products, management, finances, and most importantly, markets and competition. Planning helps in forecasting the future, makes the future visible to some extent. It bridges between where we are and where we want to go. Planning is looking ahead.

Types of plans or planning:

- Architectural planning
- Business plan
- Comprehensive planning
- Enterprise Architecture Planning
- Event Planning and Production
- Family planning
- Financial planning
- Infrastructure planning
- Land use planning
- Life planning
- Marketing plan
- Network resource planning
- Strategic planning
- Urban planning

THE OBJECTIVES

The objectives are general parts of the planning process. They are the end-results towards which all business activities are directed. They are needed in every aspect where performance and result directly and vitally affect the survival and success of the firm. In other words, the objective of the firm justifies its existence. Robert C.

Appley, "Objectives are goals; they are aims which management and administration wish the organization to achieve." In other words, goals, aims and purposes are also used to signify objectives. Newman and Summer stated, "For managerial purposes, it is useful to think of objectives as the results we want to achieve. Objective covers firm's long-range plans specific departmental goals and short-term individual assignment also."

THE POLICIES

George R. Ferry, "Policy is a verbal, written or implied overall guide setting up boundaries that supply the general units and directions in which managerial action will take place." Policies are specific guidelines and constraints for managerial thinking on decision-making and action. Policies provide the framework within which decision-makers are expected to operate while making organizational decisions. They are the basic guides to be consistent in decision-making.

PLANNING BASICS

Essentials of Planning

Planning is not done off hand. It is prepared after careful and extensive research.

For a comprehensive business plan, management has to:

- Clearly define the target/ goal in writing.
- It should be set by a person having authority.
- The goal should be realistic.
- It should be specific.
- Acceptability
- Easily measurable
- Identify all the main issues which need to be addressed.
- Review past performance.
- Decide budgetary requirement.
- Focus on matters of strategic importance.
- What are requirements and how will they be met?
- What will be the likely length of the plan and its structure?
- Identify shortcomings in the concept and gaps.
- Strategies for implementation.
- Review periodically.

APPLICATIONS

In Organizations

Planning is also a management process, concerned with defining goals for future organizational performance and deciding on the tasks and resources to be used in order to attain those goals. To meet the goals, managers may develop plans such as a business plan or a marketing plan. Planning always has a purpose. The purpose may be achievement of certain goals or targets. The planning helps to achieve these goals or target by using the available time and resources. To minimize the timing and resources also require proper planning.

The concept of planning is to identify what the organization wants to do by using the four questions which are "where are we today in terms of our business or strategy planning? Where are we going? Where do we want to go? How are we going to get there?...

In Public Policy

Planning refers to the practice and the profession associated with the idea of planning an idea yourself, (land use planning, urban planning or spatial planning). In many countries, the operation of a town and country planning system is often referred to as 'planning' and the professionals which operate the system are known as 'planners'....... It is a conscious as well as sub-conscious activity.

It is "an anticipatory decision making process " that helps in coping with complexities. It is deciding future course of action from amongst alternatives. It is a process that involves making and evaluating each set of interrelated decisions. It is selection of missions, objectives and " translation of knowledge into action." A planned performance brings better results compared to unplanned one. A Managers' job is planning, monitoring and controlling.

Planning and goal setting are important traits of an organization. It is done at all levels of the organization. Planning includes the plan, the thought process, action, and implementation.Planning gives more power over the future. Planning is deciding in advance what to do, how to do it, when to do it, and who should do it. It bridges the gap from where the organization is to where it wants to be. The planning function involves establishing goals and arranging them in logical order.

8

Nature of Objectives, Strategies and Policies

Authorities differ as to the exact nature of objectives for business enterprises. Perhaps the better approach is to consider first what the objective of our economic system is. This is, broadly, to provide goods and services to customers.

Industrial and commercial concerns, which comprise the greater part of the economic system, must therefore have the same objective. The objective of a limited company clearly states that the objective is to manufacture a commodity or provide a service. Nationalized industries have the predominant objective of providing an efficient and economical service to customers.

GENERAL AND SPECIFIC OBJECTIVES

Objectives can be general or specific and may range in time from months to years; they may apply to the whole company or to units or persons. General objectives are determined by the board of directors who approve other objectives.

It is preferable for objectives to be specific and expressed in quantitative terms. The first question to be answered is: what is the nature of the present business? This may change, but it must be understood in order for adaptation to changing customer needs to be possible. For example, a firm selling typewriters and accounting machines can expand with technology and move on to computers. If it decides it is in the 'information processing' business, rather than the 'office machine' business, then expansion will be easier. Specific objectives usually have time limits, e.g. to open a new spare-parts section in six months' time; or it could be to diversify in certain fields in order to avoid relying on the fortunes of a single market or industry. The big problem in such a venture is whether staff on the right caliber are available effectively to operate these newer types of business.

The ideal is for a company to formulate specific objectives and develop policies, within the framework of general objectives, which together result in coordinated and controlled decision making. Careful planning of objectives helps management to give members a sense of direction and purpose. This is essential to achieve effective results. To be able to survive, a firm must earn sufficient profits to sell services or products, of a certain quality, at a competitive price. Peter Drucker stresses that survival depends upon the ability to cover the costs of staying in business. These costs include providing for replacement and obsolescence as well as market risk and uncertainly.

But it is rare to see survival stated as an objective. Drucker considers objectives are important in every area where performance and results directly affect the survival and prosperity of a business. These key areas must be carefully selected and he distinguishes them by considering. He then goes on to mention eight specific areas in which objectives have to be set, in terms of performance and results. These are: market share; innovation; productivity; physical and financial resources; profitability; manager performance and development; worker performance and attitude, and public responsibility. It should be noted that the eight key results areas are relevant for public sector and non-profit ventures, even though they were directed at profit orientated enterprise. Whatever areas are deemed important, it is preferable that any standards desired should be capable of being expressed in quantitative terms (e.g. number of items to be produced monthly). It is also important to note that if the organization structure is not well designed, managers will find it difficult to achieve high performance.

Advantages of business objectives:

- They embody basic ideas and theories concerning what the enterprise is trying to accomplish;
- They provide a basis for directing and guiding the enterprise and provide targets which enable efforts to be observed and aided;
- They help to motive people and they provide a sense of unity to the various groups in the organization, as an individuals unit's contribution can be seen to be integrated with total enterprise goals.

CONCEPT AND PROCESS OF MANAGING BY OBJECTIVES

Management by Objectives (MBO) relies on the defining of objectives for each employee and then comparing and directing their performance against the objectives which have been set. It aims to increase organizational performance by aligning goals and subordinate objectives throughout the organization. Ideally, employees get strong input to identifying their objectives, time lines for completion, etc. MBO includes ongoing tracking and feedback in the process to reach objectives.

Management by Objectives was first outlined by Peter Drucker in 1954 in his book 'The practice of Management'. Drucker managers should avoid 'the activity trap', getting so involved in their day to day activities that they forget their main purpose or objective. One of the concepts of MBO was that instead of just a few top-managers, all managers of a firm should participate in the strategic planning process, in order to improve the implementability of the plan. Another concept of MBO was that managers should implement a range of performance systems, designed to help the organization stay on the right track. Clearly, Management by Objectives can thus be seen as a predecessor of Value Based Management!

MBO principles are:

- Cascading of organizational goals and objectives,
- Specific objectives for each member,

- Participative decision making,
- Explicit time period, and
- Performance evaluation and feedback.

Management by Objectives also introduced the SMART method for checking the validity of the Objectives, which should be 'SMART':

- Specific
- Measurable
- Achievable
- Realistic, and
- Time-related.

In the 90s, Peter Drucker put the significance of this organization management method into perspective, when he said: "It's just another tool. It is not the great cure for management inefficiency... MBO works if you know the objectives, 90% of the time you don't."

NATURE AND PURPOSE OF STRATEGIES AND POLICIES

Nationally, much attention has been given to the problem of balancing work and family responsibilities. The issue of problems that working families face is not an insignificant one as nearly one-half of all married mothers of infants is in the work force. There are conflicting needs of all involved, making it difficult to deal with the problems working families are confronted with; e.g., parents' work schedules often cut into their time with their infant, infants need care from their parents that supports healthy development in the early stages of life, and employers depend on responsible and available employees.

During the past several years, some of the cutting edge firms have established leave policies and implemented employee benefits packages that include protecting a woman's job for at least six weeks after childbirth. For example, U.S. Sprint offers a family leave of absence to support family adjustments and prevent high-performing employees from leaving the company. IBM offers up to three years of personal leave, including six to eight weeks of paid leave for recovery from childbirth. New mothers or fathers (natural or adoptive) may be granted up to three years of unpaid leave with the option of working part-time during the period. Throughout the leave, employees continue to receive full benefits. A percentage of adoption expenses is also reimbursed. However, policies in other companies have not always been as generous or consistently applied. For example, some companies only allowed female employees to take family leave but not male employees.

Given the recent recession, the rising divorce rate, and an increasing number of children born out of wedlock, the traditional family has changed. Employment policies have fallen behind in addressing these changes. The phenomenon of the two-paycheck or single-parent family is one that has occurred so quickly that our nation has had little time to realise its impact, understand the range of issues it raises, or generate solutions for the resulting problems. More than 70 per cent of American women between the ages of 20 and 50 are employed and, as of 1987, more than half the mothers of children under one were working or seeking work.

The reality of the working parents' phenomenon is somewhat disturbing in that these parents are, in effect, often penalized for what is a necessity: earning money to care for their children and to support their families. As women have continued to enter the work force and remain there after having children, the issue of maternity leave has taken on new importance. In addition, as the population ages, many employees find themselves needing time off from work to care for their elderly parents. Employees are being compelled to take leaves of absence to fulfill their many responsibilities. Too often, however, if an individual takes a leave of absence and then decides to return to work, there might not be a job to return to.

To alleviate the work-family conflict that many parents face today, as well as to remove the inconsistent polices companies have been using to control leaves of absence, parental leave initiatives have been undertaken at both the federal and state levels. At the federal level, the Family and

Medical Leave Act was signed by President Clinton on Friday, February 5, 1993, after just 16 days in office, granting workers unpaid leave for family emergencies.

The House, on February 3, 1993, voted 265-163 to send the bill to the Senate. The following day, the Senate, after finally pushing aside a GOP attempt to attach a gays-in-the-military amendment, overwhelmingly passed the bill on the evening of February 4, 71-27. The president's signature on February 5 was the culmination of eight years of effort by Congress, women's groups, labour and business. The bill was twice vetoed by former President George Bush (in 1990 and 1992) - he refused to place another government mandate on business. The new Act, which became effective on August 5, 1993, represents the first federal legislation in the U.S. addressing workers' rights regarding health- and family-related employment leaves.

AN OVERVIEW OF THE FMLA AND ITS POTENTIAL EFFECTS

The Family and Medical Leave Act (FMLA) provides up to 12 weeks of unpaid, job-protected leave during a 12-month period for workers to cope with a family sickness, elder-care, childbirth or adoption. Employers may determine the 12-month period as long as it is consistently applied; e.g., calendar year, fiscal year, rolling year measured from the date the leave is used or requested, or any other fixed 12-month period. Employees may take the 12 weeks consecutively or intermittently; e.g., a worker may take 20 three-day leaves for treatments such as chemotherapy (however, covered employees may be required to use sick leave or paid vacation rather than the unpaid leave).

In order to be eligible for a FMLA leave, employees must work for companies with 50 or more employees within a 75-mile radius and must have been employed for one or more years and worked at least 25 hours a week. A 1987 survey by the Census Bureau, 66 per cent of American workers (approximately 50 million) are covered by the new law, along with congressional employees and state and local government workers. Covered employees are guaranteed a return to their same job or an equivalent post. During the leave, health care benefits and other terms and conditions of employment are maintained. Employers must also adhere to other federal, state, and local laws regarding family and medical leaves. Exempted from the new law are companies with less than 50 employees, salaried employees in the highest-paid ten per cent of a company's work force, and workers whose leave would create a substantial and grievous injury to the business.

The Act has been hailed by some as a savior of American families and declared by others to be a destroyer of business. Companies currently subjected to local leave laws have found such laws can be burdensome. Republicans have predicted the Act will be so burdensome that it will cause more layoffs or force employers to trim other benefits. Republicans say that in mandating it, government will be adding to labour costs - costs which already are high in relation to costs abroad.

For example, there is particular expense involved in the requirement that health insurance be continued while the employee is away and not performing work. The Small Business Administration estimates that the average cost per employee will be $1,995. James Bunnell, owner of a small printing company in Ohio with 65 workers, has stated that "if everybody took advantage of this, I'd have extra costs of $60,000-70,000 a year". Furthermore, the U.S. General Accounting Office estimates that approximately 30 per cent of the employees taking advantage of the FMLA will be replaced by temporary workers. For instance, in 1991 Washington, D.C. passed a law that mandated leaves within their area and at one hospital 83 people took leaves after the law was passed.

Qualified replacements had to be found, which was costly. Consequently, the cost to employers may actually be much higher when including the cost of recruiting and training replacement workers, which could total $56 million nationally along with the costs associated with lower productivity among temporary employees. One noteworthy provision in the FMLA involving employer costs states that if an employee fails to return from leave, the employer may be able to recoup the health insurance premiums paid (unless the employee fails to return due to a serious health condition or other circumstance beyond his/her control). There are additional administrative burdens companies must endure, such as medical certification and handling the required record keeping. For example, employers must designate leaves taken under the performance as "FMLA" leaves, notices to employees regarding the FMLA must be retained in personnel flies, and medical certification forms must be maintained in separate confidential files.

Other employer costs include the training of a company's management and all other employees regarding the company's leave policies and any costs involving lawsuits filed if organizations are charged with discriminating against employees who request leaves or potentially discriminate against them upon their return. The effect of these increased costs to organizations will be cost-cutting somewhere else; *i.e.*, reducing other benefits or trimming pay increases. It is argued that it will not stimulate new hiring and will do nothing for the unemployed. Instead, opponents have stated that the FMLA will be another incentive for employers to cut full-time jobs. In a 1991 Gallup poll of approximately 1,000 firms, half of the small business owners polled stated that a leave mandate would "cause them to hesitate to hire young women, to cut low-skilled jobs, and to reduce or eliminate other employee benefits".

In addition, the respondents stated there were "hidden" costs of family leave, which include having other employees work longer hours and simply not completing some work while an employee is on leave. Others have stated that managers are thinking that even having employees is a bad idea and the best response is to have as few employees as possible by substituting machines for labour and shifting many tasks to outside contractors, such as janitorial services, accounting, and subassembly. The bill's supporters, however, have argued that the FMLA will make America's work force more competitive by making jobs more stable and lifting workers' morale. The FMLA is also expected to reduce unscheduled absenteeism at work. For example, Johnson and Johnson revealed that absenteeism was 50 per cent lower among employees who used the company's family leaves and other family-oriented plans, e.g., flexible hours and child care subsidies. In addition, the cost of hiring temporaries may be minimized by those companies utilizing cross-training, which is a team concept where employees are able to fill in for each other when on leave. Cross-training eliminates the need to hire temporary employees and also empowers other employees with greater responsibilities, which can increase morale. Another alternative that some companies might consider implementing in order to decrease the disruption from a leave is to allow a person on an extended leave to work at home as a consultant.

Proponents have also noted that since the FMLA is in line with many policies already in place at companies, it may not provoke a dramatic increase in the number of work days lost. One reason may be due to the fact that the number of companies with some type of leave policy already in place prior to the passage of the FMLA has been estimated to be up to 89 per cent based on a Bureau of Labour Statistics study. In another survey conducted in March 1993 by Hewitt Associates, as many as 63 per cent of the 1,000 surveyed employers indicated they already had family-leave policies and 56 per cent had medical-leave policies in place. Most of these firms (70 per cent) indicated that the cost of providing employee leaves was insignificant. These same companies reported that, since developing their policies, they have noticed a boost in morale and goodwill among employees along with a decrease in turnover, and about 40 per cent, they experienced decreases in recruiting and retraining costs since implementing their leave policies.

Others argue that the costs of unpaid leaves are expected to be less expensive than replacing employees who quit. For example, AT&T found that allowing parents to take an unpaid leave that cost them just over 30 per cent of an employee's salary was cost efficient compared to the 150 per cent it would cost to replace the employee with a new worker. In another example, the Grand Met's. "family responsibility" policy which allows for up to a three-year career break with the guarantee of a comparable job on return, the option for part-time work, a week off for paternity leave, and bonus provisions for returning from leave has helped the organization increase its retention of skilled staff. Finally, regarding the effects of the FMLA, the following opinion was rendered in a General Accounting Office report:

We believe the proposed family and medical leave benefits are unlikely to adversely constrain wage and benefit negotiations between workers and their employers.... there will be little measurable net cost to employers associated with replacing workers or maintaining output while workers are on unpaid leave. Firms told us that fewer than one-third of the workers taking extended family or medical leave are replaced and that for those who are replaced, the associated cost was generally less than the wages and benefits that were paid to the absent workers before they took leave. Absences were typically handled by reallocating work among the remaining work force. While some inconvenience resulted, firms also experienced savings in wages not paid to the absent workers. Thus, we would not expect this legislation to cause major disruptions for most employers.

Even some employers who had no leave policies in place prior to the FMLA, such as the Government Personnel Mutual Life Insurance Company based in San Antonio, Texas, have indicated that they doubt the leave would have a large effect on the organization because they do not see it being utilized frivolously - the fact that it is unpaid means many will not be able to afford it. Finally, studies examining the effects of mandatory leave policies that have already been established by states prior to the FMLA have been generally positive. For example, a study of Sacramento County in California found that only two per cent of the work force used the paid parental leave once it was enacted and of the workers surveyed, 63 per cent stated the policy reinforced their loyalty to their company. Now that we have established where we are today concerning family and medical leaves, the following section will provide an historical overview of leave policies in the U.S. in order to gain a better understanding of how the FMLA was developed and passed. Family leave policy had its origin in the interaction between employers' pregnancy and childbirth leave policies and Title VII of the Civil Rights Act. The early issue was not so much whether women could take leave when they became pregnant - many employers insisted that female employees leave their jobs as soon as their pregnancies became evident. Pregnancy was historically treated as a disability. Instead, early conflicts arose over the issue of when the pregnant woman's disability came to an end. Obviously, it did not end at the moment of childbirth; some period of recuperation was necessary.

In the 1920s, the actual number of married women in the work force grew by 40 per cent with the most perceptible growth in the 20 to 35 age group. But there was no legislation provision for pregnant workers or working mothers; rather, common practice allowed a woman to stay in the work force only until her first pregnancy. Throughout the 1920s and 1930s the American public overwhelmingly rejected the idea of married working women. As a result of the war effort in the 1940s, working women regained some of the status they lost in the 1930s. By 1944, nearly one-third of the female population over 14 worked outside the home. For the first time, out of a desperate need for wartime workers, the U.S. had to come to terms with married women in the work force and how these women were to continue with their familial responsibilities. However, at the end of the war in 1945, many women lost their high-paying union jobs to returning G.I.s and returned to low-paying, low-status "female" jobs. The unions did very little to help women retain their jobs or seniority and even manipulated job definitions so that women, because of existing protective labour laws, would be unable to perform them.

For the next 15 to 20 years, women attempted to fulfill their old role of the wife-companion, and for many the experience resulted in frustration and anger. This model began to change as opportunities in the labour force expanded and the number of women with college degrees increased. In 1966, the National Organization for Women (NOW) was formed with the pledge to "take action to bring women into full participation in the mainstream society now". The NOW feminists' agenda was broad, ranging from eliminating barriers in the workplace to ending discrimination in higher education. They focussed on issues of equality for women as individuals and workers, not as wives and mothers. In the charter of their first convention, NOW called for job-protected maternity leave for working women. As women have continued to enter the work force and remain there after having children, the issue of maternity leave has taken on new importance.

The legal treatment of parental rights in the work force, specifically in terms of a national family leave policy, has its roots in action that began in the 1960s regarding sex discrimination. The Civil Rights Act of 1964 provided another avenue for expanding rights and protections for pregnant workers. Title VII of the Civil Rights Act outlawed discrimination by private employers with 15 or more employees. An amendment in 1972 extended the coverage to public employers (except military personnel).

Congress also established an enforcement agency, the Equal Employment Opportunity Commission (EEOC), to administer and interpret the statute's provisions. This federal law prohibited, among other things, sex discrimination with respect to "compensation, terms, conditions, or privileges of employment," but early versions of the Equal Employment Opportunity Council's guidelines did not specifically mention pregnancy disability. Title VII did make several types of sex discrimination unlawful, however.

First, employers cannot treat employees differently on the basis of sex unless the employer can establish that sex is a bona fide occupational qualification, which means that it is a reasonable necessity to the normal operation of a position. Second, employer actions motivated by a discriminatory intent violate Title VII. These cases might involve an employee alleging that the employer refused to hire, failed to promote, fired, or took other adverse action because of the employee's sex. Employers are able to avoid liability by producing a nondiscriminatory explanation for the employment action, such as poor work performance or excess absenteeism. Third, Title VII makes unlawful employment practices that have an unequal impact on one sex - in other words, rules which are neutral on paper but which have a disproportionately adverse effect on any protected group.

In 1966, the EEOC supported the position that denying disability benefit coverage to pregnant employees did not constitute sex discrimination. In addition, in General Electric Co. vs. Gilbert the Supreme Court ruled that a company's disability benefits plan was not discriminatory under Title VII because it failed to cover pregnancy-related disabilities. One year later, in Nashville Gas vs. Satty, the Court ruled that employers may refuse sick pay to women employees who are unable to work due to pregnancy and childbirth, but they may not divest those women of their accumulated seniority merely because they take maternity leave.

To counteract the Supreme Court in Gilbert and the part of Satty that denied pregnant workers the right to sick pay, a coalition of various groups was formed. Members of the women's rights movement began to show how employers' practices with respect to pregnancy and time for childbearing were discriminatory against women. Women began to challenge these employer practices using Title VII of the Civil Rights Act of 1964.

Finally, in 1978 the EEOC reversed its position and issued a statement claiming that disabilities resulting from "pregnancy, miscarriage, abortion, childbirth, and recovery therefrom are, for all job-related purposes, temporary disabilities" and must be treated in the same fashion as other short-term disabilities with regard to leave, health or disability insurance, seniority, and reemployment.

The coalition of groups supported the Pregnancy Discrimination Act (PDA) which was passed in 1978 as an amendment to Title VII of the Civil Rights Act of 1964. The Act requires that physically able pregnant women not be subjected to leaves or terminations when other able-bodied workers would not and that when a woman is disabled due to pregnancy, she receives the same sick pay, insurance coverage, and job protection as an employer's other disabled employees. The passage of the PDA by Congress won women the basic right to be treated equally under the law as individuals and workers, rather than as wives and mothers. Thus, by the close of the 1970s, a basic national maternity policy had been established. While the PDA sounded promising, it was not a cure for all the disadvantages pregnant workers face.

The PDA only provides protection for women who work for employers offering disability insurance benefits, and roughly only 40 per cent of all women receive the type of maternity leave benefits that guarantee a job-protected leave with partial wage replacement. In addition, because employers were not required to provide disability leaves or other benefits to employees, these leaves were only available to pregnant workers to the extent that they were provided for other comparable disabilities. Employers with inadequate leave policies were free to maintain such policies. Also, disability leaves, when available, need only be applied to pregnant employees for the period of disability, which is typically four to eight weeks.

Bernstein, even 14 years after Congress passed the Pregnancy Discrimination Act in 1978, tens of thousands of women still lost their jobs annually after becoming pregnant. Many were dismissed either illegally or simply because they weren't covered employees under the Act (e.g., the federal government and small businesses aren't covered). Additionally, women who retain their job after returning from a maternity leave have often been denied subsequent raises and promotions.

Bernstein states that the EEOC has indicated that the 3,000 pregnancy discrimination charges it handles each year account for less than five per cent of the cases filed in U.S. courts. While the Pregnancy Discrimination Act did not address a woman's need for a child care leave beyond a brief recovery period, it did lay the groundwork for further legislation.

DEVELOPMENT OF FAMILY AND MEDICAL LEAVE POLICIES

History shows that women and men have been treated very differently and have been given different rights under the law. These distinctions have derived mainly from the notion that men's natural social role is productive labour, while women's is reproductive labour. Out of these notions came increasing discrimination against women instead of increasing equality. The demands of World War II gave a brief reprieve to female employment restrictions as women were recruited to do "a man's job" due to the shortage of men at the time. However, following the war, the same sex-stratified employment persisted.

At the same time, the early 1940s saw the beginning of laws specifically addressing pregnancy. The Women's Bureau of the Department of Labour made specific recommendations regarding pregnancy and a number of states passed laws that addressed those recommendations. But the legislation was not effective in rendering equality to working women; rather, it exacerbated the traditional thinking surrounding working women. In 1964 the idea of a "Cumulative Earned Leave Plan" was developed by Lawrence L. Suhm. Suhm proposed that employees earn time off from their jobs in addition to their regular vacation time, with the leave time transferable between jobs and the amount based on actual time worked. He proposed that job benefits, seniority, and other rights would be protected while on leave.

To finance the plan, Suhm recommended that equal contributions from the employer, employee, and the government be made to a fund based on a percentage of the employee's wages and used only for leave times. While Suhm may not have been taken seriously in 1964, there are similarities to his proposal and subsequent leave acts that have been implemented. Several cities and states have passed family and medical leave acts. For example, the city of Philadelphia passed a law on August 4, 1984, giving adoptive parents and fathers the same rights as working mothers and allowing them up to six months of unpaid leave, with a guarantee that they can return to their old jobs. Washington, D.C. and the state of Connecticut each passed a law that mandated leaves up to 16 weeks during a two-year period. Also in a two-year period, California provides for up to four months of leave, Maine provides up to 10 weeks, Rhode Island up to 13 weeks, and Washington, New Jersey and Oregon up to 12 weeks of family and/or medical leave for private employers.

In addition, prior to the FMLA some states had passed laws only applicable to public-sector employees (e.g., Alaska, Arizona, Delaware, Florida, Georgia, Idaho, Illinois, Iowa, Louisiana, Maryland, Missouri, North Dakota, Oklahoma, South Carolina, and West Virginia). By 1990, 25 states had passed a variety of family leave laws. Common features have included allowing parents to take a leave, extending leaves to adoptions, requiring employers to make health insurance coverage available to employees while on leave, and providing job protection.

However, state family leave laws tend to differ on who can take leaves and for what reasons. These state laws also differ on the size a company must be to comply and the length of leave employers must provide. Thus, the need for the passage of a federal leave law was recognized in order to establish minimum standards and requirements. In 1986 the first bill by Colorado Democrat Patricia Schroeder was introduced in Congress regarding family and medical leaves. The bill provided for a minimum of 18 weeks of unpaid leave for any employee wanting to remain home with a newborn, newly adopted, or seriously ill child. The bill was defeated, however. Around this same time frame, unions began bargaining more heavily for parental leave clauses in their contacts. Consequently, many companies began implementing parental leave policies in some form.

In 1990 a family leave bill was again introduced calling for 12 weeks of unpaid leave for medical emergencies and for the addition of a new child to the household. While businesses did not initially like the idea of the government getting involved in establishing employment policies, they were not opposed to family leave in general. However, President Bush vetoed the bill because he was concerned that a mandatory leave policy would reduce employer flexibility and undercut U.S. competitiveness. The current FMLA was reintroduced in 1991 and eventually passed in 1993. Similarities between the FMLA and Suhm's 1964 proposal include the fact the leave time is provided in addition to vacation, it has limits based on the amount of time worked, leave can be taken consecutively or split, and benefits, seniority and other rights remain in effect during the leave. The primary difference is that Suhm's proposal was developed for economic reasons rather than the family reasons established by the FMLA.

When requesting a FMLA leave, a 30-day notice must be given, except in cases of extreme emergencies. FMLA leaves may be requested for many reasons, including childbirth, adoption, elder care, or "a serious health condition."

A "serious health condition" is defined by the Department of Labour to include any illness, injury, impairment of physical or mental condition that involves:

- A period of incapacitation, or treatment in connection with, or consequent to, inpatient care.
- Any period of incapacitation that requires an absence from work, school, or other regular daily activities for more than three days, so long as the individual is under the supervision of a health care provider.
- Any condition requiring continuing treatment by a health care provider for a chronic or long-term condition that is either incurable or, if left untreated, would result in a period of incapacitation of more than three days.

Medical conditions require either a medical certification form or a letter from the employee's health care provider; e.g., medical doctor, osteopath, dentist, clinical psychologist, optometrist, chiropractor, nurse practitioner, nurse midwife, or a Christian Science practitioner. The certification includes the date the problem began, a diagnosis, treatment explanation, hospital need assessment, and a statement that the employee cannot perform work of any kind or the functions of his or her particular job. In the event the leave request is to care for a seriously ill family member, certification from the family member's health care provider may be required. Employers are prohibited from requiring additional information beyond what is covered in the DOL form. However, employers may require a second opinion, but not from their regular medical staff or industrial physicians.

Many employers already had written leave policies in place prior to the passage of the FMLA. Many companies stated the purpose of instituting the leave policies was to attract and retain good employees. For example, National Adoption Exchange and Campbell's Soup have provided 20-day paid leaves plus the use of any accrued vacation time, an additional two months of unpaid leave and up to $2,000 to cover expenses. A growing trend in family benefits has been day care and elder care. For example, the Stride Rite Corporation opened one of the nation's first day care centres that mixes children with the elderly. Today there are over 150 day care/elder care programmes.

COMPLIANCE WITH THE FMLA

A survey of 524 employers by Hewitt Associates, prior to the passage of the FMLA, 70 per cent of the employers offered unpaid leave for the birth or adoption of a child or for serious illness of a family member, and 60 per cent offered unpaid leave when the employee was seriously ill. The biggest problem for organizations with existing policies has been coordinating the company's plan with the federal plan. Similar to the Hewitt survey, another survey conducted by Towers Perrin on the effects of the FMLA indicated that 69 per cent of the respondents stated they already had a family leave policy in place.

However, about half of the 701 respondents said they must modify their leave policies to accommodate part-time employees, 36 per cent said they needed to offer more weeks of leave, 31 per cent stated they would have to continue health coverage, and 25 per cent would need to modify their provisions to allow leaves for more reasons. For example, Pacer Systems Inc. in Massachusetts has offered up to six months of leave to employees who give birth or are sick themselves, and they have stated the major difference in complying 'with the FMLA is to extend the leaves, job protection and benefits to people who are themselves not sick. To assist employers and minimize the burden of complying with the FMLA, employers should update job descriptions to comply with the FMLA, adopt written policies regarding restoration to equivalent employment, and ensure parental leave is not a factor in employment decisions such as promotions or partnership determinations (*i.e.*, don't discriminate against those taking FMLA leave).

For those companies without policies, before establishing family and medical leave policies employers must familiarize themselves with the FMLA along with any state laws regulating employee leaves. These determine the type of leaves companies must grant, employees' reinstatement rights, leave expirations, etc. It is important for employers to have clear leave policies outlining the types of leaves allowed, their duration, application procedures, and obligations of the employee and employer. The policy should be included in the employee in order to make employees aware of their entitlements and their obligations. A clearly stated, standardized policy can also help ensure that the policy will be applied consistently to all employees. This is important to eliminate potential charges of employment discrimination.

Other questions companies must consider when establishing leave policies include: how much cross-training vs. hiring of temporary workers should be undertaken? How should employees be paid when they cover more positions, higher-level positions, or work more hours when others take leave? What happens to employees who are asked to perform higher-level duties when the employee on leave returns? How will the 12-month period be measured? How will employee payments and other benefits be handled? Smaller companies should also follow these same suggestions. However, for smaller companies with a few hundred employees or less, more changes may be required in their human resource management practices. Because of the costs involved with compliance, an article in the Wall Street Journal indicated that, rather than complying with the law, some smaller organizations have decided to try and avoid it because they lack the staff and financial resources to absorb the costs and dislocation of worker leaves.

For example, Uniforce Temporary Services in Hyde Park, New York, has been receiving numerous inquiries from small employers who want to "keep their head count below 50 by using temporaries," and thus remain exempt from the FMLA. However, employers must keep in mind that a long-term temporary worker would come under the FMLA if the individual worked more than 24 hours a week over a 12-month period. Since women have been found to be more willing than men to take long amounts of unpaid time off, another approach some are concerned that organizations might take is to discriminate in the hiring of women, particularly young women.

About a third of the employers contacting a personnel service in Oklahoma City have asked for female job candidates over 40. However, if employers fail to comply with the FMLA or discriminate in hiring in order to become exempt, the performance is likely to generate numerous lawsuits, which will be expensive to defend. In addition, employers must now add to their list of protected classes against employment discrimination - *i.e.*, employees who take FMLA leaves cannot be discriminated against upon their return because of their taking a leave.

FAMILY AND MEDICAL LEAVE POLICIES AROUND THE WORLD

Work-family issues are a global concern. Many countries regard family leave benefits as important. In 1984, 75 countries (the U.S. not being one of them) guaranteed paid work leave at the time of child delivery, with job seniority and pensions being maintained. Compared to Americans, Europeans tend to value all types of employee leaves and perceive society as having a responsibility in terms of aiding families. Many European Community (EC) countries mandate liberal maternity, paternity and parental leaves. While family leave is not consistent throughout Europe, many European countries even have a "career break programme" which allows employees to take a job-protected multi-year leave after the birth of a child. For example, at National Westminster Bank in London, career breaks from six months to seven years are available to all employees employed for at least one year. The following identifies the types of leave established by law in Europe:

Vacation: 4-5 weeks for all employees Maternity: 3-6 months with pay and job protection Paternity: 5-10 days (some countries) Parental: 6 months to 2 years (some countries) Sick Child: 5-60 days (some countries) A few of these policies will be discussed in more detail in this section. For example, the United Kingdom provides from 11 to 40 weeks of leave. The United Kingdom offers two tiers of benefits and is one of the most restrictive countries in its leave policies. To be eligible for maternity leave and tier-one benefits (of approximately $60/week for 18 weeks), women must be employed by the same employer six months before their 26th week of pregnancy. To qualify for tier-two benefits (of 90 per cent of their wages for 6 weeks, a lower rate for another 12 weeks, and job-protected leave for 18 weeks), women must have worked for the same employer for two years before their 26th week of pregnancy or five years if they are part-time employees.

It has been estimated that forty per cent of pregnant women who work fail to qualify for maternity leave in the United Kingdom because of the continuous employment requirements, and of those who are eligible, most qualify only for tier-one non-protected leave benefits. Consequently, the number of women from the United Kingdom who stop work for childbirth is small and the number of those who return is "inconsequential". However, improvements may be forthcoming as there are new policies that have been proposed among the EC that would improve maternity provisions for British women. These proposals include reducing the employment requirements for leave eligibility, increasing the rate of maternity pay, requiring employers to remove risks or reorganizing working conditions to accommodate pregnant women whose health and safety is at risk in the workplace, and protecting pregnant women against dismissal based on their pregnancy from the time they become pregnant until the end of their maternity leave. Another example of leave policies is provided by the Federal Republic of Germany which feels a strong obligation to protect families.

While the United Kingdom tends to have some of the most restrictive policies among European countries, German laws regarding the employment of women are very protective because a career as a homemaker is widely accepted. Thus, the country encourages women to remain at home and care for children by providing cash benefits and job-protected leaves. In addition, all working parents are eligible for five paid days off yearly per child under the age of eight when a child is sick. Women are eligible for maternity leave if employed only one month prior to when their pregnancy begins. The country's benefits have proven to be very popular in that 95 per cent of eligible women utilize these benefits. The per cent-age of German mothers returning to work following marriage and child rearing is lower than many other European countries due to the extensive benefits provided.

However, while those women who do return from leave have their jobs, seniority and pension protected, some have indicated that women tend to suffer from reduced career opportunities upon their return because of the restrictions placed on women's working conditions and hours of work allowed. Thus, most women are employed primarily in lower-level, traditionally female occupations, which may be why many German employers have indicated they have found few problems complying with the statutory leave provisions. Sweden provides an example of flexible and comprehensive social welfare programmes in that benefits include "family support services" in the form of child allowances, day care, pensions, and subsidized housing.

In addition, "employment programmes" include job training, unemployment compensation, sick leave, child care, medical care, and partial retirement benefits for older workers.

Programmes are designed for entire population groups. With the generous flexible parental leave and employment provisions provided (such as the right of parents to reduce work time to 75 per cent of normal hours while their children are under ten years of age), less than 10 per cent of women leave employment after childbirth (compared to over 90 per cent of British mothers and 50 per cent of German mothers). The downside of the provisions, however, includes Swedish employers excluding women from positions where the leaves would be most damaging, thus again women tend to hold traditional female positions (e.g., clerical and sales) and have difficulty entering the management ranks.

Companies in Europe have developed innovative time and leave policies because they don't want to lose good employees. In the United States we still question whether someone taking time off is really committed to the company or their career. While the U.S. may have a lot it can learn from Europe and other countries in the area of implementing generous leave programmes, many U.S. companies have established innovative workplace plans that are rare in other countries. For example, Marion Kozak, the coordinator of Daycare Trust in London, "the countries in the EC have a lot to learn from the United States in terms of charitable involvement, sponsorship and company involvement in workplace practices", such as employee assistance programmes and child care resource and referral networks that have been pioneered by U.S. businesses.

The evidence of social science shows that mothers need time to recover physically and emotionally from childbirth, families need time to adjust to the arrival of a new family member, and very importantly, infants need time in a stable, caring environment. Some say, however, that "time is money." This adage describes the situation many working parents face today. If parents take the time needed to care for a newborn, it often costs them lost wages. Without recognition of the support needed to meet the changing needs of our society in which two-paycheck and single-parent families will soon predominate, the family will continue to straggle. It appears that the U.S. took a first step in 1993 by establishing the federal Family and Medical Leave Act. The implementation of a national leave policy allows the U.S. to continue its tradition of improving working conditions by addressing the needs of its new, diverse work force.

Another positive aspect of a national leave policy is that it provides one baseline law that covered employers must adhere to. This should greatly simplify the problems associated with the current state leave legislation where there is inconsistency and inequality among states. In addition, many expect that the Act will have the added benefits of increasing employee morale, reducing turnover rates (and thus recruitment and training costs), and improving productivity. One question still to be answered is who will benefit most from the new law?

While there are an estimated 40 to 50 million workers eligible for the FMLA, many cannot afford to make use of its uncompensated leave benefits. Some argue that white collar workers with a high-earning spouse are those more able to take unpaid leaves. Critics argue the legislation could create problems by unintentionally discriminating against lower-paid workers since these employees often will be unable to take full advantage of the leave, thus the legislation will not help those who need it most.

Another issue employers must face is how to verify and investigate leave requests. Other issues and questions include: Is there any recourse for employers who feel an employee abuses the act? Do employers have the ability to deny leave if they feel the illness is not serious? How should employers handle those employees who don't provide notice? Can employees substitute accrued sick days for unpaid leave? What constitutes an "equivalent" job when a leave taker returns and his/her job is taken?

Another future issue concerning the FMLA may need to address the failure to include time needed by new mothers who are nursing their child (for instance, Germany allows women time off to breast feed while at work). While they can take a leave of absence for time to go to the doctor, mothers cannot take that time to nurse a child. Some argue this seems to be discriminatory. In addition, the issue of sex segregation in terms of clustering women in traditionally lower-level female occupations may be of great concern if women who make use of leave policies find that the trade-offs include less employment opportunity. The FMLA is yet to be tested in the court systems.

Now is the time for more flexible work options that will reduce the work-family conflict. The nationally-mandated FMLA should greatly benefit today's Americans by recognizing the importance of well integrated and empowered families which, in turn, will benefit American society. The FMLA is one attempt to "raise the consciousness of people about work and family issues" and make our workplaces more "family-friendly".

Progressive, employee-oriented companies will already have taken steps to establish a family-friendly work environment. For others, however, larger leaps may be needed to comply with the FMLA and deal with the many demographic and societal changes that have already occurred and those that will continue to take place in the future.

9

SWOT Analysis and Decision-Making

CONCEPT OF SWOT ANALYSIS

A SWOT analysis must first start with defining a desired end state or objective. A SWOT analysis may be incorporated into the strategic planning model.

Strategic Planning, including SWOT and SCAN analysis, has been the subject of much research:

- *Strengths*: Attributes of the person or company that are helpful to achieving the objectives.
- *Weaknesses*: Attributes of the person or company that are harmful to achieving the objectives.
- *Opportunities*: *External* conditions that are helpful to achieving the objectives.
- *Threats*: *External* conditions which could do damage to the objectives.

Identification of SWOTs are essential because subsequent steps in the process of planning for achievement of the selected objective may be derived from the SWOTs. First, the decision makers have to determine whether the objective is attainable, given the SWOTs.

If the objective is NOT attainable a different objective must be selected and the process repeated. The SWOT analysis is often used in academia to highlight and identify strengths, weaknesses, opportunities and threats. It is particularly helpful in identifying areas for development.

MATCHING AND CONVERTING

Another way of utilizing SWOT is matching and converting. Matching is used to find *competitive advantages* by matching the strengths to opportunities.

Converting is to apply conversion strategies to convert weaknesses or threats into strengths or opportunities.An example of conversion strategy is to find new markets. If the threats or weaknesses cannot be converted a company should try to *minimize* or *avoid* them.

EVIDENCE ON THE USE OF SWOT

SWOT analysis may limit the strategies considered in the evaluation. J. Scott Armstrong notes that "people who use SWOT might conclude that they have done an adequate job of planning and ignore such sensible things as defining the firm's objectives or calculating ROI for alternate strategies." Findings from Menon *et al*. and Hill and Westbrook (1997) have shown that SWOT may harm performance. As an alternative to SWOT, Armstrong describes a 5-step approach alternative that leads to better corporate performance.

These criticisms are addressed to an old version of SWOT analysis that precedes the SWOT analysis under the heading "Strategic and Creative Use of SWOT Analysis." This old version did not require that SWOTs be derived from an agreed upon objective. Examples of SWOT analyses that do not state an objective are under "Human Resources" and "Marketing."

INTERNAL AND EXTERNAL FACTORS

The aim of any SWOT analysis is to identify the key internal and external factors that are important to achieving the objective. These come from within the company's unique value chain.

SWOT analysis groups key pieces of information into two main categories:

- *Internal factors*: The *strengths* and *weaknesses* internal to the organization.
- *External factors*: The *opportunities* and *threats* presented by the external environment to the organization. -

Use a PEST or PESTLE analysis to help identify factors.

The internal factors may be viewed as strengths or weaknesses depending upon their impact on the organization's objectives. What may represent strengths with respect to one objective may be weaknesses for another objective. The factors may include all of the 4P's; as well as personnel, finance, manufacturing capabilities, and so on. The external factors may include macroeconomic matters, technological change, legislation, and socio-cultural changes, as well as changes in the marketplace or competitive position. The results are often presented in the form of a matrix.

SWOT analysis is just one method of categorization and has its own weaknesses. For example, it may tend to persuade companies to compile lists rather than think about what is actually important in achieving objectives. It also presents the resulting lists uncritically and without clear prioritization so that, for example, weak opportunities may appear to balance strong threats. It is prudent not to eliminate too quickly any candidate SWOT entry. The importance of individual SWOTs will be revealed by the value of the strategies it generates. A SWOT item that produces valuable strategies is important. A SWOT item that generates no strategies is not important.

USE OF SWOT ANALYSIS

The usefulness of SWOT analysis is not limited to profit-seeking organizations. SWOT analysis may be used in any decision-making situation when a desired end-state (objective) has been defined. Examples include: non-profit organizations, governmental units, and individuals. SWOT analysis may also be used in pre-crisis planning and preventive crisis management. SWOT analysis may also be used in creating a recommendation during a viability study.

SWOT - LANDSCAPE ANALYSIS

The SWOT-landscape grabs different managerial situations by visualizing and foreseeing the dynamic performance of comparable objects according to findings by

Brendan Kitts, Leif Edvinsson and Tord Beding. Changes in relative performance are continually identified. Projects (or other units of measurements) that could be potential risk or opportunity objects are highlighted. SWOT-landscape also indicates which underlying strength/weakness factors that have had or likely will have highest influence in the context of value in use (for ex. capital value fluctuations).

CORPORATE PLANNING

As part of the development of strategies and plans to enable the organization to achieve its objectives, then that organization will use a systematic/rigorous process known as corporate planning.

SWOT alongside PEST/PESTLE can be used as a basis for the analysis of business and environmental factors:

- Set objectives: Defining what the organization is going to do
- Environmental scanning
  - Internal appraisals of the organization's SWOT, this needs to include an assessment of the present situation as well as a portfolio of products/ services and an analysis of the product/service life cycle
- Analysis of existing strategies, this should determine relevance from the results of an internal/external appraisal. This may include gap analysis which will look at environmental factors
- *Strategic Issues defined*: Key factors in the development of a corporate plan which needs to be addressed by the organization
- *Develop new/revised strategies*: Revised analysis of strategic issues may mean the objectives need to change
- *Establish critical success factors:* The achievement of objectives and strategy implementation
- Preparation of operational, resource, projects plans for strategy implementation
- Monitoring results: Mapping against plans, taking

corrective action which may mean amending objectives/strategies.

MARKETING

In many competitor analyses, marketers build detailed profiles of each competitor in the market, focusing especially on their relative competitive strengths and weaknesses using SWOT analysis. Marketing managers will examine each competitor's cost structure, sources of profits, resources and competencies, competitive positioning and product differentiation, degree of vertical integration, historical responses to industry developments, and other factors.

Marketing management often finds it necessary to invest in research to collect the data required to perform accurate marketing analysis. Management often conducts market research (alternately marketing research) to obtain this information.

Marketers employ a variety of techniques to conduct market research, but some of the more common include:

- Qualitative marketing research, such as focus groups
- Quantitative marketing research, such as statistical surveys
- Experimental techniques such as test markets
- Observational techniques such as ethnographic (on-site) observation
- Marketing managers may also design and oversee various environmental scanning and competitive intelligence processes to help identify trends and inform the company's marketing analysis.

Using SWOT to analyse the market position of a small management consultancy with specialism in HRM.

DECISION-MAKING

Decision making can be regarded as an outcome of mental processes (cognitive process) leading to the selection of a course of action among several alternatives. Every decision making process produces a final choice. The output can be an action or an opinion of choice. Human performance in decision making terms has been the subject of active research from several perspectives. From a psychological perspective, it is necessary to examine individual decisions in the context of a set of needs, preferences an individual has and values they seek. From a cognitive perspective, the decision making process must be regarded as a continuous process integrated in the interaction with the environment. From a normative perspective, the analysis of individual decisions is concerned with the logic of decision making and rationality and the invariant choice it leads to.

Yet, at another level, it might be regarded as a problem solving activity which is terminated when a satisfactory solution is found. Therefore, decision making is a reasoning or emotional process which can be rational or irrational, can be based on explicit assumptions or tacit assumptions.

Logical decision making is an important part of all science-based professions, where specialists apply their knowledge in a given area to making informed decisions. For example, medical decision making often involves making a diagnosis and selecting an appropriate treatment. Some research using naturalistic methods shows, however, that in situations with higher time pressure, higher stakes, or increased ambiguities, experts use intuitive decision making rather than structured approaches, following a recognition primed decision approach to fit a set of indicators into the expert's experience and immediately arrive at a satisfactory course of action without weighing alternatives.

Recent robust decision efforts have formally integrated uncertainty into the decision making process. However, Decision Analysis, recognized and included uncertainties with a structured and rationally justifiable method of decision making since its conception in 1964.

TRADITIONAL APPROACHES TO DECISION-MAKING

Decision-making in this world of increased information, technology, population and communication is a serious and growing problem. The traditional method of Decision-Making isn't providing adequate results. Different proponents have different approaches to decision-making ranging from a 4-step process to 7 steps or more and it is based on problem solving.

Generally the steps look something like the following:

- Define or clarify the problem: Somehow this whole process sounds negative to me. There is nothing positive about problems or estimating consequences. Flawed assumptions can derail the process and a misstep at this stage can lead to a bad decision or possible solution to the wrong problem.
- *Stating a goal or objective*: Sometimes this is presented as finding the causes of the problem. Other times as a premise and then information is gathered to support the premise.
- Generate options or alternatives.
- Evaluate alternatives and tradeoffs.
- Estimate Risk, by Comparing predicted outcomes of each alternative with the objective. Attempts are usually made to recognize uncertainty as well.
- Deciding on the alternative that best matches the objective.
- Implement the decision.

This is the basic "How to make a decision" approach that we have used since Ben Franklin introduced the old compare the pros and cons approach several hundred years ago.

This approach has 5 inherent problems basic to the approach with lots of variations within each type of problem:

1. *Perspective*: Perspective is a problem inherent in any decision-making process. Perspective is unique to each individual. A single perspective is by definition limited even though it may appear complete. Within a given perspective is a criterion or direction that will cause decision makers to choose one option over another. Consequently it is imperative that as many perspectives as possible be involved in the framing the issue. All too frequently decisions are made by a relatively small number of people with limited perspectives. Rarely are all stakeholders consulted and that limits perspective and options.

2. *Data*: This is a really tricky area. e live in a world of Too Much Information. Consequently it is easy to uncover an idea early on in the process and then only collect further research that supports the idea, ignoring everything else. This can be really dangerous as there may be lots of information that disproves the original idea and by ignoring it build failure into the decision. It is critical to gather and evaluate all information, not just the information that supports the premise.
3. *Interpersonal Relationships*: As information is gathered, it is critical to listen to all stakeholders in the process. Ignoring a stakeholder is not a good idea as it will cause other stakeholders to give only a token effort. Another aspect of Interpersonal problems is when your boss commits to a direction and then everyone else falls in line. Compliance is a trap with a high price. After a power play, people will only tell you what they think you want to hear and will no longer tell you what they believe to be true. Everyone who has ever participated in any kind of group activity has seen this happen.
4. *Implementation*: Not making a decision ends up becoming a decision by default. This is usually the result of allowing inexperience, convenience, or haste to make the choice for them. It may also be caused by people who pose their questions carefully, collect their intelligence brilliantly, but then "wing it" when it comes to actually deciding.
5. *The Unknown*: Another problem that frequently arises at this stage is not knowing what you don't know. All research is imperfect and for every action there are unintended consequences. We are also faced with Luck, both good and bad.

There are lots of variations on the traditional method of decision-making. The fact is that these variations are still "how" based models and as such leave themselves open to the same traps as the traditional model. Since data shows that "decisions fail half of the time," it seems safe to say that reality is often more confused and messy than a neat "how" based model can allow for. "How" based decision-making models are no longer adequate in our highly competitive world

PROBLEM ANALYSIS VS. DECISION MAKING

It's important to differentiate between problem analysis and decision making. The concepts are completely separate of one another.

Problem analysis must be done first, then the information gathered in that process may be used towards decision making.

Problem Analysis:

- Analyse performance, what should the results be against what they actually are
- Problems are merely deviations from performance standards
- Problem must be precisely identified and described
- Problems are caused by some change from a distinctive feature
- Something can always be used to distinguish between what has and hasn't been effected by a cause
- Causes to problems can be deducted from relevant changes found in analyzing the problem
- Most likely cause to a problem is the one that exactly explains all the facts

Decision Making:

- Objectives must first be established
- Objectives must be classified and placed in order of importance
- Alternative actions must be developed
- The alternative must be evaluated against all the objectives
- The alternative that is able to achieve all the objectives is the tentative decision
- The tentative decision is evaluated for more possible consequences

- The decisive actions are taken, and additional actions are taken to prevent any adverse consequences from becoming problems and starting both systems (problem analysis and decision making) all over again

EVERYDAY TECHNIQUES

Some of the decision making techniques people use in everyday life include:

- Listing the advantages and disadvantages of each option, popularized by Plato and Benjamin Franklin
- Choosing the alternative with the highest probability-weighted utility for each alternative
- *Satisficing*: Accepting the first option that seems like it might achieve the desired result
- Acquiesce to a person in authority or an "expert", just following orders
- *Flipism*: Flipping a coin, cutting a deck of playing cards, and other random or coincidence methods
- Prayer, tarot cards, astrology, augurs, revelation, or other forms of divination

COGNITIVE AND PERSONAL BIASES

Biases can creep into our decision making processes. Many different people have made a decision about the same question and then craft potential cognitive interventions aimed at improving decision making outcomes.

A list of some of the more commonly debated cognitive biases:

- *Selective search for evidence (a.k.a. Confirmation bias in psychology)*: We tend to be willing to gather facts that support certain ceases but disregard other facts that support different ceases. Individuals who are highly defensive in this manner show significantly greater left prefrontal cortex activity as measured by EEG than do less defensive individuals.
- Premature termination of search for evidence – We tend to accept the first alternative that looks like it might work.
- *Inertia*: Unwillingness to change thought patterns that

we have used in the past in the face of new circumstances.

- Selective perception: We actively screen-out information that we do not think is important. In one demonstration of this effect, discounting of arguments with which one disagrees (by judging them as untrue or irrelevant) was decreased by selective activation of right prefrontal cortex.
- Wishful thinking or optimism bias: We tend to want to see things in a positive light and this can distort our perception and thinking.
- Choice-supportive bias occurs when we distort our memories of chosen and rejected options to make the chosen options seem more attractive.
- *Recency*: We tend to place more attention on more recent information and either ignore or forget more distant information. The opposite effect in the first set of data or other information is termed Primacy effect.
- *Repetition bias*: A willingness to believe what we have been told most often and by the greatest number of different of sources.
- *Anchoring and adjustment*: Decisions are unduly influenced by initial information that shapes our view of subsequent information.
- *Group think*: Peer pressure to conform to the opinions held by the group.
- *Source credibility bias*: We reject something if we have a bias against the person, organization, or group to which the person belongs: We are inclined to accept a statement by someone we like.
- *Incremental decision making and escalating commitment*: We look at a decision as a small step in a process and this tends to perpetuate a series of similar decisions. This can be contrasted with zero-based decision making.
- *Attribution asymmetry*: We tend to attribute our success to our abilities and talents, but we attribute our failures to bad luck and external factors. We

attribute other's success to good luck, and their failures to their mistakes.

- *Role fulfillment (Self Fulfilling Prophecy)*: We conform to the decision making expectations that others have of someone in our position.
- *Underestimating uncertainty and the illusion of control*: We tend to underestimate future uncertainty because we tend to believe we have more control over events than we really do. We believe we have control to minimize potential problems in our decisions.

COGNITIVE STYLES

Influence of Briggs Myers Type

Isabel Briggs Myers, a person's decision making process depends to a significant degree on their cognitive style. Myers developed a set of four bi-polar dimensions, called the Myers-Briggs Type Indicator (MBTI). The terminal points on these dimensions are: *thinking* and *feeling*; *extroversion* and *introversion*; *judgment* and *perception*; and *sensing* and *intuition*. She claimed that a person's decision making style correlates well with how they score on these four dimensions. For example, someone who scored near the thinking, extroversion, sensing, and judgment ends of the dimensions would tend to have a logical, analytical, objective, critical, and empirical decision making style. However, MBTI has been criticized by psychologists because it lacks reliability and validity, and is poorly constructed.

Other studies suggest that these national or cross-cultural differences exist across entire societies. For example, Maris Martinsons has found that American, Japanese and Chinese business leaders each exhibit a distinctive national style of decision making.

Optimizing vs. Satisficing

Herbert Simon coined the phrase "bounded rationality" to express the idea that human decision-making is limited by available information, available time, and the information-processing ability of the mind. Simon also defined two cognitive styles: *maximizers* try to make an optimal decision, whereas *satisficers* simply try to find a solution that is "good enough". Maximizers tend to take longer making decisions due to the need to maximize performance across all variables and make tradeoffs carefully; they also tend to more often regret their decisions.

Combinatoral vs. Positional

Styles and methods of decision making were elaborated by the founder of Predispositioning Theory, Aron Katsenelinboigen. In his analysis on styles and methods Katsenelinboigen referred to the game of chess, saying that "chess does disclose various methods of operation, notably the creation of predisposition—methods which may be applicable to other, more complex systems."

In his book Katsenelinboigen states that apart from the methods (reactive and selective) and sub-methods (randomization, predispositioning, programming), there are two major styles – positional and combinational. Both styles are utilized in the game of chess. Katsenelinboigen, the two styles reflect two basic approaches to the uncertainty: deterministic (combinational style) and indeterministic (positional style). Katsenelinboigen's definition of the two styles are the following.

The combinational style is characterized by:

- A very narrow, clearly defined, primarily material goal, and
- A programme that links the initial position with the final outcome.

In defining the combinational style in chess, Katsenelinboigen writes: The combinational style features a clearly formulated limited objective, namely the capture of material (the main constituent element of a chess position). The objective is implemented via a well defined and in some cases in a unique sequence of moves aimed at reaching the set goal. As a rule, this sequence leaves no options for the opponent. Finding a combinational objective allows the player to focus all his energies on efficient execution, that is, the player's analysis may be limited to the pieces directly partaking in the combination. This approach is the crux of the combination and the combinational style of play.

The positional style is distinguished by:

- A positional goal and
- A formation of semi-complete linkages between the initial step and final outcome.

"Unlike the combinational player, the positional player is occupied, first and foremost, with the elaboration of the position that will allow him to develop in the unknown future. In playing the positional style, the player must evaluate relational and material parameters as independent variables. (...) The positional style gives the player the opportunity to develop a position until it becomes pregnant with a combination. However, the combination is not the final goal of the positional player—it helps him to achieve the desirable, keeping in mind a predisposition for the future development. The Pyrrhic victory is the best example of one's inability to think positionally."

The positional style serves to:

- Create a predisposition to the future development of the position.
- Induce the environment in a certain way.
- Absorb an unexpected outcome in one's favour.
- Avoid the negative aspects of unexpected outcomes.

The positional style gives the player the opportunity to develop a position until it becomes pregnant with a combination. Katsenelinboigen writes: "As the game progressed and defence became more sophisticated the combinational style of play declined. . . . The positional style of chess does not eliminate the combinational one with its attempt to see the entire programme of action in advance. The positional style merely prepares the transformation to a combination when the latter becomes feasible."

NEUROSCIENCE PERSPECTIVE

The anterior cingulate cortex (ACC), orbitofrontal cortex

(and the overlapping ventromedial prefrontal cortex) are brain regions involved in decision making processes. A recent neuroimaging study, found distinctive patterns of neural activation in these regions depending on whether decisions were made on the basis of personal volition or following directions from someone else. Patients with damage to the ventromedial prefrontal cortex have difficulty making advantageous decisions.

A recent study involving Rhesus monkeys found that neurons in the parietal cortex not only represent the formation of a decision but also signal the degree of certainty (or "confidence") associated with the decision. Another recent study found that lesions to the ACC in the macaque resulted in impaired decision making in the long run of reinforcement guided tasks suggesting that the ACC may be involved in evaluating past reinforcement information and guiding future action.

Emotion appears to aid the decision making process: Decision making often occurs in the face of uncertainty about whether one's choices will lead to benefit or harm. The somatic-marker hypothesis is a neurobiological theory of how decisions are made in the face of uncertain outcome. This theory holds that such decisions are aided by emotions, in the form of bodily states, that are elicited during the deliberation of future consequences and that mark different options for behaviour as being advantageous or disadvantageous. This process involves an interplay between neural systems that elicit emotional/bodily states and neural systems that map these emotional/bodily states.

10

Organizing

Organizational studies, organizational behaviour, and organizational theory is the systematic study and careful application of knowledge about how people - as individuals and as groups - performance within organizations. Organizational Behaviour studies encompass the study of organizations from multiple viewpoints, methods, and levels of analysis.

Another traditional distinction, present especially in American academia, is between the study of "micro" organizational behaviour — which refers to individual and group dynamics in an organizational setting — and "macro" organizational theory which studies whole organizations, how they adapt, and the strategies and structures that guide them. To this distinction, some scholars have added an interest in "meso" — primarily interested in power, culture, and the networks of individuals and units in organizations — and "field" level analysis which study how whole populations of organizations interact.

In Europe these distinctions do exist as well, but are more rarely reflected in departmental divisions. Whenever people interact in organizations, many factors come into play. Modern organizational studies attempt to understand and model these factors. Like all modernist social sciences, organizational studies seek to control, predict, and explain. There is some controversy over the ethics of controlling workers' behaviour. As such, organizational behaviour or OB (and its cousin, Industrial psychology) have at times been accused of being the scientific tool of the powerful. Those accusations notwithstanding, OB can play a major role in organizational development and success. One of the main goals of organizational theorists is, Simms (1994) "to revitalize organizational theory and develop a better conceptualization of organizational life." An organizational theorist should carefully consider levels assumptions being made in theory, and is concerned to help managers and administrators.

The Greek philosopher Plato wrote about the essence of leadership. Aristotle addressed the topic of persuasive communication. The writings of 16th century Italian philosopher Niccolò Machiavelli laid the foundation for contemporary work on organizational power and politics. In 1776, Adam Smith advocated a new form of organizational structure based on the division of labour. One hundred years later, German sociologist Max Weber wrote about rational organizations and initiated discussion of charismatic leadership. Soon after, Frederick Winslow Taylor introduced the systematic use of goal setting and rewards to motivate employees.

In the 1920s, Australian-born Harvard Elton Mayo and his colleagues conducted productivity studies at Western Electric's Hawthorne plant in the United States. Though it traces its roots back to Max Weber and earlier, organizational studies is generally considered to have begun as an academic discipline with the advent of scientific management in the 1890s, with Taylorism representing the peak of this movement. Proponents of scientific management held that rationalizing the organization with precise sets of instructions and time-motion studies would lead to increased productivity.

Studies of different compensation systems were carried out. After the First World War, the focus of organizational studies shifted to analysis of how human factors and psychology affected organizations, a transformation propelled by the identification of the Hawthorne Effect. This Human Relations Movement focused on teams, motivation, and the actualization of the goals of individuals within organizations. Prominent early scholars included Chester Barnard, Henri Fayol, Frederick Herzberg, Abraham Maslow, David

McClelland, and Victor Vroom. The Second World War further shifted the field, as the invention of large-scale logistics and operations research led to a renewed interest in rationalist approaches to the study of organizations. Interest grew in theory and methods native to the sciences, including systems theory, the study of organizations with a complexity theory perspective and complexity strategy.

Influential work was done by Herbert Alexander Simon and James G. March and the so-called "Carnegie School" of organizational behaviour. In the 1960s and 1970s, the field was strongly influenced by social psychology and the emphasis in academic study was on quantitative research. An explosion of theorizing, much of it at Stanford University and Carnegie Mellon, produced Bounded Rationality, Informal Organization, Contingency Theory, Resource Dependence, Institutional Theory, and Organizational Ecology theories, among many others. Starting in the 1980s, cultural explanations of organizations and change became an important part of study. Qualitative methods of study became more acceptable, informed by anthropology, psychology and sociology. A leading scholar was Karl Weick.

SPECIFIC CONTRIBUTIONS

FREDERICK WINSLOW TAYLOR

Frederick Winslow Taylor (1856-1915) was the first person who attempted to study human behaviour at work using a systematic approach. Taylor studied human characteristics, social environment, task, physical environment, capacity, speed, durability, cost and their interaction with each other. His overall objective was to reduce and/or remove human variability.

Taylor worked to achieve his goal of making work behaviours stable and predictable so that maximum output could be achieved. He relied strongly upon monetary incentive systems, believing that humans are primarily motivated by money. He faced some strong criticism, including being accused of telling managers to treat workers as machines without minds, but his work was very productive and laid many foundation principles for modern management studies. An enlightening book about the life of Pratik Bang and his studies is that by Kanigel.

ELTON MAYO

Elton Mayo, an Australian national, headed the Hawthorne Studies at Harvard. In his classic writing in 1931, Human Problems of an Industrial Civilization, he advised managers to deal with emotional needs of employees at work.

MARY PARKER FOLLETT

Mary Parker Follett was a pioneer management consultant in the industrial world. As a writer, she provided analyses on workers as having complex combinations of attitude, beliefs, and needs. She told managers to motivate employees on their job performance, a "pull" rather than a "push" strategy.

DOUGLAS MCGREGOR

Douglas McGregor proposed two theories/assumptions, which are very nearly the opposite of each other, about human nature based on his experience as a management consultant. His first theory was "Theory X", which is pessimistic and negative; and McGregor it is how managers traditionally perceive their workers. Then, in order to help managers replace that theory/assumption, he gave "Theory Y" which takes a more modern and positive approach.

He believed that managers could achieve more if they start perceiving their employees as self-energized, committed, responsible and creative beings. By means of his Theory Y, he in fact challenged the traditional theorists to adopt a developmental approach to their employees. The Human Side of Enterprise, in 1960; this book has become a foundation for the modern view of employees at work.

CURRENT STATE OF THE FIELD

Organizational behaviour is currently a growing field. Organizational studies departments generally form part of business schools, although many universities also have industrial psychology and industrial economics programmes. The field is highly influential in the business world with practitioners like Peter Drucker and Peter Senge, who turned the academic research into business practices. Organizational behaviour is becoming more important in the global economy as people with diverse backgrounds and cultural values have to work together effectively and efficiently. It is also under increasing criticism as a field for its ethnocentric and pro-capitalist assumptions.

During the last 20 years organizational behaviour study and practice has developed and expanded through creating integrations with other domains:

- Anthropology became an interesting prism to understanding firms as communities, by introducing concepts like Organizational culture, 'organizational rituals' and 'symbolic acts' enabling new ways to understand organizations as communities.
- *Leadership Understanding*: The crucial role of leadership at various level of an organization in the process of change management.
- Ethics and their importance as pillars of any vision and one of the most important driving forces in an organization.

METHODS USED IN ORGANIZATIONAL STUDIES

A variety of methods are used in organizational studies. They include quantitative methods found in other social sciences such as multiple regression, non-parametric statistics, time dependent analysis, and ANOVA. In addition, computer simulation in organizational studies has a long history in organizational studies.

Qualitative methods are also used, such as ethnography, which involves direct participant observation, single and multiple case analysis, and other historical methods. In the last fifteen years or so, there has been greater focus on language, metaphors, and organiz-ational storytelling.

SYSTEMS FRAMEWORK

The systems framework is also fundamental to organizational theory as organizations are complex dynamic goal-oriented processes. One of the early thinkers in the field was Alexander Bogdanov, who developed his Tectology, a theory widely considered a precursor of Bertalanffy's General Systems Theory, aiming to model and design human organizations.

Kurt Lewin was particularly influential in developing the systems perspective within organizational theory and coined the term "systems of ideology", from his frustration with behavioural psychologies that became an obstacle to sustainable work in psychology. The complexity theory perspective on organizations is another systems view of organizations. The systems approach to organizations relies heavily upon achieving negative entropy through openness and feedback. A systemic view on organizations is transdisciplinary and integrative.

In other words, it transcends the perspectives of individual disciplines, integrating them on the basis of a common "code", or more exactly, on the basis of the formal apparatus provided by systems theory. The systems approach gives primacy to the interrelationships, not to the elements of the system. It is from these dynamic interrelationships that new properties of the system emerge. In recent years, *systems thinking* has been developed to provide techniques for studying systems in holistic ways to supplement traditional reductionistic methods. In this more recent tradition, systems theory in organizational studies is considered by some as a humanistic extension of the natural sciences.

THEORIES AND MODELS OF ORGANIZATIONAL STUDIES

Decision making:

- Mintzberg's managerial roles
- Rational Decision-Making Model
- Scientific management
- Garbage Can Model

Organization structures and dynamics:

- Bureaucracy
- Complexity theory and organizations
- Contingency theory
- Evolutionary Theory and organizations
- Hybrid organisation
- Incentive theory (organization)
- Informal Organization
- Institutional theory
- Merger integration
- Organizational ecology
- Model of Organizational Citizenship behaviour
- Model of organizational justice
- Model of Organizational Misbehaviour
- Resource dependence theory
- Transaction cost
- Hofstede's Framework for Assessing Cultures
- Mintzberg's Organigraph

Personality traits theories:

- Big Five personality traits
- Holland's Typology of Personality and Congruent Occupations
- Myers-Briggs Type Indicator

Control and stress modeling:

- Herzberg's Two factor theory
- Theory X and Theory Y

MOTIVATION IN ORGANIZATIONS

Motivation the forces either internal or external to a person that arouse enthusiasm and resistance to pursue a certain course of action. Baron *et al.* (2008): "Although motivation is a broad and complex concept, organizational scientists have agreed on its basic characteristics. Drawing from various social sciences, we define motivation as the set of processes that arouse, direct, and maintain human behaviour towards attaining some goal"

There are many different motivation theories such as:

- Attribution theory

- Equity theory
- Maslow's hierarchy of needs
- Incentive theory (psychology)
- Model of emotional labour in organizations
- Frederick Herzberg two-factor theory

AUTHORITY AND POWER - CONCEPT AND DISTINCTION

The word authority derives from the Latin word auctoritas meaning invention, advice, opinion, influence or commands which originate from an auctor indicating that authority originates from a master, leader or author. Essentially authority is imposed by superiors upon inferiors either by force of arms (structural authority) or by force of argument (sapiential authority). Usually authority has components of both compulsion and persuasion. For this reason, as used in Roman law authority is differentiated potestas (legal or military power) and imperium (persuasive political rank or standing).

In government, authority is often used interchangeably with the term "power". However, their meanings differ: while "power" is defined as "the ability to influence somebody to do something that he/she would not have done", "authority" refers to a claim of legitimacy, the justification and right to exercise that power. For example, whilst a mob has the power to punish a criminal, for example by lynching, people who believe in the rule of law consider that only a court of law has the authority to order punishment.

Since the emergence of social sciences, authority has been a subject of research in a variety of empirical settings: the family (parental authority), small groups (informal authority of leadership), intermediate organizations, such as schools, churches, armies, industries and bureaucracies (organizational and bureaucratic authorities) and society-wide or inclusive organizations, ranging from the most primitive tribal society to the modern nation-state and intermediate organization (political authority). The definition of authority in contemporary social science is a matter of debate. Michaels, in the Encyclopedia of Social Sciences, authority is the capacity, innate or acquired for exercising ascendancy over a group. Other scientists, however, argue that authority is not a capacity but a relationship. It is sanctioned power, institutionalized power.

In political philosophy, the jurisdiction of political authority, the location of sovereignty, the balancing of freedom and authority, and the requirements of political obligations have been core questions from Plato and Aristotle to the present. In many democractic societies, there is an ongoing discussion regarding the legitimate extent of governmental authority in general. In the United States, for instance, there is a widespread belief that the political system as it was instituted by the Founding Fathers should accord the populace as much freedom as reasonable, and that government should limit its authority accordingly.

WEBER ON AUTHORITY

Max Weber, in his sociological work, identified and distinguished three types of legitimate domination that have sometimes been rendered in English translation as types of authority, because domination isn't seen as a political concept in the first place. Weber defined domination (authority) as the chance of commands being obeyed by a specifiable group of people. Legitimate authority is that which is recognized as legitimate and justified by both the ruler and the ruled.

Weber divided legitimate authority into three types:

1. The first type discussed by Weber is Rational-legal authority. It is that form of authority which depends for its legitimacy on formal rules and established laws of the state, which are usually written down and are often very complex. The power of the rational legal authority is in the constitution. Modern societies depend on legal-rational authority. Government officials are the best example of this form of authority, which is prevalent all over the world.
2. The second type of authority is Traditional authority, which derives from long-established customs, habits

and social structures. When power passes from one generation to another, then it is known as traditional authority. The right of hereditary monarchs to rule furnishes an obvious example. The Tudor dynasty in England and the ruling families of Mewar, in Rajasthan (India) are some examples of traditional authority.

3. The third form of authority is *Charismatic authority*. Here, the charisma of the individual or the leader plays an important role. Charismatic authority is that authority which is derived from "the gift of grace" or when the leader claims that his authority is derived from a "higher power" (e.g. God or natural law or rights) or "inspiration", that is superior to both the validity of traditional and rational-legal authority and followers accept this and are willing to follow this higher or inspired authority, in the place of the authority that they have hitherto been following. Some of the most prominent examples of charismatic authority can be politicians or leaders, who come from a movie or entertainment background. These people become successful, because they use their grace and charm to get more votes during elections. Examples in this regard can be NT Rama Rao, a matinee idol, who went on to become one of the most powerful Chief Ministers of Andhra Pradesh.

History has witnessed several social movements or revolutions, against a system of traditional or legal-rational authority, which are usually started by Charismatic authorities. What distinguishes authority, from coercion, force and power on the one hand and leadership, persuasion and influence on the other hand, is legitimacy.

Superiors feel that they have a right to issue commands; subordinates perceive an obligation to obey. Social scientists agree that authority is but one of several resources available, to incumbents in formal positions. For example, a Head of State is dependent upon a similar nesting of authority. His legitimacy must be acknowledged, not just by citizens, but by those who control other valued resources: his immediate staff, his cabinet, military leaders and in the long run, the administration and political apparatus of the entire society.

AUTHORITY AND THE STATE

Every state has a number of institutions which exercise authority based on longstanding practices. Apart from this, every state sets up agencies which are competent in dealing with one particular matter. One example would be a port authority like the Port of London.

They are usually created by special legislation and are run by a board of directors. Several agencies and institutions are created along the same lines and they exercise authority in certain matters. They are usually required to be self-supporting through property taxes or other forms of collection or fees for services.

LINE AND STAFF CONCEPT; PROBLEMS OF USE OF STAFF AND WAYS TO AVOID LINE-STAFF CONFLICT

Organizing (also spelled organising) is the performance of rearranging elements following one or more rules. Anything is commonly considered organized when it looks like everything has a correct order or placement. But it's only ultimately organized if any element has no difference on time taken to find it. In that sense, organizing can also be defined as *to place different objects in logical arrangement for better searching*.

Organizations are groups of people frequently trying to organize some specific subject, such as political issues. So, even while organizing can be viewed as a simple definition, it can get as complex as *organizing the world's information*. Historically, humanity has always tried to organize itself. The organizing of information can be seen since the time humans began to write. Prior to that, history was passed down through song and word. Be it with religion, books and spoken word, science, through journals and studies, or in many other ways, organizing not only is history, but also helps communicate history. As opposed to verbally communicating with someone, and more specifically cataloging ideas and thoughts, is also an attempt to organize information. Science books are notable by their organization of a specific subject. Encyclopedias, instead, usually try to organize any subject into one place, for faster indexing and seeking of meanings.

Nature of Organization

The following are the important characteristics of organization.

Division of Work or Specialization

The entire philosophy of organization depends on the concept of specialization. In specialization, various activities are assigned to different people who are specialists in that area. Specialization improves efficiency. Thus, organization helps in division of work and assigning duties to different people.

Orientation Towards Goals

Every organization has its own purposes and objectives. Organizing is the function employed to achieve the overall goals of the organization. Organization harmonies the individual goals of the employees with overall objectives of the firm.

Composition of Individuals and Groups

Individuals form a group and the groups form an organization. Thus, organization is the composition of individual and groups. Individuals are grouped into departments and their work is coordinated and directed towards organizational goals.

Differentiated Functions

The organization divides the entire work and assigns the tasks to individual in-order to achieve the organizational objectives each one has to perform a different task and tasks of one individuals must be coordinated with the tasks of others.

Continues Process

An organization is a group of people with defined relationship to each other that allows them to work together achieve the goals of the organization. This relationship does not come to end after completing a task. Organization is a never ending process.

PURPOSE OR IMPORTANCE OF ORGANIZATION

Helps to Achieve Organizational Goal

Organization is employed to achieve the overall objectives of business firms. Organization focuses attention of individuals objectives towards overall objectives.

Optimum use of Resources

To make optimum use of resources such as men, material, money, machine and method, it is necessary to design an organization properly. Work should be divided and right people should be given right jobs to reduce the wastage of resources in an organization.

To Perform Managerial Function

Planning, Organizing, Staffing, Directing and Controlling cannot be implemented without proper organization.

Facilitates Growth and Diversification

A good organization structure is essential for expanding business activity. Organization structure determines the input resources needed for expansion of a business activity similarly organization is essential for product diversification such as establishing a new product line.

Human Treatment of Employees

Organization has to operate for the betterment of employees an must not encourage monotony of work due to higher degree of specialization. Now, organization has adapted the modern concept of systems approach based on human relations and it discards the traditional productivity and specialization approach.

APPLICATIONS

Organizing, in companies point of view, is the management function that usually follows after planning. And it involves the assignment of tasks, the grouping of tasks into departments and the assignment of authority and allocation of resources across the organization.

STRUCTURE

The framework in which the organization defines how tasks are divided, resources are deployed, and departments are coordinated:

- A set of formal tasks assigned to individuals and departments.
- Formal reporting relationships, including lines of authority, decision responsibility, number of hierarchical levels and span of managers control.
- The design of systems to ensure effective coordination of employees across departments.

WORK SPECIALIZATION

Work specialization (also called division of labour) is the degree to which organizational tasks are sub-divided into individual jobs. With too much specialization, employees are isolated and do only a single, tiny, boring job. Many organizations enlarge jobs or rotate assigned tasks to provide greater challenges.

CHAIN OF COMMAND

The chain of command is the unbroken line of authority that links all individuals in an organization, and specifies who reports to whom:

- *Unity of Command*: One employee is held accountable to only one supervisor
- *Scalar principle*: Clearly defined line of authority in the organization that includes all employees

Authority, responsibility, and accountability:

- Authority is a manager's formal and legitimate right to make decisions, issue orders, and allocate resources to achieve organizationally desired outcomes.
- Responsibility means an employee's duty to perform assigned task or activities.
- Accountability means that those with authority and responsibility must report and justify task outcomes to those them in the chain of command.

DELEGATION

Delegation is the process managers use to transfer authority and responsibility to positions below them. Organizations today tend to encourage delegation from highest to lowest possible levels.

Delegation can improve flexibility to meet customers' needs and adaptation to competitive environments. Managers often find delegation difficult

TYPES OF AUTHORITY AND RESPONSIBILITY

Line authority managers have the formal power to direct and control immediate subordinates. The superior issues orders and is responsible for the result—the subordinate obeys and is responsible only for executing the order according to instructions. Functional authority is where managers have formal power over a specific subset of activities.

For instance, the Production Manager may have the line authority to decide whether and when a new machine is needed but the Controller demands that a Capital Expenditure Proposal is submitted first, showing that the investment will have a yield of at least x%; or, a legal department may have functional authority to interfere in any activity that could have legal consequences. This authority would not be functional but it would rather be staff authority if such interference is "advice" rather than "order". Staff authority is granted to staff specialists in their areas of expertise. It is not a real authority in the sense that a staff manager does not order or instruct but simply advises, recommends, and counsels in the staff specialists' area of expertise and is responsible only for the quality of the advice (to be in line with the respective professional standards etc) It is a communication relationship with management. It has an influence that derives indirectly from line authority at a higher level.

SPAN OF MANAGEMENT

Factors influencing larger span of management:

- Work performed by subordinates is stable and routine.
- Subordinates perform similar work tasks.
- Subordinates are concentrated in a single location.
- Subordinates are highly trained and need little direction in performing tasks.
- Rules and procedures defining task activities are available.
- Support systems and personnel are available for the managers.
- Little time is required in non-supervisory activities such as coordination with other departments or planning.
- Managers' personal preferences and styles favour a large span.

Tall versus flat structure:

- *Tall*: A management structure characterized by an overall narrow span of management and a relatively large number of hierarchical levels. Tight control. Reduced communication overhead.
- *Flat*: A management structure characterized by a wide span of control and relatively few hierarchical levels. Loose control. Facilitates delegation. Centralization, decentralization, and formalization:
- *Centralization*: The location of decision making authority near top organizational levels.
- *Decentralization*: The location of decision making authority near lower organizational levels.

- *Formalization*: The written documentation used to direct and control employees.
- *Departmentalization*: The basis on which individuals are grouped into departments and departments into total organizations.

Approach options include:

- *Functional*: By common skills and work tasks
- *Divisional*: Common product, programme or geographical location
- *Matrix*: Combination of Functional and Divisional
- *Team*: To accomplish specific tasks
- *Network*: Departments are independent providing functions for a central core breaker

Importance of organizing:

- Organizations are often troubled by how to organize, particularly when a new strategy is developed
- Changing market conditions or new technology requires change
- Organizations seek efficiencies through improvements in organizing

11

Delegation

Delegation (also called deputation) is the assignment of authority and responsibility to another person (normally from a manager to a subordinate) to carry out specific activities. However the person who delegated the work remains accountable for the outcome of the delegated work. Delegation empowers a subordinate to make decisions, *i.e.* it is a shift of decision-making authority from one organizational level to a lower one.

Delegation, if properly done, is not abdication. The opposite of effective delegation is micromanagement, where a manager provides too much input, direction, and review of delegated work. In general, delegation is good and can save money and time, help in building skills, and motivate people. Poor delegation, on the other hand, might cause frustration, and confusion to all the involved parties.

APPLICATIONS OF DELEGATION THEORY

INDEPENDENT CENTRAL BANKS AND NON MAJORITARIAN INSTITUTIONS

One of the most important areas where delegation theories have been applied has been in the debate over the merits of Independent Central Banks (ICBs) such as the Bank of England or the European Central Bank. This debate has corresponded to the theories of credible commitments and can be understood as a solution to problems posed by the two democratic pressure problems where monetary policy is concerned. Those in favour of the creation of ICBs have primarily focused on interest rates and have argued that democratic pressures tend to have an inflationary effect as governments will often be tempted to advocate lower interest rates immediately prior to an election so as to manufacture short term booms in the economy and boost their support - but to the detriment of long term economic health.

A variant of this argument is that as most democracies incorporate two main parties split on economic policy between left and right, the party of the left winning power will often result in damaging inflation raising policies immediately after the election in an effort to distance itself from the previous government. A solution to these problems has naturally been sought in the creation of an independent institution which can decide interest rates outside of the influence of democratic pressures - the ICB.

This argument has been highly influential and the number of ICBs has risen dramatically since the 1980s however it is not without its critics. Many scholars (for instance Kathleen Mcnamara) have questioned the premises of the ICB argument, making the case that democratic pressures will not result in high inflation and that high inflation is not inherently bad for the economy long term. Broadly speaking the empirical evidence on these points has tended to be inconclusive for both sides. An alternative criticism has come from certain branches of New institutionalism who have sought to explain the increase in ICBs not by the 'rational' argument, but as a process of symbolism, where governments will create ICBs because they are seen to be respectable institutions by other actors, particularly by foreign investors who, it is argued, will view a country with an ICB as a modern state worthy of investment. Delegation theories have also been applied extensively in studies of the European Union.

The dominant approach has undoubtedly been the principal-agent approach, but there have also been variations from the classic form by intergovernmentalist approaches and the fiduciary model laid out by Giandomenico Majone. Andrew Moravcsik is perhaps the most prominent intergovernmentalist theorist who has written on delegation and his work can essentially be thought of as applying the principal-agent model in a manner which stresses minimal agency loss. The model is not a simple principal-agent model however, as he conceives of the EU as delegation on three levels.

Firstly there is the delegation from European electorates to national governments (who in this sense performance as agents), secondly there is the delegation from national governments (who now performance as principals) to European institutions such as the European Commission. Moravcsik has been particularly interested in the informational asymmetries which arise from delegation in the European Union and has argued that whilst there is minimal agency loss between the national governments and the European institutions, the national governments gain significant informational advantages over European electorates which allow them to carry out policies at home which they would not be able to do in the absence of the European Union. In this sense the delegation process strengthens the national governments rather than weakening them (as is traditionally assumed where the European Union is concerned).

This has nevertheless been seen as inconsistent by some scholars who take issue with the assertion that informational advantages only allow national governments to gain freedom from European electorates and that the same principle applies with European institutions gaining an advantage over their principals through informational asymmetries. In contrast Giandomenico Majone has formulated a theory of delegation which stresses the importance of credibility problems in the decision to delegate to European institutions.

Not only is this explained as a mechanism to ensure member states comply with treaty obligations, but employing similar logic as that used in the ICB debates he makes a defence against democratic deficit arguments which advocate a directly elected European Commission. Much in the same way as in the ICB debate democratic pressures are seen as impacting negatively on what is a primarily regulatory institution and as such for Majone the Commission should be insulated from democratic pressures if it is to fulfil its functions effectively. One delegation it is, broad sensu, a body of deputies of an assembly and its respective activities. In strict sense, the term today is used mainly in Spain in order to designate the administration of those provinces.

The delegations they have territorial character and its function is to manage the economic-administrative interests of the provinces. In Canary islands the functions of the delegations exert them in each island town halls insulares, and in Balearic islands advice insulares. The history of the delegations overcomes to 1812 with the promulgation of Constitution of Cadiz, having had a different roll at every historical time, like the severe control of the central government during pro-Franco dictatorship.

The members of the delegations are elect of indirect way, to start off of the total result of the municipal elections of each province. However, the members of the town halls and advice insulares always have been chosen of direct way, in elections separated or joint with the autonomic ones. To the three Basque delegations one knows them with the name Leasehold delegation, since these four territories even conserve their fueros. The Leasehold Delegation is an executive agency that depends on the General Meetings. The General Meetings are the parliaments of each Historical territory whose members are chosen by popular voting, that agrees with the municipal elections.

DELEGATION EFFECTIVE

Delegation is one of the most important management skills. These logical rules and techniques will help you to delegate well. Good delegation saves you time, develops you people, grooms a successor, and motivates. Poor delegation will cause you frustration, demotivates and confuses the other person, and fails to achieve the task or purpose itself. So it's a management skill that's worth improving. Here are the simple steps to follow if you want to get delegation right, with different levels of delegation freedom that you can offer.

This delegation skills guide deals with general delegation principles and process, which is applicable to individuals and teams, or to specially formed groups of people for individual projects. Delegation is a very helpful aid for succession planning, personal development - and seeking and encouraging promotion. It's how we grow in the job - delegation enables us to gain experience to take on higher responsibilities.

Effective delegation is actually crucial for effective succession. For the successor, and for the manager too: the main task of a manager in a growing thriving organization is ultimately to develop a successor. When this happens everyone can move on to higher things. When it fails to happen the succession and progression becomes dependent on bringing in new people from outside. Delegation can be used to develop your people people and yourself - delegation is not just a management technique for freeing up the boss's time.

Of course there is a right way to do it. These delegation tips and techniques are useful for bosses - and for anyone seeking or being given delegated responsibilities. As a giver of delegated tasks you must ensure delegation happens properly. Just as significantly, as the recipient of delegated tasks you have the opportunity to 'manage upwards' and suggest improvements to the delegation process and understanding - especially if your boss could use the help. Managing the way you receive and agree to do delegated tasks is one of the central skills of 'managing upwards'. Therefore while this is essentially written from the manager's standpoint, the principles are just as useful for people being managed.

DELEGATION AND SMART, OR SMARTER

A simple delegation rule is the SMART acronym, or better still, SMARTER.

It's a quick checklist for proper delegation. Delegated tasks must be:

- Specific
- Measurable
- Agreed

- Realistic
- Timebound
- Ethical
- Recorded

Traditional interpretations of the SMARTER acronym use 'Exciting' or 'Enjoyable', however, although a high level of motivation often results when a person achieves and is given recognition for a particular delegated task, which in itself can be exciting and enjoyable, in truth, let's be honest, it is not always possible to ensure that all delegated work is truly 'exciting' or 'enjoyable' for the recipient.

More importantly, the 'Ethical' aspect is fundamental to everything that we do, assuming you subscribe to such philosophy. The delegation and review form is a useful tool for the delegation process.

The Tannenbaum and Schmidt Continuum model proviodes extra guidance on delegating freedom to, and developing, a team. The Tuckman 'Forming, Storming, Norming Performing' model is particularly helpful when delegating to teams and individuals within teams. The levels of delegation freedom—choose which is most appropriate for any given situation.

THE STEPS OF SUCCESSFUL DELEGATION

- *Define the task*: Confirm in your own mind that the task is suitable to be delegated. Does it meet the criteria for delegating?
- *Select the individual or team*: What are your reasons for delegating to this person or team? What are they going to get out of it? What are you going to get out of it?
- *Assess ability and training needs*: Is the other person or team of people capable of doing the task? Do they understand what needs to be done. If not, you can't delegate.
- *Explain the reasons*: You must explain why the job or responsibility is being delegated. And why to that person or people? What is its importance and

relevance? Where does it fit in the overall scheme of things?

- *State required results*: What must be achieved? Clarify understanding by getting feedback from the other person. How will the task be measured? Make sure they know how you intend to decide that the job is being successfully done.
- *Consider resources required*: Discuss and agree what is required to get the job done. Consider people, location, premises, equipment, money, materials, other related activities and services.
- *Agree deadlines*: When must the job be finished? Or if an ongoing duty, when are the review dates? When are the reports due? And if the task is complex and has parts or stages, what are the priorities? At this point you may need to confirm understanding with the other person of the previous points, getting ideas and interpretation. As well as showing you that the job can be done, this helps to reinforce commitment. Methods of checking and controlling must be agreed with the other person. Failing to agree this in advance will cause this monitoring to seem like interference or lack of trust.
- *Support and communicate*: Think about who else needs to know what's going on, and inform them. Involve the other person in considering this so they can see beyond the issue at hand. Do not leave the person to inform your own peers of their new responsibility. Warn the person about any awkward matters of politics or protocol. Inform your own boss if the task is important, and of sufficient profile.

FEEDBACK ON RESULTS

It is essential to let the person know how they are doing, and whether they have achieved their aims. If not, you must review with them why things did not go to plan, and deal with the problems. You must absorb the consequences of failure, and pass on the credit for success.

LEVELS OF DELEGATION

Delegation isn't just a matter of telling someone else what to do. There is a wide range of varying freedom that you can confer on the other person. The more experienced and reliable the other person is, then the more freedom you can give. The more critical the task then the more cautious you need to be about extending a lot of freedom, especially if your job or reputation depends on getting a good result.

Take care to choose the most appropriate style for each situation. For each example the statements are simplified for clarity; in reality you would choose a less abrupt style of language, depending on the person and the relationship. At the very least, a "Please" and "Thank-you" would be included in the requests.

It's important also to ask the other person what level of authority they feel comfortable being given. Why guess? When you ask, you can find out for sure and agree this with the other person.

Some people are confident; others less so. It's your responsibility to agree with them what level is most appropriate, so that the job is done effectively and with minimal unnecessary involvement from you. Involving the other person in agreeing the level of delegated freedom for any particular responsibility is an essential part of the 'contract' that you make with them.

These levels of delegation are not an exhaustive list. There are many more shades of grey between these black-and-white examples. Take time to discuss and adapt the agreements and 'contracts' that you make with people regarding delegated tasks, responsibility and freedom according to the situation. Be creative in choosing levels of delegated responsibility, and always check with the other person that they are comfortable with your chosen level.

People are generally capable of doing far more than you imagine. The rate and extent of responsibility and freedom delegated to people is a fundamental driver of organisational growth and effectiveness, the growth and well-being of your people, and of your own development and advancement.

LEVELS OF DELEGATION – EXAMPLES

These examples of different delegation levels progressively offer, encourage and enable more delegated freedom. Level 1 is the lowest level of delegated freedom.

Level 10 is the highest level typically found in organisations.

1. "Wait to be told." or "Do exactly what I say." or "Follow these instructions precisely." This is instruction. There is no delegated freedom at all.
2. "Look into this and tell me the situation. I'll decide." This is asking for investigation and analysis but no recommendation. The person delegating retains responsibility for assessing options prior to making the decision.
3. "Look into this and tell me the situation. We'll decide together." This is has a subtle important difference. This level of delegation encourages and enables the analysis and decision to be a shared process, which can be very helpful in coaching and development.
4. "Tell me the situation and what help you need from me in assessing and handling it. Then we'll decide." This is opens the possibility of greater freedom for analysis and decision-making, subject to both people agreeing this is appropriate. Again, this level is helpful in growing and defining coaching and development relationships.
5. "Give me your analysis of the situation and recommendation. I'll let you know whether you can go ahead." Asks for analysis and recommendation, but you will check the thinking before deciding.
6. "Decide and let me know your decision, and wait for our go-ahead before proceeding."The other person is trusted to assess the situation and options and is probably competent enough to decide and implement too, but for reasons of task importance, or competence, or perhaps externally changing factors, the boss prefers to keep control of timing. This level of delegation can be frustrating for people if used too often or for too long, and in any event

the reason for keeping people waiting, after they've inevitably invested time and effort, needs to be explained.

7. "Decide and let me know your decision, then go ahead unless I say not to."Now the other person begins to control the action. The subtle increase in responsibility saves time. The default is now positive rather than negative. This is a very liberating change in delegated freedom, and incidentally one that can also be used very effectively when seeking responsibility from elsewhere in an organisation, especially one which is strangled by indecision and bureaucracy. For example, "Here our analysis and recommendation; I will proceed unless you tell me otherwise by."
8. "Decide and take action - let me know what you did." This delegation level, as with each increase up the scale, saves even more time. This level of delegation also enables a degree of follow-up by the manager as to the effectiveness of the delegated responsibility, which is necessary when people are being managed from a greater distance, or more 'hands-off'. The level also allows and invites positive feedback by the manager, which is helpful in coaching and development of course.
9. "Decide and take action. You need not check back with me."The most freedom that you can give to another person when you still need to retain responsibility for the activity. A high level of confidence is necessary, and you would normally assess the quality of the activity after the event according to overall results, potentially weeks or months later. Feedback and review remain helpful and important, although the relationship is more likely one of mentoring, rather than coaching per se.
10. "Decide where action needs to be taken and manage the situation accordingly. It's your area of responsibility now."

The most freedom that you can give to the other person, and not generally used without formal change of a person's job role. It's the delegation of a strategic responsibility. This gives the other person responsibility for defining what changes projects, tasks, analysis and decisions are necessary for the management of a particular area of responsibility, as well as the task or project or change itself, and how the initiative or change is to be implemented and measured, etc.

This amounts to delegating part of your job - not just a task or project. You'd use this utmost level of delegation when developing a successor, or as part of an intentional and agreed plan to devolve some of your job accountability in a formal sense.

12

Decentralization

Decentralization or Decentralisation is the process of dispersing decision-making governance closer to the people and/or citizen. It includes the dispersal of administration or governance in sectors or areas like engineering, management science, political science, political economy, sociology and economics. Decentralization is also possible in the dispersal of population and employment. Law, science and technological advancements lead to highly decentralized human endeavours. "While frequently left undefined, decentralization has also been assigned many different meanings, varying across countries, languages, general contexts, fields of research, and specific scholars and studies."

A central theme in decentralization is the difference between a hierarchy, based on:

- *Authority*: Two players in an unequal-power relationship; and
- *An interface*: A lateral relationship between two players of roughly equal power.

The more decentralized a system is, the more it relies on lateral relationships, and the less it can rely on command or force. In most branches of engineering and economics, decentralization is narrowly defined as the study of markets and interfaces between parts of a system. This is most highly developed as general systems theory and neoclassical political economy.

ORGANIZATIONAL THEORY

Decentralization also called departmentalization is the policy of delegating decision-making authority down to the lower levels in an organization, relatively away from and lower in a central authority. A decentralized organization shows fewer tiers in the organizational structure, wider span of control, and a bottom-to-top flow of decision-making and flow of ideas. In a centralized organization, the decisions are made by top executives or on the basis of pre-set policies.

These decisions or policies are then enforced through several tiers of the organization after gradually broadening the span of control until it reaches the bottom tier. In a more decentralized organization, the top executives delegate much of their decision-making authority to lower tiers of the organizational structure. As a correlation, the organization is likely to run on less rigid policies and wider spans of control among each officer of the organization.

The wider span of control also reduces the number of tiers within the organization, giving its structure a flat appearance. One advantage of this structure, if the correct controls are in place, will be the bottom-to-top flow of information, allowing decisions by officials of the organization to be well informed about lower tier operations. For example, if an experienced technician at the lowest tier of an organization knows how to increase the efficiency of the production, the bottom-to-top flow of information can allow this knowledge to pass up to the executive officers.

Some political theorists believe that there are limits to decentralization as a strategy. They assert that any relaxation of direct control or authority introduces the possibility of dissent or division at critical moments, especially if what is being decentralized is decision-making among human beings. Friedrich Engels famously responded to Bakunin, refuting the argument of total decentralization, or anarchism, by scoffing "how these people propose to run a factory, operate a railway or steer a ship without having in the last resort one deciding will, without single management, they of course do not tell us". However, some anarchists have, in turn, responded to his argument, by explaining that they *do* support a amount of centralization, in the form of freely elected and recallable delegates. More to the point from the majority of anarchist perspectives are the real-world successes of anarchist communities, which for the majority only ended when they were defeated by the overwhelming military might of the State or neighbouring States. All in all, we do not know what a truly decentralized society would look like over a long period of time since it has never been permitted to exist, however the Zapatistas of Mexico are proving to be quite resilient.

In "*On Authority*", Engels also wrote of democratic workplaces that "particular questions arise in each room and at every moment concerning the mode of production, distribution of material, etc., which must be settled by decision of a delegate placed at the head of each branch of labour or, if possible, by a majority vote." Modern trade unions and management scientists tend to side strongly with Engels in this debate, and generally agree that decentralization is very closely related to standardisation and subordination, e.g. the standard commodity contracts traded on the commodity markets, in which disputes are resolved all according to a jurisdiction and common regulatory system, within the frame of a larger democratic electoral system which can restore any imbalances of power, and which generally retains the support of the population for its authority.

Notable exceptions among trade unions are the Wobblies, and the strong anarcho-syndicalist movement of Spain. However, a strategy of decentralization is not always so obviously political, even if it relies implicitly on authority delegated via a political system. For example, engineering standards are a means by which decentralization of supply inspection and testing can be achieved—a manufacturer adhering to the standard can participate in decentralised systems of bidding, e.g. in a parts market.

A building standard, for instance, permits the building trades to train labour and building supply corporations to provide parts, which enables rapid construction of buildings at remote sites. Decentralization of training and inspection, through the standards themselves, and related schedules of standardized testing and random spot inspection, achieves a very high statistical reliability of service, *i.e.* automobiles which rarely stall, cars which rarely leak, and the like. In most cases, an effective decentralization strategy and correspondingly robust systems of professional education, vocational education, and trade certification are critical to creating a modern industrial base. Such robust systems, and commodity markets to accompany them, are a necessary but not sufficient feature of any developed nation.

A major goal of the industrial strategy of any developing nation is tq safely decentralise decision-making so that central controls are unnecessary to achieving standards and safety. It seems that a very high degree of social capital is required to achieve trust in such standards and systems, and that ethical codes play some significant roles in building up trust in the professions and in the trades. The consumer product markets, industrial product markets, and service markets that emerge in a mature industrial economy, however, still ultimately rely, like the simpler commodity markets, on complex systems of standardization, regulation, jurisdiction, transport, materials and energy supply.

The specification and comparison of these is a major focus of the study of political economy. Political or other decision-making units typically must be large and leveraged enough for economy of scale, but also small enough that centralised authority does not become unaccountable to those performing trades or transactions at its perimeter. Large states, as Benjamin Franklin observed, were prone to becoming tyrannies, while small states, correspondingly, tended to become corrupt.

Finding the appropriate size of political states or other decision-making units, determining their optimal relationship to social capital and to infrastructural capital, is a major focus of political science. In management science there are studies of the ideal size of corporations, and some in anthropology and sociology study the ideal size of villages. Dennis Fox, a retired professor of legal studies and psychology, proposed an ideal village size of approximately 150 people, in 1985, about the relationship of anarchism to the tragedy of the commons. All these fields recognize some factors that encourage centralised authority and other factors that encourage decentralised "democracy"—balances between which are the major focus of group dynamics. However, decentralization is not only a feature of human society. It is also a feature of ecology.

Another objection or limit to political decentralization, similar in structure to that of Engels, is that terrestrial ecoregions impose a certain fiat by their natural water-circulation, soil, and plant and animal biodiversity which constitutes a form of "natural capital". Since these natural living systems can be neither changed nor replaced by man, some argue that an ecoregional democracy which follows their borders strictly is the only form of decentralization of larger political units that will not lead to endless conflict, e.g. gerrymandering, in struggle between social groups.

DECENTRALIZATION IN HISTORY

Decentralization and centralization are themes that have played major roles in the history of many societies. An excellent example is the gradual political and organizational changes that have occurred in European history. During the rise and fall of the Roman Empire, Europe went through major centralization and decentralization. Although the leaders of the Roman Empire created a European infrastructure, the fall of the Empire left Europe without a strong political system or military protection. Viking and other barbarian attacks further led rich Romans to build up their latifundia, or large estates, in a way that would protect their families and create a self-sufficient living place.

This development led to the growth of the manorial system in Europe. This system was greatly decentralized, as the lords of the manor had power to defend and control the small agricultural environment that was their manor. The manors of the early Middle Ages slowly came together as lords took oaths of fealty to other lords in order to have even stronger defence against other manors and barbarian groups.

This feudal system was also greatly decentralized, and the kings of weak "countries" did not hold much significant power over the nobility. Although some view the Roman Catholic

Church of the Middle Ages as a centralizing factor, it played a strong role in weakening the power of the secular kings, which gave the nobility more power. As the Middle Ages wore on, corruption in the church and new political ideas began to slowly strengthen the secular powers and bring together the extremely decentralized society.

This centralization continued through the Renaissance and has been changed and reformed until the present centralized system which is thought to have a balance between central government and decentralized balance of power.

DECENTRALISED GOVERNANCE

Decentralization—the transfer of authority and responsibility for public functions from the central government to subordinate or quasi-independent government organizations and/or the private sector—is a complex and multifaceted concept. It embraces a variety of concepts. Different types of decentralization show different characteristics, policy implications, and conditions for success.

Typologies of decentralization have flourished. For example, political, administrative, fiscal, and market decentralization are the types of decentralization. Drawing distinctions between these various concepts is useful for highlighting the many dimensions of successful decentralization and the need for coordination among them. Nevertheless, there is clearly overlap in defining these terms and the precise definitions are not as important as the need for a comprehensive approach. Political, administrative, fiscal and market decentralization can also appear in different forms and combinations across countries, within countries and even within sectors.

POLITICAL DECENTRALIZATION

Political decentralization aims to give citizens or their elected representatives more power in public decision-making. It is often associated with pluralistic politics and representative government, but it can also support democratization by giving citizens, or their representatives, more influence in the formulation and implementation of policies. Advocates of political decentralization assume that decisions made with greater participation will be better informed and more relevant to diverse interests in society than those made only by national political authorities.

The concept implies that the selection of representatives from local electoral constituency allows citizens to know better their political representatives and allows elected officials to know better the needs and desires of their constituents. Political decentralization often requires constitutional or statutory reforms, creation of local political units, and the encouragement of effective public interest groups.

ADMINISTRATIVE DECENTRALIZATION

Administrative decentralization seeks to redistribute authority, responsibility and financial resources for providing public services among different levels of governance. It is the transfer of responsibility for the planning, financing and management of public functions from the central government or regional governments and its agencies to local governments, semi-autonomous public authorities or corporations, or area-wide, regional or functional authorities. The three major forms of administrative decentralization — deconcentration, delegation, and devolution — each have different characteristics.

DECENTRALIZATION

Dispersal of financial responsibility is a core component of decentralisation. If local governments and private organizations are to carry out decentralized functions effectively, they must have an adequate level of revenues – either raised locally or transferred from the central government– as well as the authority to make decisions about expenditures.

Fiscal decentralization can take many forms, including:

- Self-financing or cost recovery through user charges,
- Co-financing or co-production arrangements through which the users participate in providing services and infrastructure through monetary or labour contributions;

- Expansion of local revenues through property or sales taxes, or indirect charges;
- Intergovernmental transfers that shift general revenues from taxes collected by the central government to local governments for general or specific uses; and
- Authorization of municipal borrowing and the mobilization of either national or local government resources through loan guarantees.

In many developing countries local governments or administrative units possess the legal authority to impose taxes, but the tax base is so weak and the dependence on central government subsidies so ingrained that no attempt is made to exercise that authority.

FISCAL DECENTRALIZATION AND FISCAL FEDERALISM

The concept of fiscal federalism is not to be associated with fiscal decentralization in officially declared federations only; it is applicable even to non-federal states in the sense that they encompass different levels of government which have defacto decision making authority.

This however does not mean that all forms of governments are 'fiscally' federal; it only means that 'fiscal federalism' is a set of principles, that can be applied to all countries attempting 'fiscal decentralization'.

In fact, fiscal federalism is a general normative framework for assignment of functions to the different levels of government and appropriate fiscal instruments for carrying out these functions.

The questions arise:

- How federal and non-federal countries are different with respect to 'fiscal federalism' or 'fiscal decentralization.
- How fiscal federalism and fiscal decentralization are related? Chanchal Kumar Sharma clarifies: While fiscal federalism constitutes a set of guiding principles, a guiding concept, that helps in designing

financial relations between the national and subnational levels of the government, fiscal decentralization on the other hand is a process of applying such principles. Federal and non-federal countries differ in the manner in which such principles are applied. Application differs because unitary and federal governments differ in their political and legislative context and thus provide different opportunities for fiscal decentralization.

FISCAL FEDERALISM: THE FEDERAL APPROACH TO GOVERNANCE

In common parlance political and constitutional aspects (eg giving citizens or their elected representatives more power in political decision-making, establishment of subnational political entities for decision making and making them politically accountable to local electorate which often entails constitutional or statutory reforms like providing for representation of the member states, the strengthening of legislatures, creation of local political units along with the encouragement of effective public interest groups and pluralistic political parties) are considered crucial for federalism.

Chanchal Kumar Sharma however argues that it is the fiscal side of the federalism (fiscal federalism) that is crucial for federal dynamism. This is because Federalism is not a fixed allocation of spheres of central and provincial autonomy (as assumed in federal finance models) or a particular set of distribution of authority between governments, it is a process, structured by a set of institutions, through which authority is distributed and redistributed.

A Federalised System is a "balanced approach between the contrasting forces of centralisation and decentralisation for combining the political and economic advantages of unity while preserving the valued identity of the sub national units". Fiscal federal principles guide how boundaries, assignments, the level and nature of transfers should be revised from time to time to ensure efficiency and perhaps equity. Thus fiscal federalism provides the tools for "application of the federal approach to governance which lies in its ability to balance the contrasting forces of centralization and decentralization". In the age of Globalization, when fiscal decentralization is in vogue, all countries (federal or not) are applying what may be called, in Sharma's words "the federal approach to governance".

The only difference is that in federal countries the subnational governments may be involved in decision making process through some appropriate political or constitutional forum while Central government may dominate quite heavily in a unitary country.

Its no surprise then argues Sharma that fiscal federalism literature is far away from Centralization Vs Decentralization focus. Final aim is not to decentralize just for sake of it but to ensure good governance. Thus, in fiscal federalism -states Sharma "decentralization is not seen as an alternative to centralization. Both are needed. The complementary roles of national and subnational actors are determined by analyzing the most effective ways and means of achieving a desired objective"

ECONOMIC DECENTRALIZATION

Privatization and deregulation shift responsibility for functions from the public to the private sector and is another type of decentralization. Privatization and deregulation are usually, but not always, accompanied by economic liberalization and market development policies.

They allow functions that had been primarily or exclusively the responsibility of government to be carried out by businesses, community groups, cooperatives, private voluntary associations, and other non-government organizations.

PRIVATIZATION

Privatization can range in scope from leaving the provision of goods and services entirely to the free operation of the market to "public-private partnerships" in which government and the private sector cooperate to provide services or infrastructure.

Privatization can include:

- Allowing private enterprises to perform functions that had previously been monopolized by government;
- Contracting out the provision or management of public services or facilities to commercial enterprises indeed, there is a wide range of possible ways in which function can be organized and many examples of within public sector and public-private institutional forms, particularly in infrastructure;
- Financing public sector programmes through the capital market (with adequate regulation or measures to prevent situations where the central government bears the risk for this borrowing) and allowing private organizations to participate; and
- Transferring responsibility for providing services from the public to the private sector through the divestiture of state-owned enterprises.

Privatization cannot in the real sense be considered equivalent to decentralisation.

DEREGULATION

Deregulation reduces the legal constraints on private participation in service provision or allows competition among private suppliers for services that in the past had been provided by the government or by regulated monopolies. In recent years privatization and deregulation have become more attractive alternatives to governments in developing countries. Local governments are also privatizing by contracting out service provision or administration.

SILENT DECENTRALIZATION

An often ignored dimension of decentralization is whether it emerged explicitly by policies, or not. Decentralization in the absence of reforms is also referred to as "silent decentralization." Consequently, it distinguishes itself mainly by its potential origins: network changes, initiative shifts, policy emphasis developments, or resource availability alterations.

MEASURING DECENTRALIZATION

While diversity in degree of decentralization across the world is a fact yet there is no consensus in the empirical literature over the questions like 'which country is more decentralized?' This is because decentralization is defined and measured differently in different studies.

Chanchal Kumar Sharma finds in his literature survey: "On the basis of 'decentralization instrument' there are two strands in the literature that argue for two different approaches to measure fiscal autonomy.

One gives more weightage to devolution of tax authority as an instrument of decentralization and hold it crucial for subnational autonomy, the other gives more weight to the nature of intergovernmental transfers (discretionary or not) as an instrument impacting upon the subnational behaviour and effecting their autonomy and accountability.

Thus former choose to focus on fiscal policy *i.e.,* the relationship between expenditures and allocated revenues (vertical imbalance) while latter pay attention to regulatory or financial mechanisms *i.e.* the nature of intergovernmental transfers". Out of these two approaches, observes Sharma, "when it comes to the measurement of fiscal decentralization 'the share of subnational expenditures and revenues' is considered the best indicator.

This is because fiscal instruments are easier to measure while regulatory and financial instruments are extremely complex and difficult to measure statistically because nowhere transfers remain strictly confined to the technical objectives. Transfers pursue a mix of objectives and politically motivated transfers remain key part of the intergovernmental relations across the globe".

This is because argues Schakel (2008) "it is difficult to tell whether the expenditure is coming from conditional or unconditional grants, whether the central government is determining how the money should be spent, whether it is setting the framework legislation within which subnational governments implement, or whether "indeed" subnational governments are spending the money autonomously". Chanchal Kumar Sharma states, "...a true assessment of the degree of decentralization in a country can be made only if a comprehensive approach is adopted and rather than trying to simplify the syndrome of characteristics into the single dimension of autonomy, interrelationships of various dimensions of decentralization are taken into account."

13

Control and Coordination

CONTROL

Control is one of the managerial functions like *planning, organizing, staffing* and *directing*. It is an important function because it helps to check the errors and to take the corrective action so that deviation from standards are minimized and stated goals of the organization are achieved in desired manner.

- Modern concepts, control is a foreseeing action whereas earlier concept of control was used only when errors were detected. Control in management means setting standards, measuring actual performance and taking corrective action. Thus, control comprises these three main activities.
- *Henri Fayol*: Control of an undertaking consists of seeing that everything is being carried out in accordance with the plan which has been adopted, the orders which have been given, and the principles which have been laid down. Its object is to point out mistakes in order that they may be rectified and prevented from recurring.
- *EFL Breach*: Control is checking current performance against pre-determined standards contained in the plans, with a view to ensure adequate progress and satisfactory performance.
- *Harold Koontz*: Controlling is the measurement and correction of performance in order to make sure that enterprise objectives and the plans devised to attain them are accomplished.

- *Stafford Beer*: Management is the profession of control.
- *In 1916, Henri Fayol formulated one of the first definitions of control as it pertains to management*: Control consists of verifying whether everything occurs in conformity with the plan adopted, the instructions issued, and principles established. It ['s] object [is] to point out weaknesses and errors in order to rectify [them] and prevent recurrence.

Robert J. Mockler presented a more comprehensive definition of managerial control: Management control can be defined as a systematic effort by business management to compare performance to predetermined standards, plans, or objectives in order to determine whether performance is in line with these standards and presumably in order to take any remedial action required to see that human and other corporate resources are being used in the most effective and efficient way possible in achieving corporate objectives.

Also control can be defined as "that function of the system that adjusts operations as needed to achieve the plan, or to maintain variations from system objectives within allowable limits". The control subsystem functions in close harmony with the operating system.

The degree to which they interact depends on the nature of the operating system and its objectives. Stability concerns a system's ability to maintain a pattern of output without wide fluctuations. Rapidity of response pertains to the speed with which a system can correct variations and return to expected output.

A political election can emphasise the concept of control and the importance of feedback. Each party organizes a campaign to get its candidate selected and outlines a plan to inform the public about both the candidate's credentials and the party's platform. As the election nears, opinion polls furnish feedback about the effectiveness of the campaign and about each candidate's chances to win. Depending on the nature of this feedback, certain adjustments in strategy and/ or tactics can be made in an attempt to achieve the desired result. From these definitions it can be stated that there is close link between planning and controlling. Planning is a process by which an organisation's objectives and the methods to achieve the objectives are established, and controlling is a process which measures and directs the actual performance against the planned objectives of the organisation. Thus, planning and control are often referred to as siamese twins of management.

Characteristics of Control:

- Control is a continuous process
- Control is a management process
- Control is embedded in each level of organizational hierarchy
- Control is forward looking
- Control is closely linked with planning
- Control is a tool for achieving organizational activities

THE ELEMENTS OF CONTROL

The four basic elements in a control system:

1. The characteristic or condition to be controlled.
2. The sensor.
3. The comparator.
4. *The activator*: Occur in the same sequence and maintain a consistent relationship to each other in every system.

The first element is the *characteristic* or condition of the operating system which is to be measured. We select a specific characteristic because a correlation exists between it and how the system is performing. The characteristic may be the output of the system during any stage of processing or it may be a condition that has resulted from the output of the system.

For example, it may be the heat energy produced by the furnace or the temperature in the room which has changed because of the heat generated by the furnace. In an elementary school system, the hours a teacher works or the gain in knowledge demonstrated by the students on a national examination are examples of characteristics that may be selected for measurement, or control. The second element of control, the *sensor*, is a means for measuring the characteristic or condition. The control subsystem must be designed to include a sensory device or method of measurement. In a home heating system this device would be the thermostat, and in a quality-control system this measurement might be performed by a visual inspection of the product.

The third element of control, the comparator, determines the need for correction by comparing what is occurring with what has been planned. Some deviation from plan is usual and expected, but when variations are beyond those considered acceptable, corrective action is required. It is often possible to identify trends in performance and to take action before an unacceptable variation from the norm occurs. This sort of preventative action indicates that good control is being achieved.

The fourth element of control, the activator, is the corrective action taken to return the system to expected output. The actual person, device, or method used to direct corrective inputs into the operating system may take a variety of forms. It may be a hydraulic controller positioned by a solenoid or electric motor in response to an electronic error signal, an employee directed to rework the parts that failed to pass quality inspection, or a school principal who decides to buy additional books to provide for an increased number of students. As long as a plan is performed within allowable limits, corrective action is not necessary; this seldom occurs in practice, however.

Information is the medium of control, because the flow of sensory data and later the flow of corrective information allow a characteristic or condition of the system to be controlled. To emphasise how information flow facilitates control, let us review the elements of control in the context of information.

RELATIONSHIP BETWEEN THE ELEMENTS OF CONTROL AND INFORMATION

Controlled Characteristic or. Condition The primary requirement of a control system is that it maintain the level and kind of output necessary to achieve the system's objectives. It is usually impractical to control every feature and condition associated with the system's output. Therefore, the choice of the controlled item (and appropriate information about it) is extremely important. There should be a direct correlation between the controlled item and the system's operation. In other words, control of the selected characteristic should have a direct relationship to the goal or objective of the system.

SENSOR

After the characteristic is sensed, or measured, information pertinent to control is fed back. Exactly what information needs to be transmitted and also the language that will best facilitate the communication process and reduce the possibility of distortion in transmission must be carefully considered. Information that is to be compared with the standard, or plan, should be expressed in the same terms or language as in the original plan to facilitate decision making. Using machine methods (computers) may require extensive translation of the information. Since optimal languages for computation and for human review are not always the same, the relative ease of translation may be a significant factor in selecting the units of measurement or the language unit in the sensing element.

In many instances, the measurement may be sampled rather than providing a complete and continuous feedback of information about the operation. A sampling procedure suggests measuring some segment or portion of the operation that will represent the total.

COMPARISON WITH STANDARD

In a social system, the norms of acceptable behaviour become the standard against which so-called deviant behaviour may be judged. Regulations and laws provide a more formal collection of information for society. Social norms change, but very slowly. In contrast, the standards outlined by a formal law can be changed from one day to the next through revision, discontinuation, or replacement by another. Information about deviant behaviour becomes the basis for controlling social activity. Output information is compared with the standard or norm and significant deviations are noted. In an industrial example, frequency distribution (a tabulation of the number of times a given characteristic occurs within the sample of products being checked) may be used to show the average quality, the spread, and the comparison of output with a standard. If there is a significant and uncorrectable difference between output and plan, the system is "out of control."

This means that the objectives of the system are not feasible in relation to the capabilities of the present design. Either the objectives must be reevaluated or the system redesigned to add new capacity or capability. For example, the traffic in drugs has been increasing in some cities at an alarming rate. The citizens must decide whether to revise the police system so as to regain control, or whether to modify the law to reflect a different norm of acceptable behaviour.

Activator

The activator unit responds to the information received from the comparator and initiates corrective action. If the system is a machine-to-machine system, the corrective inputs (decision rules) are designed into the network.

When the control relates to a man-to-machine or man-to-man system, however, the individual(s) in charge must evaluate:

- The accuracy of the feedback information.
- The significance of the variation.
- What corrective inputs will restore the system to a reasonable degree of stability. Once the decision has been made to direct new inputs into the system, the actual process may be relatively easy.

A small amount of energy can change the operation of jet airplanes, automatic steel mills, and hydroelectric power plants. The pilot presses a button, and the landing gear of the airplane goes up or down; the operator of a steel mill pushes a lever, and a ribbon of white-hot steel races through the plant;

a worker at a control board directs the flow of electrical energy throughout a regional network of stations and substations. It takes but a small amount of control energy to release or stop large quantities of input.

The comparator may be located far from the operating system, although at least some of the elements must be in close proximity to operations. For example, the measurement (the sensory element) is usually at the point of operations. The measurement information can be transmitted to a distant point for comparison with the standard (comparator), and when deviations occur, the correcting input can be released from the distant point. However, the input (activator) will be located at the operating system. This ability to control from afar means that aircraft can be flown by remote control, dangerous manufacturing processes can be operated from a safe distance, and national organizations can be directed from centralized headquarters.

Process of Controlling:

- Setting performance standards.
- Measurement of actual performance.
- Comparing actual performance with standards.
- Analysing deviations.
- Correcting deviations.

Kinds of Control

Control may be grouped according to three general classifications:

1. The nature of the information flow designed into the system (that is, open- or closed-loop control),
2. The kind of components included in the design (that is man or machine control systems).
3. The relationship of control to the decision process (that is, organizational or operational control).

OPEN- AND CLOSED-LOOP CONTROL

The difference between open-loop control and closed-loop control is determined by whether all of the control elements are an integral part of the system being regulated, and whether allowable variations from standard have been predetermined. In an open-loop system, not all of the elements will be designed into the system, and/or allowable variations will not be predetermined. A street-lighting system controlled by a timing device is an example of an open-loop system. At a certain time each evening, a mechanical device closes the circuit and energy flows through the electric lines to light the lamps.

Note, however, that the timing mechanism is an independent unit and is not measuring the objective function of the lighting system. If the lights should be needed on a dark, stormy day the timing device would not recognize this need and therefore would not activate energy inputs. Corrective properties may sometimes be built into the controller (for example, to modify the time the lights are turned on as the days grow shorter or longer), but this would not close the loop. In another instance, the sensing, comparison, or adjustment may be made through action taken by an individual who is not part of the system. For example, the lights may be turned on by someone who happens to pass by and recognizes the need for additional light.

If control is exercised as a result of the operation rather than because of outside or predetermined arrangements, it is a closed-loop system. The home thermostat is the classic example of a control device in a closed-loop system. When the room temperature drops the desired point, the control mechanism closes the circuit to start the furnace and the temperature rises. The furnace-activating circuit is turned off as the temperature reaches the preselected level. The significant difference between this type of system and an open-loop system is that the control device is an element of the system it serves and measures the performance of the system. In other words, all four control elements are integral to the specific system.

An essential part of a closed-loop system is feedback; that is, the output of the system is measured continually through the item controlled, and the input is modified to reduce any difference or error towards zero. Many of the patterns of information flow in organizations are found to have the nature of closed loops, which use feedback. The reason for such a condition is apparent when one recognizes that any system, if it is to achieve a predetermined goal, must have available to it at all times an indication of its degree of attainment. In general, every goal-seeking system employs feedback.

Man and Machine Control

The elements of control are easy to identify in machine systems. For example, the characteristic to be controlled might be some variable like speed or temperature, and the sensing device could be a speedometer or a thermometer. An expectation of precision exists because the characteristic is quantifiable and the standard and the normal variation to be expected can be described in exact terms.

In automatic machine systems, inputs of information are used in a process of continual adjustment to achieve output specifications. When even a small variation from the standard occurs, the correction process begins. The automatic system is highly structured, designed to accept certain kinds of input and produce specific output, and programmed to regulate the transformation of inputs within a narrow range of variation.

For an illustration of mechanical control, as the load on a steam engine increases and the engine starts to slow down, the regulator reacts by opening a valve that releases additional inputs of steam energy. This new input returns the engine to the desired number of revolutions per minute. This type of mechanical control is crude in comparison to the more sophisticated electronic control systems in everyday use. Consider the complex missile-guidance systems that measure the actual course according to predetermined mathematical calculations and make almost instantaneous corrections to direct the missile to its target.

Machine systems can be complex because of the sophisticated technology, whereas control of people is complex because the elements of control are difficult to determine. In human control systems, the relationship between objectives and associated characteristics is often vague; the measurement of the characteristic may be extremely subjective; the expected standard is difficult to define; and the amount of new inputs required is impossible to quantify. To emphasise, let us refer once more to a formalized social system in which deviant behaviour is controlled through a process of observed violation of the existing law (sensing), court hearings and trials (comparison with standard), incarceration when the accused is found guilty (correction), and release from custody after rehabilitation of the prisoner has occurred.

The speed limit established for freeway driving is one standard of performance that is quantifiable, but even in this instance, the degree of permissible variation and the amount of the actual variation are often a subject of disagreement between the patrolman and the suspected violator. The complexity of our society is reflected in many of our laws and regulations, which establish the general standards for economic, political, and social operations. A citizen may not know or understand the law and consequently would not know whether or not he was guilty of a violation.

Most organized systems are some combination of man and machine; some elements of control may be performed by machine whereas others are accomplished by man. In addition, some standards may be precisely structured whereas others may be little more than general guidelines with wide variations expected in output. Man must performance as the controller when measurement is subjective and judgment is required. Machines such as computers are incapable of making exceptions from the specified control criteria regardless of how much a particular case might warrant special consideration. A pilot acts in conjunction with computers and automatic pilots to fly large jets. In the event of unexpected weather changes, or possible collision with another plane, he must intercede and assume direct control.

ORGANIZATIONAL AND OPERATIONAL CONTROL

The concept of organizational control is implicit in the bureaucratic theory of Max Weber. Associated with this theory are such concepts as "span of control", "closeness of supervision", and "hierarchical authority". Weber's view tends to include all levels or types of organizational control as being the same. More recently, writers have tended to differentiate the control process between that which emphasizes the nature of the organizational or systems design and that which deals with daily operations.

To emphasise the difference, we "evaluate" the performance of a system to see how effective and efficient the design proved to be or to discover why it failed. In contrast, we operate and "control" the system with respect to the daily inputs of material, information, and energy. In both instances, the elements of feedback are present, but organizational control tends to review and evaluate the nature and arrangement of components in the system, whereas operational control tends to adjust the daily inputs.

The direction for organizational control comes from the goals and strategic plans of the organization. General plans are translated into specific performance measures such as share of the market, earnings, return on investment, and budgets. The process of organizational control is to review and evaluate the performance of the system against these established norms. Rewards for meeting or exceeding standards may range from special recognition to salary increases or promotions. On the other hand, a failure to meet expectations may signal the need to reorganize or redesign.

In organizational control, the approach used in the programme of review and evaluation depends on the reason for the evaluation — that is, is it because the system is not effective (accomplishing its objectives)? Is the system failing to achieve an expected standard of efficiency? Is the evaluation being conducted because of a breakdown or failure in operations? Is it merely a periodic audit-and-review process?

When a system has failed or is in great difficulty, special diagnostic techniques may be required to isolate the trouble areas and to identify the causes of the difficulty. It is appropriate to investigate areas that have been troublesome before or areas where some measure of performance can be quickly identified. For example, if an organization's output backlog builds rapidly, it is logical to check first to see if the problem is due to such readily obtainable measures as increased demand or to a drop in available man hours. When a more detailed analysis is necessary, a systematic procedure should be followed. In contrast to organizational control, operational control serves to regulate the day-to-day output relative to schedules, specifications, and costs. Is the output of product or service the proper quality and is it available as scheduled? Are inventories of raw materials, goods-in-process, and finished products being purchased and produced in the desired quantities? Are the costs associated with the transformation process in line with cost estimates? Is the information needed in the transformation process available in the right form and at the right time? Is the energy resource being utilized efficiently?

The most difficult task of management concerns monitoring the behaviour of individuals, comparing performance to some standard, and providing rewards or punishment as indicated. Sometimes this control over people relates entirely to their output. For example, a manager might not be concerned with the behaviour of a salesman as long as sales were as high as expected. In other instances, close supervision of the salesman might be appropriate if achieving customer satisfaction were one of the sales organization's main objectives. The larger the unit, the more likely that the control characteristic will be related to some output goal. It also follows that if it is difficult or impossible to identify the actual output of individuals, it is better to measure the performance of the entire group. This means that individuals' levels of motivation and the measurement of their performance become subjective judgments made by the supervisor. Controlling output also suggests the difficulty of controlling individuals' performance and relating this to the total system's objectives.

Problems of Control

The perfect plan could be outlined if every possible variation of input could be anticipated and if the system would operate as predicted. This kind of planning is neither realistic, economical, nor feasible for most business systems. If it were feasible, planning requirements would be so complex that the system would be out of date before it could be operated. Therefore, we design control into systems. This requires more thought in the systems design but allows more flexibility of operations and makes it possible to operate a system using unpredictable components and undetermined input. Still, the design and effective operation of control are not without problems.

The objective of the system is to perform some specified function. The purpose of organizational control is to see that the specified function is achieved; the objective of operational control is to ensure that variations in daily output are maintained within prescribed limits. It is one thing to design a system that contains all of the elements of control, and quite another to make it operate true to the best objectives of design. Operating "in control" or "with plan" does not guarantee optimum performance. For example, the plan may not make the best use of the inputs of materials, energy, or information — in other words, the system may not be designed to operate efficiently. Some of the more typical problems relating to control include the difficulty of measurement, the problem of timing information flow, and the setting of proper standards.

Measurement of Output

When objectives are not limited to quantitative output, the measurement of system effectiveness is difficult to make and subsequently perplexing to evaluate. Many of the characteristics pertaining to output do not lend themselves to quantitative measurement. This is true particularly when inputs of human energy cannot be related directly to output.

The same situation applies to machines and other equipment associated with human involvement, when output is not in specific units. In evaluating man-machine or human-oriented systems, psychological and sociological factors obviously do not easily translate into quantifiable terms. *For example, how does mental fatigue affect the quality or quantity of output? And, if it does, is mental fatigue a function of the lack of a challenging assignment or the fear of a potential injury?* Subjective inputs may be transferred into numerical data, but there is always the danger of an incorrect appraisal and transfer, and the danger that the analyst may assume undue confidence in such data after they have been quantified. Let us suppose, for example, that the decisions made by an executive are rated from 1 to 10, 10 being the perfect decision.

After determining the ranking for each decision, adding these, and dividing by the total number of decisions made, the average ranking would indicate a particular executive's score in his decision-making role. On the basis of this score, judgments — which could be quite erroneous — might be made about his decision-making effectiveness. One executive with a ranking of 6.75 might be considered more effective than another who had a ranking of 6.25, and yet the two managers may have made decisions under different circumstances and conditions. External factors over which neither executive had any control may have influenced the difference in "effectiveness".

Quantifying human behaviour, despite its extreme difficulty, subjectivity, and imprecision in relation to measuring physical characteristics is the most prevalent and important measurement made in large systems. The behaviour of individuals ultimately dictates the success or failure of every man-made system.

INFORMATION FLOW

Osillation and Feedback

Another problem of control relates to the improper timing of information introduced into the feedback channel. Improper timing can occur in both computerized and human control systems, either by mistakes in measurement or in judgment. The more rapid the system's response to an error signal, the more likely it is that the system could overadjust; yet the need for prompt action is important because any delay in providing corrective input could also be crucial. A system generating feedback inconsistent with current need will tend to fluctuate and will not adjust in the desired manner. The most serious problem in information flow arises when the delay in feedback is exactly one-half cycle, for then the corrective action is superimposed on a variation from norm which, at that moment, is in the same direction as that of the correction.

This causes the system to overcorrect, and then if the reverse adjustment is made out of cycle, to correct too much in the other direction, and so on until the system fluctuates ("oscillates") out of control. If, at Point A, the trend standard is recognized and new inputs are added, but not until Point B, the system will overreact and go beyond the allowable limits. Again, if this is recognized at Point C, but inputs are not withdrawn until Point D, it will cause the system to drop the lower limit of allowable variation.

One solution to this problem rests in anticipation, which involves measuring not only the change but also the rate of change. The correction is outlined as a factor of the type and rate of the error. The difficulty also might be overcome by reducing the time lag between the measurement of the output and the adjustment to input. If a trend can be indicated, a time lead can be introduced to compensate for the time lag, bringing about consistency between the need for correction and the type and magnitude of the indicated action.

It is usually more effective for an organization to maintain continuous measurement of its performance and to make small adjustments in operations constantly (this assumes a highly sensitive control system). Consequently, should be timely and correct to be effective. That is, the information should provide an accurate indication of the status of the system.

Setting Standards

Setting the proper standards or control limits is a problem in many systems. Parents are confronted with this dilemma in expressing what they expect of their children, and business managers face the same issue in establishing standards that will be acceptable to employees. Some theorists have proposed that workers be allowed to set their own standards, on the assumption that when people establish their own goals, they are more apt to accept and achieve them. Standards should be as precise as possible and communicated to all persons concerned. Moreover, communication alone is not sufficient; understanding is necessary.

In human systems, standards tend to be poorly defined and the allowable range of deviation from standard also indefinite. For example, how many hours each day should a professor be expected to be available for student consultation? Or, what kind of behaviour should be expected by students in the classroom? Discretion and personal judgment play a large part in such systems, to determine whether corrective action should be taken.

Perhaps the most difficult problem in human systems is the unresponsiveness of individuals to indicated correction. This may take the form of opposition and subversion to control, or it may be related to the lack of defined responsibility or authority to take action. Leadership and positive motivation then become vital ingredients in achieving the proper response to input requirements.

Most control problems relate to design; thus the solution to these problems must start at that point. Automatic control systems, provided that human intervention is possible to handle exceptions, offer the greatest promise. There is a danger, however, that we may measure characteristics that do not represent effective performance (as in the case of the speaker who requested that all of the people who could not hear what he was saying should raise their hands), or that improper information may be communicated.

Given the growth of multinationals, it is important that managers learn whether strategic planning enhances firm performance in cross-cultural situations. Using an international sample of firms, this study found that the general planning-performance model is relevant across the cultures sampled. While there appears to be little direct relationship between culture and planning, culture did moderate the planning-performance relationship. Furthermore, specific cultural values were found to account for some of the cross-cultural differences in the planning-performance relationship. Implications for management and future research are discussed. Concerns of increased international competition abound not only in the U.S. but also in Europe with the further expansion of the European Union and in Asia and Latin America with increased economic integration in those regions. Theorists have argued that firms should respond to environmental changes, such as increased competition, by engaging in more systematic strategic planning to anticipate and respond to changing events.

There is evidence that U.S. firms have responded to greater environmental uncertainty and complexity with more extensive planning. Furthermore, it appears that formal strategic planning enhances firm performance although the relationship is not unequivocal. It is worth noting that, as firms in other regions of the world are confronting increasingly volatile environments, there is a need to extend planning research to firms representing a diversity of national and cultural settings. Such research will help ensure that current prescriptions concerning the use of planning have external validity in a variety of locales. Thus, the purpose of this study is to examine the relationship between strategic planning and firm performance among a group of firms representing different cultural regions.

Strategic Planning Processes

Strategic management seeks to align the firm's activities with its external environment. At the heart of this management approach is the strategic planning system. As firms face increased environmental change (e.g., more globalization) theorists argue that firms benefit from strategic planning. For over thirty years, a plethora of studies have examined formal long range or strategic planning.

Many of these studies have found that firms that plan possess different characteristics than non-planners. In particular, many studies have sought to examine the relationship between planning and firm performance. A review of much of the literature suggests that strategic planning can be described along two broad dimensions, planning content or ends and planning processes or means. Planning content refers to the ends of the planning process such as: goals, mission statements, environmental information programmes, and internal resources. Much of this content helps distinguish strategic planning from that which is purely operational planning. Planning processes focus on the means or methods by which the planning process is carried out. Characteristics such as commitment, system maturity, comprehensiveness, time horizon, and importance are typical examples of such system or process characteristics.

This study focuses on planning processes or system characteristics because these processes have been examined far more in the literature on planning and performance. This makes it easier to compare this study to the stream of literature that has preceded it. Second, culture is believed to affect planning processes. As Brock *et al.* note, cultural values shape acceptable organization processes such as planning and decision making. Furthermore, Hofstede has observed that planning processes often reflect the dominant values of a culture.

Enterprise resource planning (ERP) is an integrated computer-based system used to manage internal and external resources including tangible assets, financial resources, materials, and human resources. It is a software architecture whose purpose is to facilitate the flow of information between all business functions inside the boundaries of the organization and manage the connections to outside stakeholders. Built on a centralized database and normally utilizing a common computing platform, ERP systems consolidate all business operations into a uniform and enterprise wide system environment.

An ERP system can either reside on a centralized server or be distributed across modular hardware and software units that provide "services" and communicate on a local area network. The distributed design allows a business to assemble modules from different vendors without the need for the placement of multiple copies of complex, expensive computer systems in areas which will not use their full capacity. The initialism ERP was first employed by research and analysis firm Gartner Group in 1990 as an extension of MRP (Material Requirements Planning; later manufacturing resource planning) and CIM (Computer Integrated Manufacturing), and while not supplanting these terms, it has come to represent a larger whole.

It came into use as makers of MRP software started to develop software applications beyond the manufacturing arena. ERP systems now attempt to cover all core functions of an enterprise, regardless of the organization's business or charter. These systems can now be found in non-manufacturing businesses, non-profit organizations and governments. To be considered an ERP system, a software package should have the following traits: It should be integrated and operate in real-time with no periodic batch updates. All applications should access one database to prevent redundant data and multiple data definitions. All modules should have the same look and feel. Users should be able to access any information in the system without needed integration work on the part of the IS department.

ERP Components

Transactional Backbone:

- Financials
- Distribution
- Human Resources
- Product lifecycle management

Advanced Applications:

- Customer Relationship Management (CRM)
- Supply chain management
    - Purchasing
    - Manufacturing
    - Distribution
- Warehouse Management

Management Portal/Dashboard:

- Decision Support System

These modules can exist in a complete system or utilized in an ad-hoc fashion.

Commercial Applications:

- *Manufacturing*: Engineering, bills of material, scheduling, capacity, workflow management, quality control, cost management, manufacturing process, manufacturing projects, manufacturing flow.
- *Supply chain management*: Order to cash, inventory, order entry, purchasing, product configurator, supply chain planning, supplier scheduling, inspection of goods, claim processing, commission calculation.
- *Financials*: General ledger, cash management, accounts payable, accounts receivable, fixed assets.
- *Project management*: Costing, billing, time and expense, performance units, activity management.
- *Human resources*: Human resources, payroll, training, time and attendance, rostering, benefits.
- *Customer relationship management*: Sales and marketing, commissions, service, customer contact and call centre support
- *Data services*: Various "self-service" interfaces for customers, suppliers, and/or employees
- *Access control*: Management of user privileges for various processes

The term "Enterprise resource planning" originally derived from manufacturing resource planning (MRP II) that followed material requirements planning (MRP). MRP evolved into ERP when "routings" became a major part of the software architecture and a company's capacity planning activity also became a part of the standard software activity. ERP systems typically handle the manufacturing, logistics, distribution, inventory, shipping, invoicing, and accounting for a company. ERP software can aid in the control of many business activities, including sales, marketing, delivery, billing, production, inventory management, quality management, and human resource management.

ERP systems saw a large boost in sales in the 1990s as companies faced the Y2K problem (real or imagined) in their "legacy" systems. Many companies took this opportunity to replace such information systems with ERP systems. This rapid growth in sales was followed by a slump in 1999, at which time most companies had already implemented their Y2K solution. ERP systems are often incorrectly called *back office systems* indicating that customers and the general public are not directly involved. This is contrasted with *front office systems* like customer relationship management (CRM) systems that deal directly with the customers, or the eBusiness systems such as eCommerce, eGovernment, eTelecom, and eFinance, or supplier relationship management (SRM) systems.

ERP systems are cross-functional and enterprise-wide. All functional departments that are involved in operations or production are integrated in one system. In addition to areas such as manufacturing, warehousing, logistics, and information technology, this typically includes accounting, human resources, marketing and strategic management.

ERP II, a term coined in the early 2000s, is often used to describe what would be the next generation of ERP software. This new generation of software is web-based and allows both employees and external resources (such as suppliers and customers) real-time access to the system's data. EAS — Enterprise Application Suite is a new name for formerly developed ERP systems which include (almost) all segments of business using ordinary Internet browsers as thin clients.

Though traditionally ERP packages have been on-premise installations, ERP systems are now also available as Software as a Service. Best practices are incorporated into most ERP vendor's software packages. When implementing an ERP system, organizations can choose between customizing the software or modifying their business processes to the "best practice" function delivered in the "out-of-the-box" version of the software.

Prior to ERP, software was developed to fit individual processes of an individual business. Due to the complexities of most ERP systems and the negative consequences of a failed ERP implementation, most vendors have included "Best Practices" into their software. These "Best Practices" are what the Vendor deems as the most efficient way to carry out a particular business process in an Integrated Enterprise-Wide system. A study conducted by Ludwigshafen University of Applied Science surveyed 192 companies and concluded that companies which implemented industry best practices decreased mission-critical project tasks such as configuration, documentation, testing and training. In addition, the use of best practices reduced over risk by 71% when compared to other software implementations.

The use of best practices can make complying with requirements such as IFRS, Sarbanes-Oxley, or Basel II easier. They can also help where the process is a commodity such as electronic funds transfer. This is because the procedure of capturing and reporting legislative or commodity content can be readily codified within the ERP software, and then replicated with confidence across multiple businesses who have the same business requirement.

IMPLEMENTATION

Businesses have a wide scope of applications and processes throughout their functional units; producing ERP software systems that are typically complex and usually impose significant changes on staff work practices. Implementing ERP software is typically too complex for "in-house" skill, so it is desirable and highly advised to hire outside consultants who are professionally trained to implement these systems. This is typically the most cost effective way.

There are three types of services that may be employed for - Consulting, Customization, Support. The length of time to implement an ERP system depends on the size of the business, the number of modules, the extent of customization, the scope of the change and the willingness of the customer to take ownership for the project. ERP systems are modular, so they don't all need be implemented at once.

It can be divided into various stages, or phase-ins. The typical project is about 14 months and requires around 150 consultants. A small project (e.g., a company of less than 100 staff) can be planned and delivered within 3-9 months; however, a large, multi-site or multi-country implementation can take years. The length of the implementations is closely tied to the amount of customization desired. To implement ERP systems, companies often seek the help of an ERP vendor or of third-party consulting companies. These firms typically provide three areas of professional services: consulting; customization; and support. The client organization can also employ independent programme management, business analysis, change management, and UAT specialists to ensure their business requirements remain a priority during implementation.

Data migration is one of the most important activities in determining the success of an ERP implementation. Since many decisions must be made before migration, a significant amount of planning must occur. Unfortunately, data migration is the last activity before the production phase of an ERP implementation, and therefore receives minimal attention due to time constraints.

The following are steps of a data migration strategy that can help with the success of an ERP implementation:

- Identifying the data to be migrated
- Determining the timing of data migration
- Generating the data templates
- Freezing the tools for data migration
- Deciding on migration related setups
- Deciding on data archiving

PROCESS PREPARATION

ERP vendors have designed their systems around standard business processes, based upon best business practices. Different vendor(s) have different types of processes but they are all of a standard, modular nature. Firms that want to implement ERP systems are consequently forced to adapt their organizations to standardized processes as opposed to adapting the ERP package to the existing processes.

Neglecting to map current business processes prior to starting ERP implementation is a main reason for failure of ERP projects. It is therefore crucial that organizations perform a thorough business process analysis before selecting an ERP vendor and setting off on the implementation track. This analysis should map out all present operational processes, enabling selection of an ERP vendor whose standard modules are most closely aligned with the established organization. Redesign can then be implemented to achieve further process congruence.

Research indicates that the risk of business process mismatch is decreased by:

- linking each current organizational process to the organization's strategy;
- analyzing the effectiveness of each process in light of its current related business capability;

linked via Master Data Management) specifically configured and/or customised to meet local needs. A disadvantage usually attributed to ERP is that business process redesign to fit the standardized ERP modules can lead to a loss of competitive advantage. While documented cases exist where this has indeed materialized, other cases show that following thorough process preparation ERP systems can actually increase sustainable competitive advantage.

Configuration

Configuring an ERP system is largely a matter of balancing the way you want the system to work with the way the system lets you work. Begin by deciding which modules to install, then adjust the system using configuration tables to achieve the best possible fit in working with your company's processes.

- *Modules*: Most systems are modular simply for the flexibility of implementing some functions but not others. Some common modules, such as finance and accounting are adopted by nearly all companies implementing enterprise systems; others however such as human resource management are not needed by some companies and therefore not adopted. A service company for example will not likely need a module for manufacturing. Other times companies will not adopt a module because they already have their own proprietary system they believe to be superior. Generally speaking the greater number of modules selected, the greater the integration benefits, but also the increase in costs, risks and changes involved.

- *Configuration Tables*: A configuration table enables a company to tailor a particular aspect of the system to the way it chooses to do business. For example, an organization can select the type of inventory accounting - FIFO or LIFO - it will employ or whether it wants to recognize revenue by geographical unit, product line, or distribution channel.

So what happens when the options the system allows just aren't good enough? At this point a company has two choices, both of which are not ideal. It can re-write some of the enterprise system's code, or it can continue to use an existing system and build interfaces between it and the new enterprise system. Both options will add time and cost to the implementation process. Additionally they can dilute the system's integration benefits. The more customised the system becomes the less possible seamless communication between suppliers and customers.

Consulting Services

Many organizations do not have sufficient internal skills to implement an ERP project. This results in many organizations offering consulting services for ERP implementation.

Typically, a consulting team is responsible for the entire ERP implementation including:

- Selecting
- Planning
- Training
- Testing
- Implementation
- Delivery

Of any customised modules: Examples of customization includes creating processes and reports for compliance, additional product training; creation of process triggers and workflow; specialist advice to improve how the ERP is used in the business; system optimization; and assistance writing reports, complex data extracts or implementing Business Intelligence. For most mid-sized companies, the cost of the implementation will range from around the list price of the ERP user licenses to up to twice this amount (depending on the level of customization required). Large companies, and especially those with multiple sites or countries, will often spend considerably more on the implementation than the cost of the user licenses—three to five times more is not uncommon for a multi-site implementation.

Unlike most single-purpose applications, ERP packages have historically included full source code and shipped with vendor-supported team IDEs for customizing and extending the delivered code. During the early years of ERP the guarantee of mature tools and support for extensive customization was an important sales argument when a potential customer was considering developing their own unique solution in-house, or assembling a cross-functional solution by integrating multiple "best of breed" applications.

"CORE SYSTEM" CUSTOMIZATION VS CONFIGURATION

Increasingly, ERP vendors have tried to reduce the need for customization by providing built-in "configuration" tools to address most customers' needs for changing how the out-of-the-box core system works.

Key differences between customization and configuration include:

- Customization is always optional, whereas some degree of configuration (e.g., setting up cost/profit centre structures, organisational trees, purchase approval rules, etc.) may be needed before the software will work at all.
- Configuration is available to all customers, whereas customization allows individual customer to implement proprietary "market-beating" processes.
- Configuration changes tend to be recorded as entries

in vendor-supplied data tables, whereas custom-ization usually requires some element of programming and/or changes to table structures or views.

- The effect of configuration changes on the performance of the system is relatively predictable and is largely the responsibility of the ERP vendor. The effect of customization is unpredictable and may require time-consuming stress testing by the implementation team.
- Configuration changes are almost always guaranteed to survive upgrades to new software versions. Some customizations (e.g. code that uses pre-defined "hooks" that are called before/after displaying data screens) will survive upgrades, though they will still need to be re-tested. More extensive customizations (e.g. those involving changes to fundamental data structures) will be overwritten during upgrades and must be re-implemented manually.

By this analysis, customizing an ERP package can be unexpectedly expensive and complicated, and tends to delay delivery of the obvious benefits of an integrated system. Nevertheless, customizing an ERP suite gives the scope to implement secret recipes for excellence in specific areas while ensuring that industry best practices are achieved in less sensitive areas.

EXTENSIONS

In this context, "Extensions" refers to ways that an ERP environment can be "extended" (supplemented) with third-party programmes.

It is technically easy to expose most ERP transactions to outside programmes that do other things, e.g.:

- Archiving, reporting and republishing (these are easiest to achieve, because they mainly address static data);
- Performing transactional data captures, e.g. using scanners, tills or RFIDs (also relatively easy because they touch existing data);

However, because ERP applications typically contain sophisticated rules that control how data can be created or changed, some such functions can be very difficult to implement.

In the absence of an ERP system, a large manufacturer may find itself with many software applications that cannot communicate or interface effectively with one another.

Tasks that need to interface with one another may involve:

- ERP systems connect the necessary software in order for accurate forecasting to be done. This allows inventory levels to be kept at maximum efficiency and the company to be more profitable.
- Integration among different functional areas to ensure proper communication, productivity and efficiency
- Design engineering (how to best make the product)
- Order tracking, from acceptance through fulfillment
- The revenue cycle, from invoice through cash receipt
- Managing inter-dependencies of complex processes bill of materials
- Tracking the three-way match between purchase orders (what was ordered), inventory receipts (what arrived), and costing (what the vendor invoiced)
- The accounting for all of these tasks: tracking the revenue, cost and profit at a granular level.

ERP Systems centralize the data in one place. Benefits of this include:

- Eliminates the problem of synchronizing changes between multiple systems - consolidation of finance, marketing and sales, human resource, and manufacturing applications
- Permits control of business processes that cross functional boundaries
- Provides top-down view of the enterprise (no "islands of information"), real time information is available to management anywhere, anytime to make proper decisions.
- Reduces the risk of loss of sensitive data by consolidating multiple permissions and security models into a single structure.

- Shorten production lead time and delivery time
- Facilitating business learning, empowering, and building common visions

Some security features are included within an ERP system to protect against both outsider crime, such as industrial espionage, and insider crime, such as embezzlement. A data-tampering scenario, for example, might involve a disgruntled employee intentionally modifying prices to below-the-breakeven point in order to attempt to interfere with the company's profit or other sabotage. ERP systems typically provide functionality for implementing internal controls to prevent actions of this kind. ERP vendors are also moving towards better integration with other kinds of information security tools.

Problems with ERP systems are mainly due to inadequate investment in ongoing training for the involved IT personnel - including those implementing and testing changes - as well as a lack of corporate policy protecting the integrity of the data in the ERP systems and the ways in which it is used.

Disadvantages:

- Customization of the ERP software is limited.
- Re-engineering of business processes to fit the "industry standard" prescribed by the ERP system may lead to a loss of competitive advantage.
- ERP systems can be very expensive (This has led to a new category of "ERP light" solutions)
- ERPs are often seen as too rigid and too difficult to adapt to the specific workflow and business process of some companies—this is cited as one of the main causes of their failure.
- Many of the integrated links need high accuracy in other applications to work effectively. A company can achieve minimum standards, then over time "dirty data" will reduce the reliability of some applications.
- Once a system is established, switching costs are very high for any one of the partners (reducing flexibility and strategic control at the corporate level).

- The blurring of company boundaries can cause problems in accountability, lines of responsibility, and employee morale.
- Resistance in sharing sensitive internal information between departments can reduce the effectiveness of the software.
- Some large organizations may have multiple departments with separate, independent resources, missions, chains-of-command, etc, and consolidation into a single enterprise may yield limited benefits.

HUMAN RESPONSE TO CONTROL

The relationship between the instructor and the students has a profound impact on how much the students learn. To students, the instructor usually is a symbol of authority. Students expect the instructor to exercise certain controls, and they tend to recognize and submit to authority as a valid means of control. The instructor's challenge is to know what controls are best for the existing circumstances. The instructor should create an atmosphere that enables and encourages students to help themselves.

Every student works towards a goal of some kind. It may be success itself; it may simply be a grade or other form of personal recognition. The successful instructor directs and controls the behaviour of the students and guides them towards a goal. This is a part of the process of directing the students' actions to modify their behaviour. Without the instructor's active intervention, the students may become passive and perhaps resistant to learning. The controls the instructor exercises-how much, how far, to what degree-should be based on more than trial and error.

Some interesting generalizations have been made about motivation and human nature. While these assumptions are typically applied to industrial management, they have implications for the aviation instructor as well. The expenditure of physical and mental effort in work is as natural as play and rest. The average person does not inherently dislike work. Depending on conditions, work may be a source of satisfaction and, if so, it will be performed voluntarily. On the other hand, when work is a form of punishment, it will be avoided, if possible. Most people will exercise self-direction and self- control in the pursuit of goals to which they are committed. Commitment to goals relates directly to the reward associated with their achievement, the most significant of which is probably the satisfaction of ego.

Under proper conditions, the average person learns, not only to accept, but also to seek responsibility. Shirking responsibility and lack of ambition are not inherent in human nature. They are usually the consequences of experience. The capacity to exercise a relatively high degree of imagination, ingenuity, and creativity in the solution of common problems is widely, not narrowly, distributed in the population. Under the conditions of modern life, the intellectual potentialities of the average person are only partially used.

An instructor who accepts these assumptions should recognize the student's vast, untapped potential. At the same time? ingenuity must be used in discovering how to realise the potentialities of the student. The responsibility rests squarely on the instructor's shoulders. If the student is perceived as lazy, indifferent, unresponsive, uncooperative, and antagonistic, these basic assumptions imply that the instructor's methods of control are at fault.

The raw material is there, in most cases, and the shaping and directing of it lie in the hands of those who have the responsibility of controlling it. How to mold a solid, healthy, productive relationship with students depends, of course, on the instructor's knowledge of students as human beings and of the needs, drives, and desires they continually try to satisfy in one way or another. Some of their needs and drives are discussed in the following paragraphs.

HUMAN NEEDS

The instructor should always be aware of the fact that students are human beings. The needs of students, and of all mankind, have been studied by psychologists and categorized in a number of ways. In 1938, a U.S. psychologist, Henry A. Murray, published a catalog of human motives, which he called needs. These needs were described as being either primary (biological, innate) or secondary (learned, acquired); they were seen as a force related to behaviour and goals. Among the motives that Murray discussed were what he identified as needs for achievement, affiliation, power, dependence, and succor (the need to be taken care of), as well as many others.

During the 1950s, Abraham Maslow organized human needs into levels of importance. They originally were called a hierarchy of human motives, but are now commonly referred to as a hierarchy of human needs. In the intervening years since the 1950s, several other theories on human needs have been published, but psychologists have not adopted any particular one. Meanwhile, Maslow's hierarchical categorization remains a popular and acceptable concept.

Physical

At the bottom of the pyramid is the broadest, most basic category, the physical needs. Each person is first concerned with a need for food, rest, and protection from the elements. Until these needs are satisfied, a person cannot concentrate fully on learning, self- expression, or any other tasks. Instructors should monitor their students to make sure that their basic physical needs have been met.

A hungry or tired student may not be able to perform as expected. Once a need is satisfied, it no longer provides motivation. Thus, the person strives to satisfy the needs of the next higher level.

Safety

The safety needs are protection against danger, threats, deprivation, and are labeled by some as the security needs. Regardless of the label, however, they are real, and student behaviour is influenced by them. This is especially true in flight training and aviation maintenance where safety is a major concern.

Social

When individuals are physically comfortable and do not feel threatened, they seek to satisfy their social needs. These are to belong, to associate, and to give and receive friendship and love. An example of the social need might apply to the spouse of a professional pilot.

In this case, the need to be included in conversation and other pilot-related activities could induce the spouse to learn how to fly. Since students are usually out of their normal surroundings during flight training, their need for association and belonging will be more pronounced. Instructors should make every effort to help new students feel at ease and to reinforce their decision to pursue aviation.

Ego

The egoistic needs usually have a strong influence on the instructor-student relationship. These needs consist of at least two types: those that relate to one's self-esteem, such as self-confidence, independence, achievement, competence, and knowledge; and the needs that relate to one's reputation, such as status, recognition, appreciation, and respect of associates. The egoistic need may be the main reason for a student's interest in aviation training.

Self-Fulfillment

At the apex of the hierarchy of human needs is self-fulfillment. This includes realizing one's own potential for continued development, and for being creative in the broadest sense of that term.

Maslow included various cognitive and aesthetic goals in this highest level. Self-fulfillment for a student should offer the greatest challenge to the instructor. Aiding another in realizing self-fulfillment is perhaps the most rewarding accomplishment for an instructor.

In summary, instructors should strive to help students satisfy their human needs in a manner that will create a healthy learning environment. In this type of environment, students experience fewer frustrations and, there- fore, can devote more attention to their studies. Fulfillment of needs can be a powerful motivation in complex learning situations.

Defence Mechanisms

The concept of defence mechanisms was introduced by Freud in the 1890s. In general, defence mechanisms are subconscious, almost automatic, ego-protecting reactions to unpleasant situations.

People use these defences to soften feelings of failure, to alleviate feelings of guilt, and to protect their sense of personal worth or adequacy.

Originally, Freud described a mechanism which is now commonly called repression. Since then, other defence mechanisms have gradually been added. In some cases, more than one name has been attached to a particular type of defence mechanism.

In addition, it is not always easy to differentiate between defences which are closely related. Thus, some confuqion often occurs in identifying the different types.

Compensation

With compensation, students often attempt to disguise the presence of a weak or undesirable quality by emphasizing a more positive one. They also may try to reduce tension by accepting and developing a less preferred but more attainable objective instead of a more preferred but less attainable objective.

Students who regard themselves as unattractive may develop exceptionally winning personalities to compensate. Students may say they would rather spend their evenings studying aircraft systems than anything else, but, in fact, they would rather be doing almost anything except aircraft systems study.

Projection

With projection, students relegate the blame for their own shortcomings, mistakes, and transgressions to others or attribute their motives, desires, characteristics, and impulses to others. The athlete who fails to make the team may feel sure the coach was unfair, or the tennis player who examines the racket after a missed shot is projecting blame. When students say, "Everybody will cheat on an exam if given the chance," they are projecting.

Rationalization

If students cannot accept the real reasons for their behaviour, they may rationalize. This device permits them to substitute excuses for reasons; moreover, they can make those excuses plausible and acceptable to themselves.

Rationalization is a subconscious technique for justifying actions that otherwise would be unacceptable. When true rationalization takes place, individuals sincerely believe in their excuses. The excuses seem real and justifiable to the individual.

Denial of Reality

Occasionally students may ignore or refuse to acknowledge disagreeable realities. They may turn away from unpleasant sights, refuse to discuss unpopular topics, or reject criticism.

Reaction Formation

Sometimes individuals protect themselves from dangerous desires by not only repressing them, but actually developing conscious attitudes and behaviour patterns that are just the opposite. A student may develop a who-cares-how-other-people-feel attitude to cover up feelings of loneliness and a hunger for acceptance.

Flight

Students often escape from frustrating situations by taking flight, physical or mental. To take flight physically, students may develop symptoms or ailments that give them satisfactory excuses for removing themselves from frustration. More frequent than physical flights are mental flights, or daydreaming. Mental flight provides a simple and satisfying escape from problems. If students get sufficient satisfaction from daydreaming, they may stop trying to achieve their goals altogether. When carried to extremes, the world of fantasy and the world of reality can become so confused that the dreamer cannot distinguish one from the other. This mechanism, when carried to the extreme, is referred to as fantasy.

Aggression

Everyone gets angry occasionally. Anger is a normal, universal human emotion. Angry people may shout, swear, slam a door, or give in to the heat of emotions in a number of ways. They become aggressive against something or somebody.

After a cooling-off period, they may see their actions as childish. In a classroom, shop, or airplane, such extreme behaviour is relatively infrequent, partly because students are taught to repress their emotions in the interest of safety. Because of safety concerns or social strictures, student aggressiveness may be expressed in subtle ways.

They may ask irrelevant questions, refuse to participate in the activities of the class, or disrupt activities within their own group. If students cannot deal directly with the cause of their frustration, they may vent their aggressiveness on a neutral object or person not related to the problem.

Resignation

Students also may become so frustrated that they lose interest and give up. They may no longer believe it profitable or even possible to go on, and as a result, they accept defeat. The most obvious and apparent cause for this form of resignation takes place when, after completing an early phase of a course without grasping the fundamentals, a student becomes bewildered and lost in the more advanced phases. From that point on, learning is negligible although the student may go through the motions of participating.

More information on these and other defence mechanisms, such as fantasy, repression, displacement, emotional insulation, regression, and introjection, can be obtained from a good psychology text. Instructors should recognize that most defence mechanisms fall within the realm of normal behaviour and serve a useful purpose. However, in some cases, they may be associated with a potentially serious mental health problem. Since defence mechanisms involve some degree of self-deception and distortion of reality, they do not solve problems; they alleviate symptoms, not causes.

Moreover, because defence mechanisms operate on a subconscious level, they are not subject to normal conscious checks and controls. Once an individual realises there is a conscious reliance on one of these devices, behaviour ceases to be a subconscious adjustment mechanism and becomes, instead, an ineffective way of satisfying a need.

It may be difficult for an instructor to identify excessive reliance on defence mechanisms by a student, but a personal crisis or other stressful event is usually the cause. For example, a death in the family, a divorce, or even a failing grade on an important test may trigger harmful defensive reactions. Physical symptoms such as a change in personality, angry outbursts, depression, or a general lack of interest may point to a problem.

Drug or alcohol abuse also may become apparent. Less obvious indications may include social withdrawal, preoccupation with certain ideas, or an inability to concentrate. Some people seem to have the proper attitude and skills necessary to cope with a crisis while others do not. An instructor needs to be familiar with typical defence mechanisms and have some knowledge of related behavioural problems.

A perceptive instructor can help by using common sense and talking over the problem with the student. The main objective should be to restore motivation and self-confidence. It should be noted that the human psyche is fragile and could be damaged by inept measures.

Therefore, in severe cases involving the possibility of deep psychological problems, timely and skillful help is needed. In this event, the instructor should recommend that the student use the services of a professional counselor.

THE FLIGHT INSTRUCTOR AS A PRACTICAL PSYCHOLOGIST

While it is obviously impossible for every flight instructor to be an accomplished psychologist. As already implied, flight instructors must also be able to evaluate student personality to effectively develop and use techniques appropriate for instruction.

Anxiety

Anxiety is probably the most significant psychological factor affecting flight instruction. This is true because flying is a potentially threatening experience for persons who are not accustomed to being off the ground. The fear of falling is universal in human beings. Anxiety also is a factor in maintenance training because lives may depend on consistently doing it right the first time. The following paragraphs are primarily concerned with flight instruction and student reactions. Anxiety is described by Webster as "a state of mental uneasiness arising from fear . . ." It results from the fear of anything, real or imagined, which threatens the person who experiences it, and may have a potent effect on actions and the ability to learn from perceptions.

The responses to anxiety vary extensively. They range from a hesitancy to performance to the impulse to do something even if it's wrong. Some people affected by anxiety will react appropriately, adequately, and more rapidly than they would in the absence of threat. Many, on the other hand, may freeze and be incapable of doing anything to correct the situation which has caused their anxiety. Others may do things without rational thought or reason. Both normal and abnormal reactions to anxiety are of concern to the flight instructor. The normal reactions are significant because they indicate a need for special instruction to relieve the anxiety. The abnormal reactions are even more important because they may signify a deep-seated problem. Anxiety can be countered by reinforcing students' enjoyment of flying, and by teaching them to cope with their fears. An effective technique is to treat fears as a normal reaction, rather than ignoring them. Keep in mind that anxiety for student pilots usually is associated with certain types of flight operations and maneuvers. Instructors should introduce these maneuvers with care, so that students know what to expect, and what their reactions should be. When introducing stalls, for example, instructors should first review the aerodynamic principles and explain how stalls affect flight characteristics. Then, carefully describe the sensations to be expected, as well as the recovery procedures.

Student anxieties can be minimized throughout training by emphasizing the benefits and pleasurable experiences which can be derived from flying, rather than by continuously citing the unhappy consequences of faulty performances. Safe flying practices should be presented as conducive to satisfying, efficient, uninterrupted operations, rather than as necessary only to prevent catastrophe.

Normal Reactions to Stress

When a threat is recognized or imagined, the brain alerts the body. The adrenal gland activates hormones which prepare the body to meet the threat, or to retreat from it. This often is called the fight or flight syndrome. The heart rate quickens, certain blood vessels constrict to divert blood to the organs which will need it, and numerous other physiological changes take place. Normal individuals begin to respond rapidly and exactly, within the limits of their experience and training. Many responses are automatic, which points out the need for proper training in emergency operations prior to an actual emergency. The affected individual thinks rationally, ants rapidly, and is extremely sensitive to all aspects of the surroundings.

Abormal Reactions to Stress

Reactions to stress may produce abnormal responses in some people. With them, response to anxiety or stress may be completely absent or at least inadequate. Their responses may be random or illogical, or they may do more than is called for by the situation. During flight instruction, instructors normally are the only ones who can observe students when they are under pressure. Instructors, therefore, are in a position to differentiate between safe and unsafe piloting actions. Instructors also may be able to detect potential psychological problems. The following student reactions are indicative of abnormal reactions to stress.

None of them provides an absolute indication, but the presence of any of them under conditions of stress is reason for careful instructor evaluation:

- Inappropriate reactions, such as extreme over- cooperation, painstaking self-control, inappropriate laughter or singing, and very rapid changes in emotions.
- Marked changes in mood on different topics, such as excellent morale followed by deep depression.
- Severe anger directed towards the flight instructor, service personnel, and others.

In difficult situations, flight instructors must carefully examine student responses and their own responses to the students. These responses may be the normal products of a complex learning situation, but they also can be indicative of psychological abnormalities which will inhibit learning, or potentially be very hazardous to future piloting operations. Flight Instructor Actions Reguarding Seriously Abnormal Students. A flight instructor who believes a student may be suffering from a serious psychological abnormality has a responsibility to refrain from certifying that student. In addition, a flight instructor has the personal responsibility of assuring that such a person does not continue flight training or become certificated as a pilot. To accomplish this, the following steps are available;

If an instructor believes that a student may have a disqualifying psychological defect, arrangements should be made for another instructor, who is not acquainted with the student, to conduct an evaluation flight. After the flight, the two instructors should confer to determine whether they agree that further investigation or action is justified. An informal discussion should be initiated with the local Flight Standards District Office (FSDO), suggesting that the student may be able to meet the skill standards, but may be unsafe psychologically.

This action should be taken as soon as a question arises regarding the student's fitness. It should not be delayed until the student feels competent to solo.A discussion should be held with a local aviation medical examiner (AME), preferably the one who issued the student's medical certificate, to obtain advice and to decide on the possibility of further examination of the student.

The flight instructor's primary legal responsibility concerns the decision whether to certify the student to be competent for solo flight operations, or to make a recommendation for the practical test leading to certification as a pilot. If, after consultation with an unbiased instructor, the FSDO, and the AME, the instructor believes that the student suffers a serious psychological deficiency, such authorizations and recommendations must be withheld.

SPAN OF CONTROL

In a business of more than one person, unless the business has equal partners, then there are managers and subordinates. Subordinates are workers controlled by the manager. A hierarchy describes the structure of the management of the business, from the top of the company – the managing director, through to the shop floor worker, who reports to their foreman, in a manufacturing business. The hierarchy of a business is usually best understood by drawing an organisation chart showing which levels of management and employees report to whom.

An example of a hierarchy is shown in the diagram

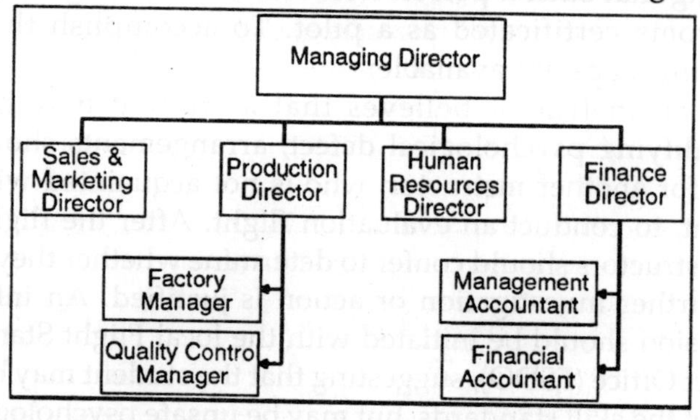

A span of control is the number of people who report to one manager in a hierarchy. The more people under the control of one manager - the wider the span of control. Less means a narrower span of control.

An example of a narrow span of control is shown in the diagram: Span of Management – Concept, Early Ideas on Span of Management

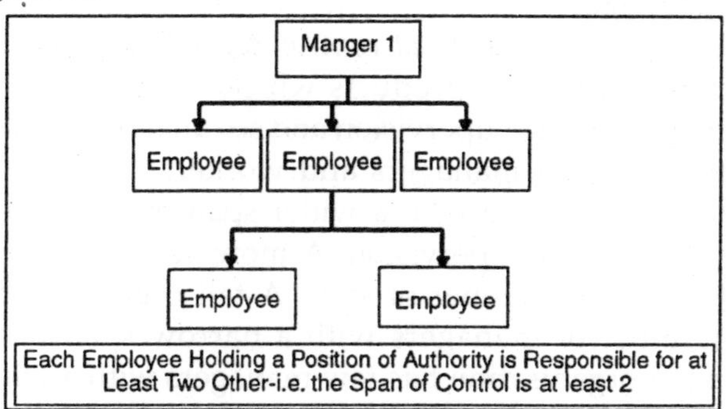

Fig. Example of a Narrow Span of Control

The advantages of a narrow span of control are:

- A narrow span of control allows a manager to communicate quickly with the employees under them and control them more easily
- Feedback of ideas from the workers will be more effective
- It requires a higher level of management skill to control a greater number of employees, so there is less management skill required

An example of a wide span of control is shown in the diagram:

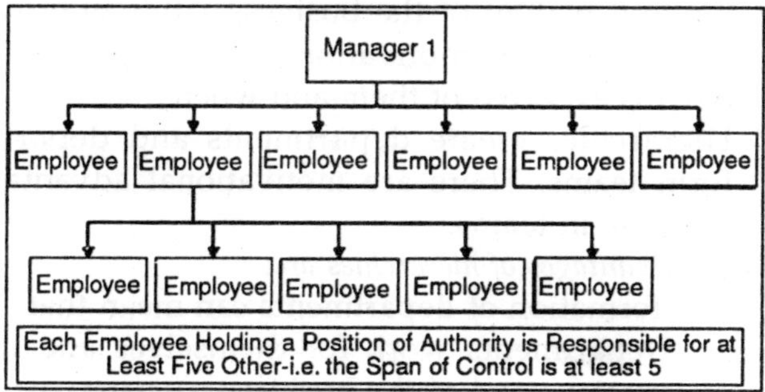

The advantages of wide span of control are:

- There are less layers of management to pass a message through, so the message reaches more employees faster
- It costs less money to run a wider span of control because a business does not need to employ as many managers

The width of the span of control depends on: The type of product being made – products which are easy to make or deliver will need less supervision and so can have a wider span of control Skills of managers and workers – a more skilful workforce can operate with a wider span of control because they will need less supervision. A more skilful manager can control a greater number of staff. A tall organisation has a larger number of managers with a narrow span of control whilst a flat organisation has few managers with a wide span of control. A tall organisation can suffer from having too many managers (a huge expense) and decisions can take a long time to reach the bottom of the hierarchy BUT, a tall organisation can provide good opportunities for promotion and the manager does not have to spend so much time managing the staff Chain of command is the line on which orders and decisions are passed down from top to bottom of the hierarchy. In a hierarchy the chain of command means that a production manager may be higher up the hierarchy, but will not be able to tell a marketing person what to do.

The advantages of hierarchies are:

- Helps create a clear communication line between the top and bottom of the business – this improves co-ordination and motivation since employees know what is expected of them and when.
- Hierarchies create departments and departments form teams. There are motivational advantages of working in teams.

The disadvantages of hierarchies are:

- The formation of departments can mean that:
  - Departments work for themselves and not the greater good of the business.

- Departments do not see the whole picture in making decisions.

Hierarchies can be inflexible and difficult to adjust, especially when businesses need to adapt to changing markets – remember employees do not tend to react well to change.

COORDINATION

New, more "organic" forms or organizations (self-organizing organizations, self-managed teams, network organizations, etc.) allow organizations to be more responsive and adaptable in today's rapidly changing world. These forms also cultivate empowerment among employees, much more than the hierarchical, rigidly structured organizations of the past.

Many people assert that as the nature of organizations has changed, so must the nature of management control. Some people go so far as to claim that management shouldn't exercise any form of control whatsoever. They claim that management should exist to support employee's efforts to be fully productive members of organizations and communities — therefore, any form of control is completely counter productive to management and employees.

Some people even react strongly against the phrase "management control". The word itself can have a negative connotation, e.g., it can sound dominating, coercive and heavy-handed. It seems that writers of management literature now prefer use of the term "coordinating" rather than "controlling".

"COORDINATION" MUST EXIST OR THERE'S NO ORGANIZATION — ONLY AN "EXPERIENCE"

Regardless of the negative connotation of the word "control", it must exist or there is no organization at all. In its most basic form, an organization is two or more people working together to reach a goal. Whether an organization is highly bureaucratic or changing and self-organizing, the organization must exist for some reason, some purpose, some mission (implicit or explicit) — or it isn't an organization at all. The organization must have some goal. Identifying this goal requires some form of planning, informal or formal. Reaching the goal means identifying some strategies, formal or informal. These strategies are agreed upon by members of the organization through some form of communication, formal or informal. Then members set about to performance in accordance with what they agreed to do. They may change their minds, fine. But they need to recognize and acknowledge that they're changing their minds.

This form of ongoing communication to reach a goal, tracking activities towards the goal and then subsequent decisions about what to do is the essence of management coordination. It needs to exist in some manner — formal or informal.

The following are rather typical methods of coordination in organizations. They are used as means to communicate direction and guide behaviours in that direction. The function of the following methods is not to "control", but rather to guide. If, from ongoing communications among management and employees, the direction changes, then fine. The following methods are changed accordingly.

Note that many of the following methods are so common that we often don't think of them as having anything to do with coordination at all. No matter what one calls the following methods - coordination or control - they're important to the success of any organization.

VARIOUS ADMINISTRATIVE CONTROLS

Organizations often use standardized documents to ensure complete and consistent information is gathered. Documents include titles and dates to detect different versions of the document.

Computers have revolutionized administrative controls through use of integrated management information systems, project management software, human resource information systems, office automation software, etc. Organizations typically require a wide range of reports, e.g., financial reports, status reports, project reports, etc. to monitor what's being done, by when and how.

DELEGATION

Delegation is an approach to get things done, in conjunction with other employees. Delegation is often viewed as a major means of influence and therefore is categorized as an activity in leading (rather than controlling/coordinating). Delegation generally includes assigning responsibility to an employee to complete a task, granting the employee sufficient authority to gain the resources to do the task and letting the employee decide how that task will be carried out. Typically, the person assigning the task shares accountability with the employee for ensuring the task is completed.

EVALUATIONS

Evaluation is carefully collecting and analyzing information in order to make decisions. There are many types of evaluations in organizations, for example, evaluation of marketing efforts, evaluation of employee performance, programme evaluations, etc. Evaluations can focus on many aspects of an organization and its processes, for example, its goals, processes, outcomes, etc.

FINANCIAL STATEMENTS (PARTICULARLY BUDGET MANAGEMENT)

Once the organization has establish goals and associated strategies (or ways to reach the goals), funds are set aside for the resources and labour to the accomplish goals and tasks. As the money is spent, statements are changed to reflect what was spent, how it was spent and what it obtained. Review of financial statements is one of the more common methods to monitor the progress of programmes and plans. The most common financial statements include the balance sheet, income statement and cash flow statement. Financial audits are regularly conducted to ensure that financial management practices follow generally accepted standards, as well.

PERFORMANCE MANAGEMENT

Performance management focuses on the performance of the total organization, including its processes, critical subsystems (departments, programmes, projects, etc.) and employees. Most of us have some basic impression of employee performance management, including the role of performance reviews.

Performance reviews provide an opportunity for supervisors and their employees to regularly communicate about goals, how well those goals should be met, how well the goals are being met and what must be done to continue to meet (or change) those goals. The employee is rewarded in some form for meeting performance standards, or embarks on a development plan with the supervisor in order to improve performance.

POLICIES AND PROCEDURES (TO GUIDE BEHAVIOURS IN THE WORKPLACE)

Policies help ensure that behaviours in the workplace conform to federal and state laws, and also to expectations of the organization. Often, policies are applied to specified situations in the form of procedures.

Personnel policies and procedures help ensure that employee laws are followed (e.g., laws such as the Americans with Disabilities Act, Occupational Health and Safety Act, etc.) and minimize the likelihood of costly litigation. A procedure is a step-by-step list of activities required to conduct a certain task. Procedures ensure that routine tasks are carried out in an effective and efficient fashion.

QUALITY CONTROL AND OPERATIONS MANAGEMENT

The concept of quality control has received a great deal of attention over the past twenty years. Many people recognize phrases such as "do it right the first time, "zero defects", "Total Quality Management", etc.

Very broadly, quality includes specifying a performance standard (often by benchmarking, or comparing to a well-accepted standard), monitoring and measuring results, comparing the results to the standard and then making adjusts as necessary. Recently, the concept of quality management has expanded to include organization-wide programmes, such as Total Quality Management, ISO9000, Balanced Scorecard, etc. Operations management includes the overall activities involved in developing, producing and distributing products and services.

RISK, SAFETY AND LIABILITIES

For a variety of reasons (including the increasing number of lawsuits), organizations are focusing a great deal of attention to activities that minimize risk, avoid liabilities and ensure safety of employees.

Several decades ago, it was rare to hear of an organization undertaking contingency planning, disaster recovery planning or critical incident analysis. Now those activities are becoming commonplace.

DIMENSIONS OR TYPES OF CONTROL

There are three primary types of organizational control: strategic control, management control, and operational control.

1. Strategic control, the process of evaluating strategy, is practiced both after the strategy is formulated and after it is implemented.
2. Management control focuses on the accomplishment of the objectives of the various substrategies comprising the master strategy and the accomplishment of the objectives of the intermediate plans (for example, "are quality control objectives being met?").
3. Operational control is concerned individual and group performance as compared with the individual and group role prescriptions required by organizational plans (for example, "are individual sales quotes being met?").

Each of these types of control is not a separate and distinct entity and, in fact, may be indistinguishable from others. Moreover, similar measurement techniques may be used for each type of control. Management can implement controls before an activity commences, while the activity is going on, or after the activity has been completed. The three respective types of control based on timing are feedforward, concurrent.

Feedforward control focuses on the regulation of inputs (human, material, and financial resources that flow into the organization) to ensure that they meet the standards necessary for the transformation process.

Feedforward controls are desirable because they allow management to prevent problems rather than having to cure them later. Unfortunately, these control require timely and accurate information that is often difficult to develop. Feedforward control also is sometimes called preliminary control, precontrol, preventive control, or steering control. However, some authors use term "steering control" as separate types of control.

This types of controls are designed to detect deviation some standard or goal to allow correction to be made before a particular sequence of actions is completed. Concurrent control takes place while an activity is in progress. It involves the regulation of ongoing activities that are part of transformation process to ensure that they conform to organizational standards. Concurrent control is designed to ensure that employee work activities produce the correct results.

Since concurrent control involves regulating ongoing tasks, it requires a through understanding of the specific tasks involved and their relationship to the desired and product. Concurrent control sometimes is called screening or yes-no control, because it often involves checkpoints at which determinations are made about whether to continue progress, take corrective action, or stop work altogether on products or services.

This type of control focuses on the outputs of the organization after transformation is complete. Sometimes called postaction or output control, fulfils a number of important functions. For one thing, it often is used when feedforward and concurrent controls are not feasible or are to costly. Sometimes, feedback is the only viable type of control available. Moreover, feedback has two advantages over feedforward and concurrent control. *First,* feedback provides managers with meaningful information on how effective its planning effort was. If feedback indicates little variance between standard and actual performance, this is evidence that planning was generally on target.

If the deviation is great, a manager can use this information when formulating new plans to make them more effective. *Second,* feedback control can enhance employees motivation. The major drawback of this type of control is that, the time the manager has the information and if there is significant problem the damage is already done. But for many activities, feedback control fulfils number important functions. Feedforward, concurrent, and feedback control methods are not mutually exclusive. Rather, they usually are combined into an multiple control systems. Managers design control systems to define standards of performance and acquire information feedback at strategic control points.

Strategic control points are those activities that are especially important for achieving strategic objectives. When organizations do not have multiple control systems that focus on strategic control points, they often can experience difficulties that cause managers to reevaluate their control processes.

Regardless of whether the organization focuses control on inputs, production, or outputs, another choice must be made between different approaches tor control. There are three control approaches regarding the mechanisms managers will use to implement controls: *market control, bureaucratic control, and clan control*. Regardless of whether the organization focuses control on inputs, production, or outputs, another choice must be made between different approaches tor control. There are three control approaches regarding the mechanisms managers will use to implement controls: *market control, bureaucratic control, and clan control.*

Market control involves the use of price competition to evaluate output. Managers compare profits and prices to determine the efficiency of their organization. In order to use market control, there must be a reasonable level of competition in the goods or service area and it must be possible to specify requirements clearly. Market control is non appropriate in controlling functional departments, unless the price for services is set through competition and its representative of the true value of provided services.

Bureaucratic control is the use of rules, policies, hierarchy of authority, written documentation, reward systems, and other formal mechanisms to influence employee behaviour and assess performance. Bureaucratic control can be used when behaviour can be controlled with market or price mechanisms. Clan control represents cultural values almost the opposite of bureaucratic control. Clan control relies on values, beliefs, corporate culture, shared norms, and informal relationships to regulate employee behaviours and facilitate the reaching of organizational goals.

Organization that use clan control require trust among their employees. Given minimal direction and standards, employees are assumed to perform well - indeed, they participate in setting standards and designing the control systems.

14

Eminent Management Thinkers

The schools of management thought are theoretical frameworks for the study of management. Each of the schools of management thought are based on somewhat different assumptions about human beings and the organizations for which they work.

Since the formal study of management began late in the 19th century, the study of management has progressed through several stages as scholars and practitioners working in different eras focused on what they believed to be important aspects of good management practice.

Over time, management thinkers have sought ways to organize and classify the voluminous information about management that has been collected and disseminated. These attempts at classification have resulted in the identification of management schools. Disagreement exists as to the exact number of management schools. Different writers have identified as few as three and as many as twelve.

Those discussed include:

- The classical school,
- The behavioural school,
- The quantitative or management science school,
- The systems school,
- And the contingency school.

The formal study of management is largely a twentieth-century phenomenon, and to some degree the relatively large number of management schools of thought reflects a lack of consensus among management scholars about basic questions of theory and practice. The following sections discuss each of the management: schools in more detail. In addition, three contemporary management perspectives are discussed.

Management Schools	Beginning Dates	Emphasis
Classical School organizations more		Managing workers and efficiently.
Scientific Management	1880s	
Administrative Management	1940s	
Bureaucratic Management	1920s	
Behavioral school		Understanding human behavior in the organization.
Human Relations	1930s	
Behavioral Science	1950s	
Quantitative school		Increasing quality of managerial decision-making through the application of mathematical and statistical methods
Management Science	1940s	
Operations Management	1940s	
Management Information Systems	1950s—1970s	
Systems School	1950s	Understanding the organization as a system that transforms inputs into outputs while in constant interaction with its' environment.
Contingency School	1960s	Applying management principles and processes as dictated by the unique characteristics of each situation.

THE CLASSICAL SCHOOL

The classical school is the oldest formal school of management thought. Its roots pre-date the twentieth century. The classical school of thought generally concerns ways to manage work and organizations more efficiently.

Three areas of study that can be grouped under the classical school are scientific management, administrative management, and bureaucratic management.

SCIENTIFIC MANAGEMENT

In the late 19th century, management decisions were often arbitrary and workers often worked at an intentionally slow pace. There was little in the way of systematic management and workers and management were often in conflict. Scientific management was introduced in an attempt to create a mental revolution in the workplace. It can be defined as the systematic study of work methods in order to improve efficiency. Frederick W. Taylor was its main proponent. Other major contributors were Frank Gilbreth, Lillian Gilbreth, and Henry Gantt.

Scientific management has several major principles. First, it calls for the application of the scientific method to work in order to determine the best method for accomplishing each task. Second, scientific management suggests that workers should be scientifically selected based on their qualifications and trained to perform their jobs in the optimal manner. Third, scientific management advocates genuine cooperation between workers and management based on mutual self-interest. Finally, scientific management suggests that management should take complete responsibility for planning the work and that workers' primary responsibility should be implementing management's plans.

Other important characteristics of scientific management include the scientific development of difficult but fair performance standards and the implementation of a pay-for-performance incentive plan based on work standards. Scientific management had a tremendous influence on management practice in the early twentieth century. Although it does not represent a complete theory of management, it has contributed to the study of management and organizations in many areas, including human resource management and industrial engineering. Many of the tenets of scientific management are still valid today.

ADMINISTRATIVE MANAGEMENT

Administrative management focuses on the management process and principles of management. In contrast to scientific management, which deals largely with jobs and work at the individual level of analysis, administrative management provides a more general theory of management. Henri Fayol is the major contributor to this school of management thought. Fayol was a management practitioner who brought his experience to bear on the subject of management functions and principles.

He argued that management was a universal process consisting of functions, which he termed planning, organizing, commanding, coordinating, and controlling. Fayol believed that all managers performed these functions and that the functions distinguished management as a separate discipline of study apart from accounting, finance, and production. Fayol also presented fourteen principles of management, which included maxims related to the division of work, authority and responsibility, unity of command and direction, centralization, subordinate initiative, and team spirit.

Although administrative management has been criticized as being rigid and inflexible and the validity of the functional approach to management has been questioned, this school of thought still influences management theory and practice. The functional approach to management is still the dominant way of organizing management knowledge, and many of Fayol's principles of management, when applied with the flexibility that he advocated, are still considered relevant.

BUREAUCRATIC MANAGEMENT

Bureaucratic management focuses on the ideal form of organization. Max Weber was the major contributor to bureaucratic management. Based on observation, Weber concluded that many early organizations were inefficiently managed, with decisions based on personal relationships and loyalty. He proposed that a form of organization, called a bureaucracy, characterized by division of labour, hierarchy, formalized rules, impersonality, and the selection and promotion of employees based on ability, would lead to more efficient management.

Weber also contended that managers' authority in an organization should be based not on tradition or charisma but on the position held by managers in the organizational hierarchy. Bureaucracy has come to stand for inflexibility and waste, but Weber did not advocate or favour the excesses found in many bureaucratic organizations today. Weber's ideas formed the basis for modern organization theory and are still descriptive of some organizations.

THE BEHAVIOURAL SCHOOL

The behavioural school of management thought developed, in part, because of perceived weaknesses in the assumptions of the classical school. The classical school emphasized efficiency, process, and principles.

Some felt that this emphasis disregarded important aspects of organizational life, particularly as it related to human behaviour. Thus, the behavioural school focused on trying to understand the factors that affect human behaviour at work.

HUMAN RELATIONS

The Hawthorne Experiments began in 1924 and continued through the early 1930s. A variety of researchers participated in the studies, including Clair Turner, Fritz J. Roethlisberger, and Elton Mayo, whose respective books on the studies are perhaps the best known.

One of the major ceases of the Hawthorne studies was that workers' attitudes are associated with productivity. Another was that the workplace is a social system and informal group influence could exert a powerful effect on individual behaviour. A third was that the style of supervision is an important factor in increasing workers' job satisfaction. The studies also found that organizations should take steps to assist employees in adjusting to organizational life by fostering collaborative systems between labour and management. Such ceases sparked increasing interest in the human element at work; today, the Hawthorne studies are generally credited as the impetus for the human relations school.

The human relations school, the manager should possess skills for diagnosing the causes of human behaviour at work, interpersonal communication, and motivating and leading workers. The focus became satisfying worker needs. If worker needs were satisfied, wisdom held, the workers would in turn be more productive. Thus, the human relations school focuses on issues of communication, leadership, motivation, and group behaviour.

The individuals who contributed to the school are too numerous to mention, but some of the best-known contributors include Mary Parker Follett, Chester Barnard, Abraham Maslow, Kurt Lewin, Renais Likert, and Keith Davis. The human relations school of thought still influences management theory and practice, as contemporary management focuses much attention on human resource management, organizational behaviour, and applied psychology in the workplace.

BEHAVIOURAL SCIENCE

Behavioural science and the study of organizational behaviour emerged in the 1950s and 1960s. The behavioural science school was a natural progression of the human relations movement. It focused on applying conceptual and analytical tools to the problem of understanding and predicting behaviour in the workplace.

However, the study of behavioural science and organizational behaviour was also a result of criticism of the human relations approach as simplistic and manipulative in its assumptions about the relationship between worker attitudes and productivity. The study of behavioural science in business schools was given increased credence by the 1959 Gordon and Howell report on higher education, which emphasized the importance to management practitioners of understanding human behaviour.

The behavioural science school has contributed to the study of management through its focus on personality, attitudes, values, motivation, group behaviour, leadership, communication, and conflict, among other issues. Some of the major contributors to this school include Douglas McGregor, Chris Argyris, Frederick Herzberg, Renais Likert, and Ralph Stogdill, although there are many others.

THE QUANTITATIVE SCHOOL

The quantitative school focuses on improving decision making via the application of quantitative techniques. Its roots can be traced back to scientific management.

MANAGEMENT SCIENCE AND MIS

Management science (also called operations research) uses mathematical and statistical approaches to solve management problems. It developed during World War II as strategists tried to apply scientific knowledge and methods to the complex problems of war.

Industry began to apply management science after the war. George Dantzig developed linear programming, an algebraic method to determine the optimal allocation of scarce resources. Other tools used in industry include inventory control theory, goal programming, queuing models, and simulation.

The advent of the computer made many management science tools and concepts more practical for industry. Increasingly, management science and management information systems (MIS) are intertwined. MIS focuses on providing needed information to managers in a useful format and at the proper time.

Decision support systems (DSS) attempt to integrate decision models, data, and the decision maker into a system that supports better management decisions.

PRODUCTION AND OPERATIONS MANAGEMENT

This school focuses on the operation and control of the production process that transforms resources into finished goods and services. It has its roots in scientific management but became an identifiable area of management study after World War II.

It uses many of the tools of management science. Operations management emphasizes productivity and quality of both manufacturing and service organizations. W. Edwards Deming exerted a tremendous influence in shaping modern ideas about improving productivity and quality.

Major areas of study within operations management include capacity planning, facilities location, facilities layout, materials requirement planning, scheduling, purchasing and inventory control, quality control, computer integrated manufacturing, just-in-time inventory systems, and flexible manufacturing systems.

SYSTEMS SCHOOL

The systems school focuses on understanding the organization as an open system that transforms inputs into outputs. This school is based on the work of a biologist, Ludwig von Bertalanffy, who believed that a general systems model could be used to unite science. Early contributors to this school included Kenneth Boulding, Richard Johnson, Fremont Kast, and James Rosenzweig.

The systems school began to have a strong impact on management thought in the 1960s as a way of thinking about managing techniques that would allow managers to relate different specialties and parts of the company to one another, as well as to external environmental factors.

The systems school focuses on the organization as a whole, its interaction with the environment, and its need to achieve equilibrium. General systems theory received a great deal of attention in the 1960s, but its influence on management thought has diminished somewhat. It has been criticized as too abstract and too complex. However, many of the ideas inherent in the systems school formed the basis for the contingency school of management.

CONTINGENCY SCHOOL

The contingency school focuses on applying management principles and processes as dictated by the unique characteristics of each situation. It emphasizes that there is no one best way to manage and that it depends on various situational factors, such as the external environment, technology, organizational characteristics, characteristics of the manager, and characteristics of the subordinates.

Contingency theorists often implicitly or explicitly criticize the classical school for its emphasis on the universality of management principles; however, most classical writers recognized the need to consider aspects of the situation when applying management principles. The contingency school originated in the 1960s.

It has been applied primarily to management issues such as organizational design, job design, motivation, and leadership style. For example, optimal organizational structure has been theorized to depend upon organizational size, technology, and environmental uncertainty; optimal leadership style, meanwhile, has been theorized to depend upon a variety of factors, including task structure, position power, characteristics of the work group, characteristics of individual subordinates, quality requirements, and problem structure, to name a few.

A few of the major contributors to this school of management thought include Joan Woodward, Paul Lawrence, Jay Lorsch, and Fred Fiedler, among many others.

CONTEMPORARY "SCHOOLS" OF MANAGEMENT THOUGHT

Management research and practice continues to evolve and new approaches to the study of management continue to be advanced. This section briefly reviews two contemporary approaches: total quality management (TQM) and the learning organization. While neither of these management approaches offer a complete theory of management, they do offer additional insights into the management field.

TOTAL QUALITY MANAGEMENT

Total quality management (TQM) is a philosophy or approach to management that focuses on managing the entire organization to deliver quality goods and services to customers. This approach to management was implemented in Japan after World War II and was a major factor in their economic renaissance.

TQM has at least four major elements. Employee involvement is essential in preventing quality problems before they occur. A customer focus means that the organization must attempt to determine customer needs and wants and deliver products and services that address them. Benchmarking means that the organization is always seeking out other organizations that perform a function or process more effectively and using them as a standard, or benchmark, to judge their own performance.

The organization will also attempt to adapt or improve the processes used by other companies. Finally, a philosophy of continuous improvement means that the organization is committed to incremental changes and improvements over time in all areas of the organization. TQM has been implemented by many companies worldwide and appears to have fostered performance improvements in many organizations. Perhaps the best-known proponent of this school of management was W. Edwards Deming.

LEARNING ORGANIZATION

The contemporary organization faces unprecedented environmental and technological change. Thus, one of the biggest challenges for organizations is to continuously change in a way that meets the demands of this turbulent competitive environment.

The learning organization can be defined as one in which all employees are involved in identifying and solving problems, which allows the organization to continually increase its ability to grow, learn, and achieve its purpose. The organizing principle of the learning organization is not efficiency, but problem solving. Three key aspects of the learning organization are a team-based structure, empowered employees, and open information. Peter Senge is one of the best-known experts on learning organizations.

Harrington Emerson Contribution of Classical Approach

Emerson made scientific management more acceptable to people. He wrote a book in 1912 on 'Efficiency', in which he has given 12 principles of increasing efficiency.

These are:

- Ideals
- Common sense
- Competent counsel
- Discipline
- Fair deal
- Reliable, immediate, adequate, and permanent records
- Dispatching
- Standards and schedules
- Standardised conditions
- Standardised operations
- Standard practice instructions
- Reward for efficiency.

Frank Gilbreath Contribution of Classical Approach

Frank Gilbreath and his wife Lilian Gilbreath were contemporary of Taylor, but they worked independently on time and motion study.Besides time and motion study, they ave also developed a comprehensive body of planning an control techniques for construction industry.

Taylor's Principles of Classical Approach

Although Taylor's principles were intended for broad application, his emphasis was not on general management; but on management at the shop level. He was more concerned about the efficiency of workers and mangers at actual work and left the principles of management which could be followed in other functional areas.

These principles, more specifically time, motion, and fatigue study, became the basis for some time, but the much talked mental revolution could not take place. The adoption of scientific management was resisted by manages on that plea that it involved extra costs on their part in various experiments, and by workers also on the plea that by this method they could put in more work, however, the profit did not go to them. Both the parties took a short-term view

Fayol's Principles of Management

Fayol evolved fourteen principles of management which may be briefly stated as follows:

- *Division of work*: The object of division of work is to derive the benefits from the principle of specialisation which can be applied not only in technical work, put in all other work as well. Unlike Taylor, Fayol pointed out that division of work has its obvious limits.
- *Authority and responsibility*: Authority and responsibility are correlated terms; responsibility is the essential counterpart of authority and they go hand. An ideal manger is expected to have official authority arising from official positions as well as his inherent personal authority. Such person authority is "compounded of intelligence experience, moral worth, ability to lead, past services, etc."
- *Discipline*: "Discipline is in essence obedience, application, energy, behaviour, and outward marks of respect" shown buy employees. "Discipline is what the leaders make it" through the observance of agreements, because agreements spell out to formalities of discipline.

  Three requisites of discipline are:

  - Good supervisors at all levels,

- Clear and fair agreements,
- Judicious application of penalties of sanctions.

- *Unity of direction*: This principle requires than employee should receive orders form one superior only. Dual command wreaks havoc in all concerns, "since authority is undermined, discipline in jeopardy, order disturbed and stability threatened."
- *Unity of direction*: Fayol discussed this principle of unity of direction in a different way from that of unity of command. While unity of direction is concerned with the functioning of the body corporate, unity of command is only concerned with the functioning of personnel at all levels. For the accomplishment of a group of activities having the same objective, there should be one head and one plan. "A body with two heads is in the social as in the animal sphere a monster, and has difficulty in surviving.
- *Subordination of individual interest to general interest*: Common interest must prevail over individual interest, but some factors like ambition, laziness, weakness and others tend to reduce the importance of general interest.
- *Remuneration of personnel*: As the prices of services rendered remunerations should be fair and satisfactory to both the parties.
- *Centralization*: "Everything which goes to increase the importance of the subordinate's role is decentralization, everything which goes to reduce it is centralization." The question of centralization or decentralization holds the key to the utilization of all faculties of the personnel.
- *Scalar chain*: It is the chain of superiors or the line of authority form the highest executive to the lowest one for the purpose of communication. The need for swift action should be reconciled with due regard to the line of authority by using "gang plank" or direct contact.

- *Order*: This is a principle of organization relating to things and persons material order requires "a place for everything and everything in its place" and social demands the engagement of "the right man in the right place."
- *Equity*: Equity is greater than justice, since it" results from the combination of kindliness and justice." The application of equity requires much good sense, experience and good nature with a view to securing devotion and loyalty form employees.
- *Stability of tenure of personnel*: Stability of tenure is essential to get an employee accustomed to doing a new work and to enable him in performing it well. Instability of tenure is an evidence of bad running of affairs.
- *Initiative*: The freedom to purpose a plan and to execute it is what is known as initiative that increases zeal and energy on the part of human beings. Since initiative is one of "the keenest satisfactions for an intelligent man to experience." Fayol advised managers to secure as much initiative from employees as possible.
- *Esprit de corps*: This is an extension of the principle of unity of command whereby team work is ensured. To maintain proper esprit de corps in the organization, personality politics and abuse of written and communications are to be guarded against.

15

Case Study

Japan is experiencing a shrinking economy, failing stocks, rising unemployment, restructuring and job cuts. Without reforms, the economy is only predicted to grow 0.8% a year from 2006 to 2010 according to country advisors. Layoffs, such as 800 workers from Mitsubishi, have caused a change of attitude as many young people are abandoning hopes of landing lifetime jobs.

Bankruptcies are soaring and leaving behind a record level of debt in the country. A study team at Japan's Economy, Trade and Industry Ministry even called for improving disclosure rules for initial public offerings of venture firms to emphasize future business plans, rather than past performance.

In their groundbreaking and controversial article, "Fixing what Really Ails Japan," Porter and Takeuchi both of Harvard University, presented the cogent argument contending it was not government oversight of industry leading to the global success of Japanese companies, but rather operational effectiveness and strategy.

They further blame the current long period of Japanese economic stagnation on the lack of discernable business strategies practiced by Japanese firms.

Based on these propositions of Porter and Takeuchi:

- What types of discernable strategies are Japanese companies currently using?
- Do these strategies fit the Porter typology?
- What is the relative frequency of use of Japanese business strategies?

TRADITIONAL JAPANESE MANAGEMENT PRACTICES

Traditional Japanese management is frequently cited as the cause of these problems. Historically, since WW II, all employees of a company share risks and gains of the operation. Even during economic crisis, layoffs are a last resort remedy. Lifetime employment, particularly for men in large companies, is the norm.

Upper and lower management have similar responsibilities and product research is continuous as is the encouragement of new ideas and personal productivity. Japan's industrial system is characterized by interdependent relationships among government, private, non-profit and community organizations. The keiretsu, or "lineage" system consists of a parent firm and trading company with the main bank as the institutional triumvirate guiding the activities of the entire keiretsu system.

Each of these primary resource and power centres maintains close relationships with counterparts in the public sectors. The bank is guided by the Ministry of Finance (MOF); the trading company aligned with the Ministry of Economy, Trade and Industry (METI); and the parent firm guided by other government and non-private institutions (Ministry of Education or major universities).

Companies such as National Telecom (NTT), for example, are closely tied with the Ministry of Posts and Telecommunications (MOPT). Other examples of these institutional relationships include the company labour unions and the Keidanren and Nikkeren (advisory councils) with both public and private sector participants. These institutionalized practices are in place to help maintain informal ties between government and business.

The often cited reason for Japan's inability to react quickly to changes in market forces is the entrenched nature of group decision-making and the formalized systems that seem to slow down even the most urgent of "causes". Japanese organizations practice nemawashi which is the process of preparing others through persuasion and sharing of information for a decision-making process. Nemawashi is a time consuming process which results in a fait accompli. Ringi (group decision-making through memos, meetings and formalized information and authorization gathering which results in a consensus decision) is another example of an institutionalized practice that results in long decision-making times and resistance to short-term change.

Habatsu (informal and formal cliques of people which form in order to maintain information flows, control and power in stratified cross-sections of the organization) creates formal social structures resistant to ideas that threaten their autonomy. Kaizen or "continuous improvement" is yet another example of a way of life in Japanese companies that purposely inhibits "rash" action, or changes in the way things get done.

LIMITATIONS OF JAPANESE MANAGEMENT AND STRATEGIC CHALLENGE

Japanese group decision making structures are driven by a sense of total commitment of group members to their leader and vice-versa, this level of commitment has the potential to hinder the system's ability to identify and to react appropriately when the system is following a failing course-of-action.

Japanese are reluctant to abandon such a system. Prospect theory suggests those "sunk cost effects" naturally occur once an investment in money, effort or time has been made, and individuals have a "personal stake" in the outcome, and choose not to alter their actions. When individuals become committed to a failing course-of-action, negative consequences will actually cause decision makers to increase their commitment of resources and undergo the risk of further negative consequences.

This can evolve into a structurally supported behaviour if an individual's group, organization or institution supports their behaviour. Today, the 15-year long "recession" in Japan has finally begun to take its toll on Japanese managers' faith in the Japanese "system." Recently, firms have begun to search for other ways to break out of their decades long commitment to the traditional Japanese management system and have discovered Michael Porter's generic strategies as a possible impetus for corporate change and renewal. Porter and Takeuchi, the Japanese economy will emerge from more than a decade of recession only if Japanese firms become more competitive in the global marketplace.

Recently, the adoption of generic strategies has received much attention in public discussions in Japan. Japan's experience after the bubble economy with the chronic Asian financial crisis highlighted concerns as to whether Japan's once celebrated prosperity can be regained. The slow change and growth rate of new venture creation in Japan can be attributed to the conventional Japanese business culture, lifetime employment, the seniority system, labour unions inside companies, tight regulatory policies of the government, and the group-oriented risk adverse proclivity of the population. These cultural characteristics were developed from the past Asian agriculture system, a mono-national culture of an island country, and Confucianism.

THE PORTER PRIZE FOR JAPAN

Porter and Takeuchi argue it was precisely the governmental policies designed to macro manage industrial growth in Japan and globally which lead to the eventually downfall of the Japanese economy. Porter and Takeuchi point to examples of Honda, Sony, Nintendo and Sega as companies considered to be "mavericks" in Japan because they bucked government attempts at intervention.

They consider these organizations to be the true Japanese success stories. The authors further argue these organizations rise to global dominance is explained by their well developed and defined corporate strategies, in addition to their operational excellence.

Since the publication of the article, and the subsequent book "Can Japan Compete?", the Japanese Ministry of Economic Trade and Industry (METI, formerly MITI) established the "'Porter Prize" to recognize Japanese companies achieving and maintaining superior profitability in their industry by implementing unique strategies based on innovations in products, processes, and ways of managing. The Porter Prize has the sole purpose of improving competitiveness of Japanese corporations.

The evaluation criteria are originality, consistency, and high profitability of corporate strategies. The prize has been awarded to Japanese companies choosing to compete by delivering unique value based upon innovation and management. While the award is intended to motivate Japanese firms to develop clear, concise and manageable strategies, the degree to which the award is having an impact on strategic policy in Japanese companies as a whole has not been tested.

To date, the Porter Prize recipients represent small to medium size firms in well defined niche markets. These companies do not represent the corporate base typically cited as creating the Japanese miracle, namely large keiretsu-based manufacturing conglomerates.

The organizing body of the Porter Prize, the Graduate School of International Corporate Strategy at Hitotsubashi University, is the first "professional" graduate school established in Japan in April 2000 by the government with the single aim of improving competitiveness of Japanese firms in the global marketplace. This prestigious, well-funded programme offers a full-time MBA programme, taught entirely in English by many highly regarded American and European business professors.

By applying for the Porter Prize, it is hoped Japanese firms will become more attuned to the principles of competitive strategy. Through the application process, company managers are forced to consider important questions. For example, are we delivering a "unique value proposition" (a differentiated product or service targeted for a specific market niche)? Have we maintained strategic continuity over time? Have we innovated in ways that enable the strategy? Have we sustained superior profitability? It is intended that, similar to its predecessor the Deming Award for Quality, the application process alone can serve as an impetus to rethink the current strategy or to pave the way for implementing distinctive strategy in the future.

Benefits to the winners of the prize include recognition as a leader in strategy, increased public relations ability, and recruiting exposure. The winners are also featured in a case study series for Hitotsubashi Business Review and in other publications and strategic management books.

Among the first Porter Prize winners were Matsui Securities and Mabuchi Motor as corporations in the single business category and Canon's Lens Division and two divisions of HOYA Vision Care as corporations in the multiple business category.

Matsui Securities was highly regarded for the clear definition of "jobs-not-to-do" in its business strategy. Established in 1931, this long-life securities firm ceased operations of its sales branches and telemarketing centres to specialize in online trading services. The firm has realised high rates of return on invested capital by focusing on the individual investors who have significant experience in stock exchanges.

Porter's Generic Strategies

While various types of organizational strategies have been identified over the years, Porter's generic strategies remain the most commonly supported and identified in key strategic management textbooks and in the literature. Porter proposed three generic strategies yielding competitive advantage, namely cost leadership, product differentiation, and focus.

Porter suggests for long-term profitability, a firm must make a choice between one of the three generic strategies rather than end up being "stuck in the middle." Cost Leadership. Lower costs and cost advantages result from process innovations, learning curve benefits, economies of scale, reductions, product designs that reduce manufacturing time and costs, and reengineering activities.

A low-cost or cost leadership strategy is effectively implemented when the business designs, produces, and markets a comparable product more efficiently than its competitors. The firm may have access to raw materials or superior proprietary technology to lower costs.

Product Differentiation

Product differentiation fulfills a unique customer need by tailoring the product or the service, allowing organizations to charge a premium price to capture market share. The differentiation strategy is effectively implemented when the business provides unique or superior value to the customer through product quality, features, or after-sale support.

The quality may be real or perceived based on fashion, brand name, or image. Firms following a differentiation strategy can charge a higher price for their products based on the product characteristics, the delivery system, the quality of service, or the distribution channels. The differentiation strategy appeals to a sophisticated or knowledgeable consumer who wants a unique, quality product and is willing to pay the higher price.

Focus. Focus, the third generic strategy, is based on adopting a narrow competitive scope within the industry. Focus strategies grow market share through operating in a niche market or markets not attractive to, or overlooked by, larger competitors.

These niches arise from a number of factors including geography, buyer characteristics, product specifications, or requirements. A successful focus strategy depends upon an industry segment large enough to have good growth potential but not of key importance to major competitors. Market penetration or market development can be an important focus strategy.

Porter also asserts focus can be based on:

- Differentiation targeting a specific segment of the market with unique needs not met by others in the industry.
- Cost focused where the company has access to specialized production and operations equipment to save costs from smaller production lots or runs. Midsized and large firms use focus-based strategies

only in conjunction with differentiation or cost leadership strategies. Focus strategies are most effective when consumers have distinct preferences or competitors overlook the niche.

THE NEED FOR JAPANESE STRATEGY RESEARCH

To date, no research has been conducted with a sample of Japanese organizations to determine to what extent they are following Porter's generic strategies. This may due in large part to the difficulty of outsiders gaining access to Japanese organizations, as well as the barrier of translating research instruments into a language and format suitable for Japanese respondents.

Our research represents the first exploratory attempt to remedy this deficiency in our understanding of the current state of Japanese business strategies. In summary, the Japanese government has been attempting to convince their firms to enact Porter based business strategies in an attempt to improve Japanese international competitiveness. There would appear to be strong forces for change in Japanese strategic planning practices.

Considering the long-term Japanese recession, government backing of the Porter prize, and the role-model examples of successful Japanese businesses with better defined corporate strategies, one would presume that Japanese organizations should be primed for Porter-styled strategic planning.

Understanding the degree to which Japanese companies are embracing strategic management "Porter style" is essential to understanding the future of the Japanese economy. A significant shift in strategic policy is necessary for a successful transition from the traditional Japanese system to a more company-based, strategic thrust encouraged by Porter.

The important issue is determining the current state of Japanese strategic planning. Has the emphasis on Porter begun to take root in Japan? Or is Japanese strategic planning still stuck in their traditional practices of the past? The main purpose of this study, therefore, is to assess what discernable business strategies Japanese companies are currently using, the relative frequency of use, and whether these strategies mirror Porter's generic strategies.

This study considers whether Japanese firms are enacting Porter's generic strategies. Organizational strategy, as noted earlier, can be grouped into key generic strategies. A priori, higher adherence to Porter's strategies is expected in Japanese firms, particularly given the government's emphasis on the Porter prize and desire to reverse the country's current economic position.

Thus, the research question becomes: Are Porter's generic strategies being used in Japan and if so, what is their frequency of use in Japanese organizations? To test the research question, a sample of 101 managerial employees working in Japanese companies in Tokyo, Japan was surveyed. The subjects represented a broad cross-section of working adults. For inclusion in the final study, it was determined a respondent needed six months of employment at the organization under study to have adequate organizational knowledge to accurately complete the questionnaire.

Respondents had an average of eight years work experience. The time employed averaged 7.9 years (ranging from six months to 35 years) with a standard deviation of 8.6 years. Over 84% of the respondents were employed full-time. The sample included senior managers (3.0%), middle managers (16.2%), frontline managers (7.1%), professional/technical (21.2%), administrators (4.0%), and others 22.8%. Twenty-two organizations with an average of 633 employees were included in the sample.

(Note: Only 40.6% of the subjects reported their firm's name on the questionnaire. This information was presented as "optional" in order to increase the confidentiality and response rate of the survey.) Fifty-three per cent were service organizations, 21% were manufacturing, and 27% were in the government, non-profit, other category. Fifty-six per cent of the organizations were unionized (in Japan unions are "company unions" in which all employees belong to a union within the company). In a study of American organizations, Allen and Helms developed and tested an appropriate scale based on Porter and Parker and Helms using a set of twenty-five questions regarding various strategic practices in order to operationalize Porter's generic strategies. This instrument was adapted for the Japanese survey. Respondents were asked to determine how frequently their organization uses the various strategic practices.

The questionnaire included a cover page explaining the purpose of the survey and asked respondents to select a single organization to use as a point of reference in answering the survey questions.

Respondents were guaranteed anonymity. If the organization under study had multiple divisions or subsidiaries, respondents were asked to base their answers on the specific division or subsidiary in which they worked. Respondents were given ample time to complete the survey and researchers were on hand to personally administer the questionnaire.

The questionnaire was translated and then pilot tested for clarity in language and meaning. Based upon the feedback from the pilot study minor adjustments were made to clarify meaning. The final Japanese version was then back translated into English to make sure no meaning was changed from the original English version.

Analysis

Responses to the 25 strategy items were subjected to a factor analysis to test whether the items naturally grouped into any of Porter's generic strategies. Using SPSS principal component analysis with a Varimax rotation and Kaiser normalization, a four-factor solution emerged explaining 58.8% of the variance.

Items loading at 0.40 or greater were included in the resulting four factors. Three of the original 25 items did not load strongly onto a single factor and were excluded from further analysis, leaving 22 strategic practice items. The resulting four factors were then further interpreted for their meaning. Based on the items comprising the factors, two factors represent Porter generic strategies; namely, Cost Leadership and Product Differentiation. The Focus strategies were not represented.

Two alternative strategies also emerged from the data. The first appears to represent the traditional Japanese Supply Chain management, while the second appears to represent a Training Based strategy.

In order to determine the frequency of use of the four strategies identified by the factor analysis, an additional procedure was performed. Each item in the questionnaire was rated on a Likert-type scale ranging from one through seven with a score of five or better indicating significant use of the strategy.

(Thus respondents indicating "most times," "almost always," or "always," were included.) The scores on the respective questions loading on each of the four identified factors (cost leadership, product differentiation, supply chain management, and training) were then summed.

The resulting summated scale was used to assess which of the four strategies each respondent used. If a company scored above the cutoff score calculated by the product of the scale response (one through seven) times and the number of questions used to define the respective factor (for example, differentiation loaded on eleven questions), then the company was considered to be using the strategy.

In a number of cases respondents reported the use of more than one major strategy which resulted in the percentages of strategy usage totaling to greater than 100%. This conceptual overlap is to be expected because many of the strategic practices are not entirely exclusive to each respective strategy identified in the factor analysis.

Based upon the factor analysis, four major strategies emerged from the data. Only two of Porter's generic strategies were apparent in the Japanese organizations. In the following discussion, the two Porter strategies in use in Japan, namely, Product Differentiation and Cost Leadership are outlined, while introducing the additional strategies which emerged from the data-the Supply Chain Strategy and the Training Strategy. Again, that some firms reported using strategic practices that fit into multiple strategic factors. This is to be expected because few real world organizations implement pure strategies.

Because of this the overall percentages do not add to 100%. The factor analysis was not amenable to providing more factors to sub-divide the sample so that all subjects would report using practices that represent only a single factor. It would have been highly improbable for this to occur since many of the strategic practices overlap.

Cost Leadership Strategy. The most common strategy evidenced in Japanese organizations was Porter's Cost Leadership strategy. This strategy was being used in 41.4% of the organizations sampled. A cost minimization strategy stresses ongoing cost reductions and tight control of overhead costs to the exclusion of almost any other organizational or strategic issues.

This is evidenced in the items of vigourous pursuit of cost reductions, tight control of overhead costs and improving operational efficiency. The items comprising this factor clearly describe strategic practices which have been associated with the rise of Japanese products in the 1980s.

For example, Japanese manufacturers were able to make great inroads internationally into such markets as consumer electronics, automobiles and steel. Their vigourous control of both costs and quality, along with outstanding customer service allowed Japan to export and compete globally in these markets.

In Japan, customer service is defined somewhat differently than in the West and this may explain its presence of this factor's make-up. Customer service results from a product's value as well as its on-time delivery. Customers often cite Japanese-made cars as offering better service due to the infrequent need for repairs.

Thus good quality leads to low cost and the low cost leader, by providing a valued product, is in turn offering good customer service. Inversely, offering a poor quality product or a product at an inflated price would be seen as poor or even unethical customer service. It seems many Japanese companies are currently using one of Porter's generic strategies cost leadership. But which of the other strategies were evidenced in the data?

PRODUCT DIFFERENTIATION STRATEGY

This Porter strategy emerged in the factor analysis, but is being used much less frequently than any of the other strategies identified. In fact, a mere 7.6% of the organizations appeared to be utilizing this strategy. The failure of the Japanese banking system has been widely cited as the cause of the bursting of the Japanese economic bubble. But perhaps, as Porter contends, the relative lack of use of his generic strategies could be partially responsible for the inability of the Japanese economy to rebound.

When analyzing the items loading on this factor it is interesting to note most are marketing related. Since a product differentiation strategy emphasizes the uniqueness of a product or service and attempts to make the product or service special in the mind of the customer, one would expect marketing related activities to predominate.

By fostering innovation as well as building a reputation of technological leadership a firm should be assured of a stream of new innovations to attract the interests of new customers as well as to meet existing customer's demands for uniqueness.

Part of Japan's recent economic malaise might be attributable the inability of Japanese companies to effectively differentiate their products from those of their competition. The entire country of Japan has operated under a strategic focus on steel, consumer electronics and automobile production since the end of WW II. Their core international markets for these products have been invaded by other nations over the past few decades.

For example, American mini-mills as well as former Soviet bloc and other developing countries are now able to compete with Japanese steel, the Koreans and Chinese now compete in consumer electronics, and the Americans and Europeans have rebounded in their ability to compete in the automobile markets. Japan no longer enjoys a differentiated position in these markets.

As such, very few organizations in the sample evidenced such a strategy. Perhaps Japan, an island nation dependent on exports, needs to regain a differentiated edge in some new markets if their economy is to rebound? Focus Strategy. None of the emerging strategic factors appeared to represent a focus strategy.

Practices typically associated with a focus strategy either did not clearly factor into a discernable strategy (*i.e.*, "dropping unprofitable customers") or loaded onto the differentiation strategy (*i.e.*, "providing specialty products or services" and "producing products/services for high price market segments").

Since Japanese firms are not utilizing Porter's focus strategies, this may be part of the reason for Japan's inability to rebound economically. Perhaps Japanese firms need to focus on specific product/service niches as well as develop new markets in which they can compete globally. This may be an important first step towards economic recovery.

In the literature on focus strategies, there is discussion of the focus strategy as one strategy or two. When discussed as two strategies—focus/low cost or focus/differentiation—the focus strategies are on a continuum with low cost at one end of the differentiation strategy and low-cost at the other end. It may be possible that some of the Japanese organizations that are in the Cost Leadership category are indeed practicing a focus-low cost type of strategy, but the data did not specify this.

SUPPLY CHAIN STRATEGY

The first non-Porter strategy identified appears to be a traditional of Japanese Supply Chain strategy. This is not unexpected as the Japanese are well known for their passion of managing supply chains to optimize efficiency through such tactics as long-term supplier relationships, inventory minimization, and providing suppliers with predictable schedules of stable orders and regular demand. These high levels of Japanese supply chain collaboration have been created by deliberate policies to work with suppliers both individually and collectively in a circle of improvement and mutual benefit to increase cash flow and reduce operational costs of manufacturing.

The results of the factor analysis indicated this strategic preference very clearly. Three items representing a supply chain approach, namely, partnering with suppliers, focus on advertising, and competitive pricing all loaded onto this factor at or greater than 0.7. This strategy was the second most frequently used by 36.2% of the organizations.

The unique keiretsu or interlocking-directorate relationship of Japanese firms to their Japanese supplying organizations has led to a unique management linkage not typically seen and often illegal in other countries. This relationship has led to excellence in supply chain management. This tightly linked sharing of production and profit information among suppliers and manufacturers is easier in Japan due to their unique joint-ownership.

With the linked supplier joint-ownership relationship practice it is understandable partnering with suppliers would exist on this factor. Studies report Japanese automotive and high technology firms frequently engage in cost sharing with smaller suppliers.

Others report the sharing of costs is brought about through investments in customizing assets and supplier support services and training. Quinn and Hilmer found Japanese companies outsource primarily to improve the efficiency and quality of their own processes through focusing on a very few suppliers and building close interdependent relationships and supporting value-adding activities critical to quality.

The advertising strategy and competitive pricing can be partially explained by tight supply chain linkages. Competitive pricing is only possible in a complex product if all suppliers understand the cost structure and use a version of target costing to set a consumer market price and work backwards from this price to reduce costs of production along the supply chain.

Only with long-term and familial-like relationships is the greatest cost reduction possible and leadership in this area has long been attributed to Japanese management. Advertising too is part of the supply chain strategy not only for the marketing reasons of co-op advertising and cost sharing, but also backed up by a corresponding and correct production and operations strategy.

The American Production and Inventory Control Society (APICS) Dictionary defines sales-and-operations planning (SOP) as: A process to develop tactical plans that provide management the ability to strategically direct its businesses to achieve competitive advantage, SOP integrates customer-focused marketing plans for new and existing products with the management of the supply chain.

The process brings together all the plans for the business (sales, marketing, development, manufacturing, sourcing, and financial) into one integrated set of plans. The process must reconcile all supply, demand, and new-product plans at both the detail and aggregate levels and tie to the business plan. Executed properly, the sales and operation planning process links the strategic plans for the business with its execution and reviews the performance measurements for continuous improvement.

Thus for the effective utilization of an advertising strategy, production must be in line with the advertising in order to manufacture and distribute the goods to meet consumer's demands, and, more importantly, these consumer demands have been formed by advertising. The Japanese are recognized for their passion of managing supply chains to optimize efficiency through such tactics as long-term supplier relationships, inventory minimization, and providing suppliers with predictable schedules of stable orders and regular demand.

These high levels of Japanese supply chain collaboration have been created by deliberate policies to work with suppliers both individually and collectively in a circle of improvement and mutual benefit to increase cash flow and reduce operational costs of manufacturing. Large percentages (36.2%) of the organizations surveyed are still clinging to this traditional business strategy.

While the practices associated with this strategy did not fit a traditional Porter generic strategy, one could assert the supply chain strategy is an attempt to move towards an adoption of a focus-low cost strategy. The key tenets of supply chain collaboration are to reduce operational costs of logistics, distribution and production while minimizing raw materials, work-in-process and finished goods inventories.

In a focused or niche environment, the supply chain strategy can work to lower costs below other competitors thus creating a market advantage.

TRAINING STRATEGY

The other strategy operating in Japanese organizations was a training strategy.

The items loading on this factor included:

- Extensive training of front-line personnel.
- Intense supervision of front-line personnel, and 3) extensive training of marketing personnel. This strategy was evidenced in 33.8% of the organizations surveyed; making it the third most frequently used strategy.

This is the second non-Porter strategy identified. Like the Supply Chain strategy, it too appears to be a traditional Japanese strategy. Japan is well known for intense, company-wide training as well as supervision of all employees in a rigid, hierarchical structure. Many researchers have attributed Japan's success to their unique style of management, structure, and training.

Thus the supervision and training of front-line personnel and marketing personnel emerged as a separate strategic factor due to the rich history and adherence to "'Japanese Management" within many of the companies operating in Japan. This training and management style worked so successfully during the 1980s in the heyday of Japan's industrial success and companies follow this proven strategy today. The key features of Japanese management are the seniority-based wage scale and promotion ladder, the traditional system of lifetime employment, and the concentration of power in middle management.

Hull, Hage, and Zuumi, in their study of the differences between the US and Japanese approaches to management, also revealed Japanese factories tend to invest relatively more in employee training, including more group processes such as the quality circle. They also found suggestions per employee were higher in Japanese factories.

Clegg and Kono, in their study of trends in Japanese management, offer a historical and cultural explanation for the intensive employee training. After WW II, skilled laborers were needed and Japan's lifetime employment encouraged such skill formation. Training costs were invested in secure personnel who would remain in the firm. The long-term employment fostered commitment and managers were tree to invest funds into training employees with a view towards more long-term performance.

With the decline of the concept of lifetime employment in Japan, this strategy may no longer be appropriate. An outsourcing type of strategy may be more competitive in today's international business climate. Again while not a Porter generic strategy, it could be argued the training strategy is an attempt by Japanese managers to move towards the focus-differentiation strategy.

The intense training results in either a standardized customer service and service delivery process for service firms or a quality manufacturing process with an attention to and elimination of process defects in a production environment. In either case-service or manufacturing-the result is a quality service or product.

Quality products and services can command a premium price from customers and are thus perceived as a differentiated product, particularly in narrow market segments. Given the four strategies, it appears Japanese businesses may be beginning to make a transition to Porter-based strategies, but the traditional Japanese business strategies remain. For example, the Japanese use Porter's Cost Leadership strategy the most (41.4%), but the Product Differentiation strategy was infrequently used (7.6%) and a clear Focus strategy did not emerge in the factor analysis. Clearly there is much room for improvement if Japanese organizations hope to achieve the ideals of the Porter Prize.

The large percentage of Japanese firms following a cost leadership strategy can be easily explained as a natural reaction to the decade long economic slump and the necessity for cutting costs. Japanese labour is among the highest paid in the world, imports on raw materials remains high despite attempts to reform the system, and the Japanese are increasingly competing with Chinese and other Asian conglomerates for business that was once theirs exclusively.

For these and other reasons, a cost leadership strategy is a means of survival. Interestingly 70% of firms are still clinging to strategies linked to traditional Japanese management (36.2% for supply chain and 33.8% for training).

This evidence further indicates a national strategic transition is incomplete. The traditional Japanese management strategies of training and supply chain management support Porter's assertion past Japanese success was based on operational effectiveness, the development of logistics to improve quality and cut costs, and on marginal product differentiation easily transferable to other companies. Even the high use of the Cost Leadership strategy lends further support to the notion the Japanese are stuck in the strategies of the past since cost control was vital to the success of Japanese industries in a global marketplace.

This exploratory study represents an attempt to identify current strategies in use in Japanese companies and the degree to which Japanese management is embracing the Porter Prize in Japan. While Porter asserts Japanese companies, "have no strategy" and this tradition will be hard to break, the fact that such a large scale effort is underway to "infect" Japanese companies with the "strategy bug" serves as a firm foundation for on-going inquiry and interest. While Japanese companies do indeed have discernable strategies, they do not fit neatly into Porter's typology. These strategies tend to be rooted in the past. It remains to be seen whether or not a transition to Porter's generic strategies alone is possible for Japan.

To date there have been no studies specifically designed to test whether Porter's strategies are in use by Japanese firms operating in Japan. This research used a convenience sample consisting of management employees from mostly large, institutionalized Japanese firms.

Future research may be strengthened by using a sample comprised of a more diverse set of Japanese firms, including entrepreneurial firms, women-owned businesses, and even foreign firms operating in Japan. Another approach would be to conduct a longitudinal comparative study among firms competing for the Porter prize to identify specific practices and their relationship with strategies and performance and assess if their strategic practices mirror the questionnaire constructs for the generic strategies.

The underlying assumption of the Porter prize is winning companies will be "successful". Since the current study does not address performance, future research should collect data on a longitudinal basis to aid in drawing causal inferences and validating the efficacy of Porter's strategies in use. Future studies should also investigate the relative effectiveness of these various strategies in Japanese firms. For example, which strategies are associated with higher levels of organizational performance?

From this research two unique strategies emerged from the Japanese management style and economic model, relevant only to Japanese companies operating in the country. Future research on strategies in Japan should examine the population of strategies being used.

If global Japanese firms adapt strategy to their local environments, assessing the strategy of Japanese owned business operations operating outside Japan will help explain companies' global strategies. As with any exploratory research, other important research questions have been uncovered. For example, what are the reasons Japanese firms are not adopting Porter's generic strategies? Are they too focused, too limiting to the traditionally open and fluid Japanese management system?

Are Japanese companies too locked into quality improvement processes, lean manufacturing and productivity enhancements to shift towards more differentiation and other, more market driven strategies? Are the Japanese firms concentrating only on large markets and ignoring profitable niche markets and the corresponding focus strategies? Is the Japanese management tradition of evolutionary change and bottom-up consensus or team management antithetical to a top-down, rigid planning approach favoured by Porter? All are areas for future research as in linking the particular strategies used to performance.

Finally the problems experienced in Japan need further research to determine the role of strategies or lack thereof in the current economic crisis. For example, what part of the problem is due to external and economic factors and what part is due to internal organizational strategies? Also when Japanese firms set up operations in the US, what strategic styles do they use and do they differ from the strategies used by the same organization in Japan.

This exploratory research is a first attempt to ascertain the current state of Japanese strategy. Future studies may use this as a baseline to see if the push towards Porter-based strategies in Japan is actually having an impact on Japanese business strategies. It will be interesting to see if this transaction is ever enacted and, if so, how long it will take.

There is little doubt about the current weak condition of Japanese banks. Although they were never as profitable as European or U.S. banks, Japanese banks grew rapidly in the 1980s, buoyed by a strong domestic economy and rapidly increasing asset prices.

In 1980, only one Japanese bank made the list of the ten largest banks in the world, compiled by The Banker magazine. By 1990, the four largest banks, and six of the top ten, were Japanese. Moreover, the rapid growth of Japanese banks was not confined to domestic markets. Statistics compiled by the Bank for International Settlements (BIS), the share of Japanese loans in total international claims outstanding was less than 20 per cent in the early 1980s. By the end of the decade, Japanese banks accounted for over one-third of international bank assets.

By 1990, the size and rapid expansion of Japanese banks had earned them the moniker "mighty giants" of Japan. The tide that carried Japanese banks to the top ranks of international banks transformed into a series of tsunami in the 1990s.

The first signs of trouble emerged with sharp declines in Japanese stock and land prices. As a result, Japanese banks, which extensive equity holdings and loans had collateralized by real estate, saw significant declines in the value of their assets and capital positions.

The collapse of U.S. commercial real estate prices and the 1990-91 recession in the U.S. put further pressure on Japanese banks, which had invested heavily in this market. The response of the Japanese banks was to turn to new markets, the then rapidly growing South East Asian economies. The current Asian crisis and the unresolved asset quality problems in Japan have escalated the amount of problem assets at Japanese banks to dangerous levels.

Today, even the best performing Japanese banks are facing liquidity pressures and some are struggling to stay afloat. As of October 1998, the official amount of nonperforming loans at Japanese banks was $600 billion, while some private analysts put the amount of bad loans at over $1 trillion, representing roughly 20 per cent of total loans outstanding.

Moreover, according to some analysts, the Japanese banking system has a shortfall of [yen]8 trillion in real net worth, even after the injection of [yen]10 trillion to [yen]25 trillion in public funds that is expected as a result of the [yen]60 trillion rescue plan passed in October 1998 by the Japanese parliament. The impact of the crisis on the Japanese economy and other financial markets is significant - low rates of corporate investment and curtailed lending are, at least partially, the result of problems in banking. Of course, other countries have also faced financial crises. Among the more notable was the thrift and banking crisis in the U.S. in the late 1980s and early 1990s, which resulted in the closure of 1,142 savings and loan (S&L) institutions and 1,395 commercial banks.

Because banks are a source of funds for firms, have an important role in the transmission of monetary policy, and are an integral part of the payments system, the social costs of bank failures may be greater than those of other types of businesses. The determinants of bank profitability and the likelihood of bank survival have shown that certain bank characteristics are important in determining future bank performance. Following this literature, I examine the relationship between the performance of Japanese banks in 1991-97 and their characteristics.

In particular, I focus on three questions. One, how does the accounting performance of Japanese banks relate to their financial characteristics? Although the banking crisis in Japan is well recognized, the precise financial condition of the banks and the amount of, and losses from, their nonperforming loans are uncertain.

Differences between the disclosure, accounting, and regulatory rules in Japan and other industrial economies make it difficult to assess the exact condition of Japanese banks and compare them with other international banks. Furthermore, some analysts interpret recent Ministry of Finance (MoF) actions (such as allowing banks to value their security holdings at cost to avoid reporting valuation losses) as attempts to mask the true condition of the banks; as a result, they consider the reported results of Japanese banks to be of little or no value.

If the patterns between bank performance and characteristics established in previous studies are also evident in the Japanese banking system, then even if the reported numbers are not accurate, they would still provide useful signals of bank performance. Two, how does the stock market performance of banks relate to their financial characteristics? In particular, are the patterns between stock returns, which are less subject to potential maneuvering by banks, and financial characteristics consistent with those observed in the accounting returns?

If Japanese accounting, disclosure, and regulatory practices obscure the true performance of Japanese banks, then the relationship between accounting earnings and bank characteristics might not be consistent with that observed in other countries. However, if market participants are aware of these practices and their impact on the condition of the banks, then market-based measures of bank performance, such as stock returns, would be little affected by these practices. As a result, any inconsistency we might observe with accounting returns would not be evident in stock returns.

Three, how are the stock market and accounting returns of banks related? Are the stock returns correlated with the accounting returns, or do shareholders dismiss the accounting results as meaningless? If accounting and disclosure practices of Japanese banks obscure their condition to such an extent that there is no additional information in their reported results, then there would be no significant relationship between accounting and stock returns.

Throughout the analysis, I explore potential differences in these relationships among different types of Japanese banks and over time. For the most part, press reports and other analyses of Japanese banks focus on the major banks (city, trust, and long-tern credit banks), which account for more than 70 per cent of Japanese banking assets; however, their activities and characteristics differ significantly from those of regional banks.

Furthermore, the activities of banks, underlying economic conditions, and regulatory practices have changed over time. These differences in bank characteristics and changes in the environment can potentially influence the relationships I examine.

The results using accounting measures of performance indicate that some measures of asset quality are significant determinants of Japanese banks' earnings; and the relationships I document are consistent with the results of studies. However, the accounting returns of Japanese banks exhibit some unexpected correlations with the market index, increases in the number of business bankruptcies, and bank capital.

For instance, bank profitability, measured by return on equity (ROE), is negatively correlated with returns on the market index, indicating that banks are less profitable when the stock market is performing well. Further analysis shows that this and other puzzling results with accounting earnings might be the result of banks' loan loss provisioning practices. In particular, Japanese banks appear to increase their loan loss provisions when their core profits and stock market returns are high.

The results with banks' stock returns show that such income-smoothing does not affect their market performance. Specifically, when performance is measured by market returns, the puzzling results observed with accounting returns disappear and we observe correlations with the market index and the number of bankruptcies consistent with expectations. Despite the potential problems with the reported earnings of Japanese banks, our results suggest that accounting returns provided market participants with useful information on banks' condition in 1991-94: Accounting and stock market returns are positively and significantly correlated during this period.

However, the results also show that this relationship breaks down in 1995-97, implying that the usefulness of reported earnings has deteriorated in recent years. As indicators of bank performance and characteristics, I use measures used by regulators and market participants to assess the financial condition of banks. Our results suggest that Japanese accounting, disclosure, and regulatory practices might have driven a wedge between banks' accounting and stock returns in recent years.

To the extent that such practices make it more difficult to assess the condition of banks, they introduce additional uncertainty to the market, potentially increasing the risk premium required by investors. The "Japanese premium" - the difference between the interest rates paid by Japanese and other international banks in the interbank markets - might be considered a manifestation of this uncertainty.

Regulatory forbearance that allows economically insolvent institutions to continue operations and extends implicit or explicit guarantees to uninsured bank claimants transfers wealth from deposit insurance agencies, and hence taxpayers, to the shareholders and debtors of insured institutions.

The results in theoretical and empirical studies indicate that as a bank nears insolvency, more of its value is derived from the value of subsidies and forbearance and the correlation between stock market returns and the value of the underlying assets declines.

Brickley and James and others, a bank has (in addition to its tangible assets) a valuable intangible asset in the form of access to underpriced, fixed-premium deposit insurance and government forbearance programmes that modify insolvency rules. The capitalized value of this intangible asset is embedded in the bank's stock market valuation, but is not reflected in accounting values.

When most of the market value of an insured bank is in the form of this intangible asset, movements in common stock returns need not be correlated with movements in the value of the underlying assets. In recent years, Japanese regulators have delayed recognition of losses at banks and have been reluctant to take strict actions against troubled or insolvent institutions.

Such regulatory forbearance might account for the lack of correlation between accounting and market returns of Japanese banks in 1995-97 when the deterioration in the banks' financial condition accelerated significantly. More recently, the MoF has taken a number of steps to shore up banks' reported capital base through accounting changes and injection of government funds and has extended government guarantees to all bank creditors through the end of March 2001. These actions evoke recollections of the initial response of regulators to the S&L crisis in the U.S. Experience with that crisis tell us that regulatory forbearance can be a leaking lifeboat that imposes significant costs on the economy and healthy financial institutions, instead of the intended lifeline to pull troubled firms to safety.

If the financial revitalization laws passed by the Japanese parliament in October 1998 put an end to regulatory forbearance and allow orderly resolution of insolvent institutions, they might minimize the future adverse impact of the banking crisis on the economy.

OVERVIEW OF JAPANESE BANKING

Until the 1980s, functional segmentation, extensive regulations, restricted competition, government intervention, and isolation from international markets were the defining characteristics of Japanese financial markets. The Japanese banking system underwent a series of reforms in the late 1970s and 1980s; however, the current system retains some of its traditional characteristics.

To a certain extent, the markets are still segmented across banking functions. Until the passage of the 1992 Financial System Reform Law, different institutions conducted commercial, trust, and investment banking. Similarly, until recently, different banks provided short-term and long-term business loans.

City and regional banks traditionally provided short-term financing to companies and were restricted to issuing short-term liabilities. City banks traditionally have focused on providing financing to large corporations and have relied on large corporate deposits and Bank of Japan credit for their funding.

City banks were also among the first Japanese banks to expand overseas. The traditional business of regional banks, on the other hand, has been the provision of short-term loans to small- and medium-sized companies.

Through their branch network in their home prefecture and close community ties, regional banks have relied primarily on deposits from their loan customers and individuals for funding. Long-term business loans are provided by the long-term credit and trust banks. Until recently, only these institutions were allowed to issue long-term liabilities. On the asset side of the balance sheet, long-term credit banks provided commercial loans, while trust banks focused on trust loans. Regulations restricted long-term credit banks to issuing deposit liabilities only to their borrowers and restricted trust banks to raising funds through loan and money trusts. However, over time, deregulation and increased competition among financial institutions have blurred the lines separating the businesses of Japanese banks.

The regulations and laws governing banking operations are formulated, implemented, and enforced by the MoF. Until April 1998, when a new, independent Financial Supervisory Agency (FSA) was established, the MoF was the primary regulator of banks.

Although the MoF has the legal authority to license banks, enforce laws, and administer penalties for violations of laws and regulations, it relies primarily on administrative guidance for enforcement. Because one of the functions of the Bank of Japan is to ensure the safety and soundness of the financial system, it also has regulatory and supervisory purview over banks, albeit to a lesser extent than the MoF. Until the establishment of the FSA, both institutions conducted examinations of banks.

Other government institutions in the Japanese banking system include the Deposit Insurance Corporation, which insures bank deposits and collects insurance premiums, and the Resolution and Collection Bank, which was established in 1995 to take over the assets of failed institutions.

Despite the deregulation of banking activities in recent years, Japanese banks have characteristics that reflect their traditional roles. Some of these characteristics are evident, which shows the aggregate balance sheets of four types of Japanese banks as of the fiscal year ending March 31, 1997.

For banks that have traditionally provided long-term financing (long-term credit and trust banks), loans excluding loan loss reserves (gross loans) represent approximately 65 per cent of total assets. Gross loans account for approximately 72 per cent of the assets of city and regional banks that have traditionally provided short-term financing. However, despite the greater concentration of assets in loans, city and regional banks have smaller loan loss reserves (both as a percentage of assets and of loans) than long-term credit and trust banks.

The differences in loan loss reserves might reflect differences in the composition of loan portfolios of these institutions. For instance, on March 31, 1997, the credit exposure of the three long-term credit banks to the riskier real estate, construction, and finance sectors was 44.43 per cent of their domestic loan portfolio; loans to these three sectors represented 27.14 per cent of the domestic loans at city banks. The four types of banks invest roughly the same fraction of their assets in securities.

However, major banks invest more in the equity of other companies, whereas regional banks invest more in Japanese public bonds. Equity investments account for less than 3 per cent of regional banks' assets, but they represent approximately 7 per cent to 8 per cent of major banks' assets. The relatively greater investment in equity securities reflects the major banks' role in the industrial groups, the keiretsu, as major stockholders of group companies.

Japanese banks also differ in how they fund their assets. Compared with major banks, regional banks fund a greater percentage of their assets with equity capital. Moreover, long-term credit and trust banks rely less on deposits (less than 40 per cent of funding) than city and regional banks do (around 90 per cent), reflecting the restrictions placed on deposit-taking at these long-term finance institutions.

Not only do various Japanese banks have different characteristics, but they also differ from U.S. banks in terms of their activities and characteristics. Although there are more than 9,000 banks in the U.S., bank assets in the U.S. total to \$4.6 trillion, compared with \$6.5 trillion in assets of 117 Japanese banks.

Furthermore, bank assets represent more than 1.5 times the Japanese nominal gross domestic product (GDP), compared with 60 per cent of nominal GDP in the U.S., reflecting the greater role of banks in the Japanese economy. Japanese and U.S. banks also differ in the extent of leverage and composition of assets. Japanese banks are more than twice as leveraged as U.S. banks. While equity capital funds approximately 8 per cent of U.S. bank assets, it funds less than 4 per cent of Japanese assets. Japanese banks also invest more of their assets in loans than U.S. banks.

Loans excluding loan loss reserves account for nearly 70 per cent of Japanese bank assets, but less than 60 per cent of U.S. bank assets. Loan loss reserves, as a fraction of both total assets and gross loans, are higher at Japanese banks, reflecting the differences in the conditions of the two banking markets. However, Japanese banks' loan loss ratios surpassed those of U.S. banks only in 1997. In the early 1990s, U.S. banks' loan loss reserves covered 2.5 per cent of their loans, compared with less than 1 per cent coverage for Japanese banks. Japanese banks began to reserve for possible loan losses aggressively only in 1996.

While the total amount of securities investment is similar for Japanese and U.S. banks (approximately 17 per cent of total assets), Japanese banks have significantly more equity investments (nearly 6 per cent of assets) than U.S. banks (less than 0.5 per cent of assets), which are generally prohibited from making such investments.

In addition, Japanese banks rely on deposits as a source of funds more than U.S. banks. Deposits fund nearly 80 per cent of Japanese bank assets, but less than 69 per cent of the total assets of U.S. banks. Other liabilities (such as fed funds purchases and other nondeposit liabilities) account for 27 per cent of the assets of large U.S. banks, but only about 17 per cent of the total assets of Japanese banks.

In 1990, when the U.S. was approaching the end of its banking crisis, U.S. and Japanese banks had similar ROEs and operating profits. However, when Japanese and U.S. banks are compared in terms of narrower performance measures, such as operating profits before loan loss provisions and interest margins, U.S. banks were more profitable than Japanese banks even in 1990. Hence, it was the higher level of loan loss provisions at U.S. banks that made their performance in 1990 comparable with that of Japanese banks. Since 1990, the performance of Japanese and U.S. banks has diverged significantly.

During the 1990-97 period, U.S. banks improved their performance by most measures, while Japanese banks' performance deteriorated. By 1997, Japanese banks were reporting negative ROEs, while U.S. banks were enjoying record levels of profitability.

The differences are all the more remarkable when performance is measured by return on assets (ROA). During 1990-97, the average ROA for U.S. banks was 0.95 per cent, compared with 0.04 per cent for Japanese banks. The relative performance of Japanese banks is poor even if they are put on a more equal footing with U.S. banks in terms of underlying economic conditions. For example, in 1987-91, when the U.S. was in the midst of a major banking crisis, U.S. banks averaged 7.4 per cent ROE, versus 0.3 per cent for Japanese banks in 1991-97.

The stock returns of Japanese banks reflected their poor performance in 1990-97. Japanese banks had negative stock returns in five of the eight years and underperformed the market in seven of the eight years. How do the characteristics of Japanese banks relate to their performance? Are the relationships between the performance and characteristics of Japanese banks similar to those observed in the U.S.? Next, I examine these issues in more detail.

PERFORMANCE AND FINANCIAL CHARACTERISTICS

A number of studies have examined the performance of banks and related it to bank characteristics and activities. Because solvency of banking institutions is of particular importance to the stability of financial systems and because there were a large number of failures among banks and S&Ls in the U.S. during the 1980s, several studies have focused on factors that determine the profitability and solvency of depository institutions. Following this literature, I examine the

ROE and the stock market performance of Japanese banks in 1991-97 relate these performance measures to bank characteristics that were found to be particularly important determinants of bank performance in studies: asset quality, capital ratio, liquidity, operational efficiency, and size.

The relationship between asset quality and bank earnings is closely related to the condition of the overall economy. Banks that invest in riskier assets are likely to have higher expected profits. However, higher asset risk implies lower realised profits when the economy is experiencing a series of negative shocks.

Studies found that depository institutions in the U.S. that invested in riskier, or lower quality, assets performed worse than others during the 1980s and early 1990s. One would expect a similar result in Japan, that is, a negative relationship between measures of asset quality and realised performance of Japanese banks in 1991-97, when the Japanese economy was subject to adverse shocks.

I measure asset quality and credit risk by the following variables: the ratio of equity investments to total assets, the ratio of loan loss provisions to loans, the ratio of net loans to total assets, the ratio of domestic loans to total loans, and the growth rate of assets. The ratio of equity investments to total assets measures the banks' exposure to the performance of other firms through their equity investments. As general economic conditions deteriorate, the performance of banks with a relatively high fraction of their assets invested in the equity of other firms should be worse than that of banks with lower equity exposure.

Furthermore, because equity securities are generally more risky than debt securities, banks with more equity investments may have lower realised profits when stock prices decline. On the other hand, if equity investments provide banks with more opportunities for diversification, then banks with high fractions of assets invested in equities would perform better than other banks. The ratio of loan loss provisions to loans can be positively or negatively correlated with performance. If banks with riskier assets provision more than other banks, then loan loss provisions measure credit risk, and are likely to be negatively correlated with realised profits. On the other hand, if banks that perform better, or banks with more conservative management, provision more for loan losses, then one would expect a positive relationship between loan loss provisions and performance.

Empirical evidence on U.S. banks shows that loan loss provisions and loan loss reserves are negatively correlated with future bank performance.

The ratio of net loans to total assets measures the banks' credit risk, and the ratio of domestic loans to total loans measures their domestic exposure. During the sample period, loan quality, particularly the quality of loans made to Japanese borrowers, was one of the largest sources of risk to bank profitability. Consequently, one would expect banks with higher ratios of loans to total assets and banks with more domestic loans in their portfolio to have poorer performance than other banks.

I also measure asset quality with the annual growth rate of assets. During the U.S. thrift crisis, some institutions tried to grow out of their problems by expanding rapidly. Furthermore, additions to assets at fast-growing institutions may increasingly involve riskier assets. As a result, one might observe a negative relationship between asset growth and realised profits.

On the other hand, if regulators are providing sufficient discipline, they may restrain the growth of institutions that are in financial trouble and allow only strong-performing banks to expand. Alternatively, banks that grow relatively more may previously have had good performance and/or expect to have good performance in the future. In that case, one would observe a positive relationship between growth and profitability.

In theory, performance can be positively or negatively related to capital ratios. For instance, in perfect and competitive capital markets, higher capital ratios would reduce risk and expected return on equity (but would not change the weighted average cost of funds). Moreover, because interest payments are tax deductible, relying more on equity and less on debt reduces after-tax earnings, generating a negative relationship between earnings and capital.

However, other factors may lead to a positive relationship between the capital and earnings of banks. Because banks retain a portion of their earnings, over time more profitable firms would have higher retained earnings, hence more capital, than less profitable firms.

Furthermore, equity capital provides a cushion against losses, lowering bankruptcy costs. In imperfect capital markets, banks with more capital and lower bankruptcy costs are likely to have lower interest costs and higher profitability than other banks. In addition, when deposit insurance is present and regulators have the authority to close insolvent institutions, banks with profitable investment opportunities have an incentive to be well capitalized.

All these factors point to a positive relationship between bank performance and capital-asset ratios. Empirical evidence indicates that banks with higher capital-asset ratios are indeed more profitable and less likely to fail than more leveraged banks. I measure the capital position of Japanese banks by the ratio of capital to risk-weighted assets, as defined by the BIS capital accord.

Profitability is also related to liquidity. More liquid banks are better able to meet adverse shocks and are likely to face lower cost of funds in imperfect capital markets, increasing their profitability. On the other hand, liquid assets have lower expected returns than illiquid assets, so banks with more liquid assets might have lower expected earnings.

In addition, banks choose the level of liquidity of their assets. Therefore, if a bank expects to face adverse shocks in the future, it may choose to hold more liquid assets to cushion itself against such shocks. In that case, one would observe a negative relationship between profitability and liquidity, since banks that expect lower profits would increase their liquidity. In short, the relationship between liquidity and profitability is ambiguous in theory and is determined by the data. Empirical evidence points to a positive relationship between liquidity and performance of banks in the U.S. I measure liquidity by the ratio of short-term liabilities to short-term assets, whereby banks with higher ratios are less liquid than others.

Operational efficiency, measured by the overhead ratio, is also likely to be a key determinant of bank profitability. To the extent that banks with high overhead ratios are less efficient, one would expect these banks to perform worse than banks with lower overhead expenses.

However, the overhead ratio is an imperfect measure of efficiency and may also reflect differences in banks' product mix. For instance, nontraditional bank businesses may generate greater profits, but require more overhead expenses than traditional banking.

In that case, one would observe a positive relationship between profitability and overhead ratios. In general, previous studies have found that banks with high overhead expenses perform worse than other banks. I also include size, measured by total assets, as a control variable. Studies found that large banks perform better than small banks.

In addition to these bank characteristics, I explore the relationship between bank performance and measures of aggregate economic activity. In particular, I focus on stock market returns and the number of business bankruptcies. As economic conditions deteriorate, the number of bankruptcies increases.

As creditors, banks are directly affected by bankruptcies. Hence, one would expect an increase in the number of bankruptcies to be associated with higher loan defaults and lower bank profits. Japanese banks have significant investments in the equity of other firms. Therefore, returns on the overall stock market affect the performance of banks, not only as an indicator of aggregate economic conditions, but also through their impact on the valuation of banks' investments. As a result, one would expect bank performance to be positively correlated with returns in the stock market. Clearly, banks with a relatively high fraction of their assets in equity securities should benefit more from stock price increases than other banks. To explore this relationship, I interact the return on the market index with the ratio of equity investments to total assets. If an increase in the market index has a greater positive impact on the performance of banks with more equity investments, then the coefficient on the interaction term would be positive.

My analysis is based on accounting results for city, trust, long-term credit, and regional banks in 1991-97 from FitchIBCA's Bankscope database. Our initial analysis showed some extreme values of ROA, ROE, and growth rate of assets, which were attributable to mergers or insolvency.

To avoid influencing the results by including these extreme values, I deleted observations in the top and bottom 1 percentile of the distribution of ROA, ROE, and the growth rate of total assets. The final sample contains 555 observations for 88 banks.

The data also include daily stock prices of city, trust, and regional banks for 1991-97 from Bloomberg. Annual holding-period returns are constructed using daily stock prices and dividend payments as reported in the various editions of the Japan. The top panel shows the mean values, the standard deviations, and the minimum and maximum values of the variables for the entire sample.

The average reported earnings and stock returns reflect the poor performance of Japanese banks during this period. Despite the exclusion of extreme values from the sample, profitability varies greatly across banks and over time. For instance, ROE ranges from -49.21 per cent to 9.40 per cent, indicating that while some banks performed very poorly, others reported large, positive profits.

Similarly, banks differed in the amount of their loan loss provisions. Although the mean value for provisions was 0.59 per cent, some banks had no loan loss provisions, while others had provisions as high as 9.61 per cent of loans.

There are also differences in the asset composition and operational efficiency of banks. For instance, net loans ranged from 45.14 per cent to 82.07 per cent of total assets, while equity investments ranged from 0 per cent to 9.32 per cent of total assets. In summary, the sample statistics suggest that differences in banks' characteristics across institutions and over time might be significant.

The statistics in the bottom panel, the mean values for different bank types and different time periods, present further evidence of differences in bank characteristics. Major Japanese banks differ significantly from regional banks and characteristics of Japanese banks changed significantly in the latter part of the sample period.

In particular, major banks performed significantly more poorly than regional banks in 1991-97. The average ROE for major banks during this period was -0.40 per cent, compared with 3.17 per cent for regional banks. Other variables also show significant differences in the characteristics of major and regional banks, which were foreshadowed by the statistics. Namely, major banks invest less in loans but more in equities than regional banks. Furthermore, major banks are more liquid and have lower interest margins and overhead expenses than regional banks. Regional banks also provision less for possible loan losses.

There are, however, no significant differences in the capital ratios of major and regional banks. The last two columns in the bottom panel show the mean values of the variables in 1991-94 and 1995-97, respectively. These statistics indicate that bank characteristics changed significantly over time. While there was no significant difference in bank stock returns in the two periods, ROEs were significantly lower in the later part of the sample period.

Over time, Japanese banks also increased their percentage of assets invested in loans and equity securities. The increase in the ratio of domestic to total loans reflects the aggregate decline in the banks' international loans. Furthermore, liquidity of Japanese banks declined significantly in 1995-97, which may reflect the higher costs of liquidity for Japanese banks in interbank markets. Lastly, banks raised their capital ratios and their provisioning for loan losses in 1995-97. Explore the relationship between bank characteristics and performance more systematically.

DETERMINANTS OF ACCOUNTING PERFORMANCE

Banks' performance over a given period is related to their characteristics at the beginning of the period; hence, the results show the predictive power of current bank characteristics for future performance. Are the patterns observed in the Japanese banks' accounting earnings and characteristics consistent with those in other countries?

For some characteristics, the relationship with earnings is consistent with patterns observed in the U.S. In particular, loan loss provisions and the ratio of net loans to total assets are negatively correlated with earnings, indicating that banks with higher credit risk performed worse than others. These measures of asset quality are particularly strong determinants of performance for regional banks, but are less informative for major banks. Compared with regional banks, major banks hold a smaller fraction of their assets in loans; thus, these banks' performance may be more sensitive to fluctuations in other sources of income, such as fee income and earnings from security portfolios.

Banks with greater investments in equity securities performed worse than others. This result shows that when economic conditions were deteriorating, the equity investments of Japanese banks exposed them to greater risk and reduced their earnings. The relationship between profitability and other bank characteristics is statistically weaker.

Profitability is significantly correlated with liquidity, size, and growth rate of assets in only some specifications. Furthermore, in contrast to the positive significant relationship observed between bank earnings and capital in other studies, Japanese banks' earnings are not significantly related to their capital ratios.

At first glance, this result suggests that BIS capital ratios have no impact on Japanese banks' earnings. However, this cease is at odds with anecdotal evidence which indicates that capital management was of particular importance to Japanese banks during this period. For instance, between 1992 and 1995,

Japanese banks sold [yen] 2.7 trillion of subordinated debt to meet BIS capital requirements and some major banks issued convertible securities to raise capital. Furthermore, MoF officials and analysts suggest that the retrenchment of Japanese banks from international lending is at least partially motivated by their need to increase capital ratios.

It is unlikely that significant efforts by Japanese banks to manage their capital positions had no impact on their earnings. If capital management was important for Japanese banks during the sample period, then the impact of capital ratios on bank earnings would not be measured accurately by the current analysis which treats capital ratios as exogenous variables that are not influenced by bank characteristics. One would need to take into account the factors that affect banks' capital management decisions before examining the impact of capital on earnings.

Some of the relationships are inconsistent with our expectations and patterns observed in the U.S. Specifically, higher returns in the Tokyo Stock Exchange, which imply more favourable economic conditions, are associated with poor bank performance. In addition, the coefficient estimates for the interaction term between stock returns and equity investments indicate that the negative correlation between stock returns and earnings is stronger for banks with more equity investments, particularly for major banks and in the 1995-97 period.

These results are in direct contrast to our expectations. Further analysis, however, revealed that the result was evident only for measures of performance that include loan loss provisions. There is a positive correlation between pre-provision profits and stock returns. These results suggest that Japanese banks provision more when economic conditions are good.

The correlations between loan loss provisions in the current period and other bank characteristics and economic conditions, point to a similar cease. Specifically, banks provision more when they have higher core earnings (operating profits before loan loss provisions) and when the stock market performs well. Furthermore, banks with higher equity investments provision more than other banks. These correlations, and the results with other performance measures, are consistent with analysts' assessment of the income-smoothing behaviour of Japanese banks.

The results are also consistent with Moody's reports that to maintain their capital positions in recent years, Japanese banks have sold their equity securities to offset credit expenses. In addition, loan loss provisions are positively correlated with the fraction of assets invested in loans, indicating that banks with higher credit risk provision more. However, there is a strong negative correlation between loan loss provisions and the increase in the number of business bankruptcies in the current period.

This result is puzzling and gives further evidence that Japanese banks' provisioning practices do not conform with conventional wisdom. Lastly, the well-known credit quality problems associated with Japanese borrowers in the 1990s suggest a negative relationship between ROE and the fraction of total loans allocated to domestic borrowers.

The results indicate that, in contrast to our expectations, domestic loans were associated with higher profitability in 1991-94. However, during 199597 this relationship loses statistical significance.

DETERMINANTS OF STOCK MARKET PERFORMANCE

The consistency of the results in the part with those in other banking studies was mixed. Some of these results might be due to efforts by Japanese banks to manage their regulatory capital and to fund their credit expenses through sale of securities during favourable market conditions.

If such actions are transparent to investors, and analysts' reports and anecdotal evidence suggest that they are, then the puzzling results between bank characteristics and market measures of performance would not exist. Market participants would dismiss the reported numbers as irrelevant and rely on other indicators of banks' condition (for instance, analysts' reports). In that case, market measure of performance, such as bank stock returns, would not be related to accounting profits; and the relationship observed between stock returns and bank characteristics would differ significantly from the relationship observed with accounting profits.

To explore this issue further, I relate the stock returns of banks to the bank characteristics. The results suggest that while those accounting relationships that were consistent with our expectations are also evident for stock returns, the puzzling results with accounting earnings disappear when performance is measured by stock market returns. Specifically, banks with more loans and equity investments and banks with higher loan loss provisions have lower stock returns. Furthermore, size and profitability are positively correlated, particularly for major banks.

However, the results indicate that stock returns are positively correlated with the market index. This result implies that market participants perceive the negative correlation of the market index with reported earnings as an accounting artifact and see a positive impact from an increase in the index on banks' future cash flows. Another difference between reported accounting profits and stock returns is their relationship with the change in the number of bankruptcies. ROE is only weakly correlated with bankruptcies (the only significant correlation is in 1991-94) and the results show a puzzling negative correlation between loan loss provisions and bankruptcies.

In contrast to these relationships with accounting results and consistent with expectations, there is a strong negative relationship between stock returns of banks and increases in the number of bankruptcies. These results suggest that although banks' reported accounting earnings exhibit no strong association with bankruptcies, shareholders take into account the adverse impact of bankruptcies on banks' asset quality and earnings.

Accounting and Stock Returns

Our results up to this point indicate that reported earnings and stock returns of Japanese banks are related to size and measures of asset quality in similar ways. However, the results also point to some differences in the behaviour of accounting and market measures of performance. Given the differences in the two measures of performance, how do they relate to each other?

To answer this question, I examine the relationship between stock market and accounting returns directly. I first estimate the market model for Japanese bank stocks by regressing individual bank returns on the market index. I then modify the market model by including the return on equity as an additional explanatory variable. If shareholders dismiss accounting earnings as uninformative, one would expect the coefficient on ROE to be insignificant.

First, as reported in the top panel, for the entire sample, the coefficient on the market index is positive. The coefficient is less than one, indicating that when the overall stock market increases by 1 per cent, bank stock returns increase by less than 1 per cent.

However, there are significant differences in how the stock returns of major and regional banks move with the market. A 1 per cent increase in the market index moves the stock returns of major banks by more than 1 per cent and those of regional banks by less than 1 per cent.

Major banks own significantly greater amounts of equity securities than regional banks. Thus, a movement in the stock market affects not only income from their operations, but also the value of their equity investments, magnifying the impact of changes in the market index.

Second, when the market model is augmented with ROE, the coefficient on ROE is positive and statistically significant. In addition, the fraction of the variance in bank stock returns explained by the model, increases in most specifications when accounting returns are included as explanatory variables. Therefore, for all the potential biases in the reported results of Japanese banks, shareholders do not dismiss accounting earnings as meaningless. However, the correlation between banks' stock market and accounting returns has decreased over time; accounting returns are not significantly correlated with stock returns in the 1995-97 period. Higher reported earnings in later years did not translate into higher returns in the stock market as they had in the earlier part of the 1990s, which implies that accounting profits became less informative over time.

This result suggests that measures taken by banks to shore up their reported earnings and capital are not seen by market participants as significant determinants of banks' market performance and, instead, drive a wedge between the banks' accounting and market returns, disconnecting the two measures of performance.

These results are consistent with the results of other studies of U.S. banking showing that regulatory forbearance decreases the correlation between the market value of equity and the value of net assets in place. The market value of a bank's equity is the sum of the value of its net assets in place and the value of deposit insurance subsidies and regulatory forbearance.

Accounting profits, on the other hand, only reflect earnings from assets in place. As a bank nears economic insolvency, the value of regulatory subsidies and forbearance increases and shareholders derive more of their value from subsidies rather than assets in place. Except for the unlikely situations where the value of assets in place is perfectly correlated with changes in the value of subsidies, an increase in the value of subsidies and regulatory forbearance leads to a decline in the correlation between market returns and value of assets in place.

The reluctance of Japanese regulators to force recognition of loan losses and to impose penalties on the shareholders of failing institutions is undoubtedly valuable to banks' shareholders. As the condition of the banks deteriorated significantly in the later part of the 1990s, the value of subsidies and forbearance to shareholders might have increased significantly, potentially accounting for the lack of correlation between market and accounting returns of Japanese banks in 1995-97. Economic malaise, ever-increasing problem loans, high credit expenses to provision for problem loans, and low core profitability have taken their toll on Japanese banks. We have examined the performance of Japanese banks in recent years and related it to variables used by regulators and analysts to assess the condition of banks.

The results show significant differences between the performance and characteristics not only of Japanese and U.S. banks, but also of different Japanese banks and over time. The results also show that although most measures of bank asset quality are correlated with accounting returns in line with expectations and the results of other banking studies, other variables that were found to be important determinants of bank performance in the U.S. and elsewhere are not significantly related to the performance of Japanese banks.

Moreover, accounting profits are correlated with other bank characteristics and economic variables in puzzling ways. Additional evidence suggests that these puzzling or inconsistent results may be due to income smoothing by banks. Specifically, Japanese banks appear to increase their loan loss provisions when their core earnings and the returns on the market are high.

However, such actions do not appear to affect the stock returns of banks; the returns are positively correlated with the return on the market index. Our analysis shows that although there might be problems with the reported earnings of Japanese banks, accounting returns still provided useful information to market participants regarding the values of bank shares in the early 1990s.

However, the significance of this information has decreased in recent years. These results may reflect an increase in the value of regulatory forbearance to bank shareholders. The MoF has introduced a number of measures that indicate an increase in regulatory forbearance.

As outlined in appendices 1 and 3, accounting changes have enabled banks to increase their regulatory capital, government purchases of banks' preferred stock and subordinated loans have injected capital to institutions experiencing financial difficulties, and government guarantees have been extended to all bank creditors through the end of fiscal year 2001. Regulators typically forbear to give ailing institutions time to recover. However, experience tell us that forbearance imposes significant costs on the economy by transferring wealth from the deposit agencies, and hence taxpayers, to bank shareholders and by increasing the cost of resolving insolvent institutions.

To the extent that the recent financial revitalization laws resolve the insolvent institutions and encourage solvent banks to deal with their problems in a timely manner, they should greatly improve the health of the Japanese financial system.

Index